When Reading Begins

noticing

how strange
we look but do not
see
until
someone invites
then suddenly
we
with new eyes
see
a clear simplicity
within complexity
from one brief
invitation
we see

to what else are we blind

—A. Cole 1991

When Reading Begins

The Teacher's Role in Decoding, Comprehension, and Fluency

Ardith Davis Cole

HEINEMANN
Portsmouth, NH

Heinemann
A division of Reed Elsevier Inc.
361 Hanover Street
Portsmouth, NH 03801–3912
www.heinemann.com

Offices and agents throughout the world

Library of Congress Cataloging-in-Publication Data
Cole, Ardith Davis.
When reading begins : the teacher's role in decoding, comprehension, and fluency / Ardith Davis Cole.
p. cm.
Includes bibliographical references and index.
ISBN 0-325-00663-6 (alk. paper)
1. Individualized reading instruction—United States. 2. Reading (Elementary)—United States. I. Title.
LB1573.45.C65 2004
372.416—dc22 2003023528

Editor: Lois Bridges
Production: Elizabeth Valway
Cover design: Judy Arisman
Interior photos: Mary Bream and Ardith Cole
Cover photo of Ardith Cole and Odette Jennings: Patrick Jennings
Composition: House of Equations, Inc.
Manufacturing: Steve Bernier

Printed in the United States of America on acid-free paper
08 07 06 05 04 ML 1 2 3 4 5

This book is dedicated to
the newest members of our wonderful family,

Ashleigh Cole and Makenzie Young.

Contents

Figures

Acknowledgments

I entered the investigative journey into teacher scaffolding well over a decade ago when I was teaching first grade at a small city school. It wasn't long before I had our entire primary staff involved. We were a tight clan! Because we trusted each other, the teachers invited me to "Come on in and videotape me! I don't mind!" I am grateful to all those colleagues.

Linda Schott, the first-grade colleague who endured my obsessions, joined me for a multitude of enlightening discussions, and allowed me to investigate her own scaffolding practices via multiple, videotaped recordings. It was Linda who invited me into her first grade this past June to capture some last-minute, scaffolding-in-action photos, many of which now grace this book. Thanks so much, Linda, for then and now. And thanks also to those cooperative Southard first graders who share the pictures with Linda.

Heartfelt thanks also go to my own first-grade students who were always so cooperative when their teacher turned on the camcorder yet one more time. What beautiful memories those videos captured.

Between those first investigations and the writing of this book, I have met so many gracious human beings. My close friend and colleague, Mary Shea, helped me collect early, informal video footage from other schools. So did Kathy Fuller. I am truly grateful to all those teachers who invited us to videotape their scaffolding acts.

Professional conversations with myriad colleagues continue to stretch my thinking. Just this year, when I explained my conception of micro and macro processing to Mary Shea, she introduced me to the mindful work of Judith Irwin. Thank you, Mary and Judith Irwin.

Indeed, the writing of our profession's experts has helped light the fires that continue to guide my journey and keep my inspirations fueled—especially the research and theory of Ken and Yetta Goodman, Marie Clay, Gay Su Pinnell, Irene Fountas, Don Holdaway, L. S. Vygotsky, Jerome Bruner, Martin Buber, Nel Noddings, and Frank Smith. Just before this book was finished, Peter Duckett's first-grade eye movement research added an important concept to my own work, and I appreciate his patience with all my last-minute interrogations.

As my small piece of classroom research expanded to include teachers from other schools, Dick Salzer, an early childhood professor at the University of Buffalo, frequently invited me to download on his doorstep. Dick eventually led me and my project to UB's reading department. It was Michael Kibby, Chair of Reading, who finally said, "Ms. Cole, where on earth are you going with all this? Will you publish it? Are you going to write a book? Do you plan on a Ph. D.? If so, you're already halfway there." Thanks to Michael, my advisor, the eventual answer to that question became "All of the above!" Also thanks to Michael, there are more interesting quasi-quantitative data in this book—data that better substantiates the section on differentiated instruction.

Thanks also goes to UB's Sam Weintraub and Doug Clements, who threw lifesavers to me several times on my swim upstream. And Ron Gentile provided some alternative fuel from the psychology department.

Furthermore, I'm sincerely indebted to Jerry Harste (Indiana University), who introduced me to the work of Michael Halliday. Frustrated by one facet of my analysis, I presented the dilemma to Jerry. "There are only three cueing systems, but many of the teachers' scaffolding behaviors don't fall into graphophonics, semantics, or syntactics. What should I do with these other behaviors?" I asked. When I described those outliers to Jerry he immediately responded, "You need Michael Halliday's 'pragmatics'!" It was that fork in the road that helped direct my observations, analysis, and conclusions onto new and fascinating ground.

When I entered the last, but more formal leg of the research journey at UB, seven generous first-grade teachers and their students volunteered to be videotaped during scaffolding. Three were from a suburban district and four were from an inner-city district. How gracious they were to allow me to enter their classrooms, to answer my ongoing questions, and to view and discuss with me what I'd captured on tape! I am forever grateful.

Furthermore, I could not have made this journey without the support of my close friends and family: Elaine Garan, who endures my obsessions and continues to be my brilliant mentor and steadfast friend; Mary and Eric Bream, who offered to "help count" when I was running out of steam; my son, Brad, who loves math and statistics, and who asked the right question at the right time: "Mom, how can I help?" Leigh-Ann Hildreth, who was my grad student, my eventual elementary school colleague, and the patient, knowledgeable first-grade teacher who transcribed all of the voiced scaffolding from fourteen of the videotapes; family members Cam, Carolyn, Jen, and Delanie, who helped me log our family's literacy experiences in my book. It took all of us!

But it also took some of my Port Townsend friends when, at the last minute, everyone thought the cover should include my face. I quickly called Patrick Jennings, who is, coincidentally, a Scholastic author. He and his wife, Alison, said their four-year-old daughter, Odette, would love to be in my scaffolding picture. So I am on the cover, thanks to photographer Patrick and sweet little Odette (who actually began pointing to words during the photo session—YES!).

People sometimes ask, "Why did you write those other books first? Why did you wait for so long to write this one?"

My answer: "It just wasn't time for it."

It took a trek to Nepal last year for the universe to offer it up. That is, in the middle of the night in a sleeping bag inside a tent at Everest Base Camp, I awoke to find an outline developing in my brain. In the morning, I sat outside in the sunshine with the peaks of Mt. Everest high above and wrote the outline for this book inside my travel journal.

At that time, *Knee to Knee, Eye to Eye* had been accepted for publication, and *Better Answers* was to be published at the end of that month. Another book seemed out of the question, so I waited as long as my patience allowed, and then I sent the *When Reading Begins* proposal, along with the Everest outline, to Lois Bridges, my good friend and insightful editor. From that moment on, Lois became the wind beneath this manuscript's wings. Her gracious "pragmatic" support gave me strength and courage. Indeed, I will always be grateful that the universe waited, because Lois Bridges so thoroughly and sensitively understands, not only the cueing systems and reading, but also young children, teachers, and obsessive authors, all of which made her the perfect editor for this book. Lois, thank you for the special person you are to all of us.

But before I finish, I want to thank Heinemann for believing in my work enough to publish two Cole books within one year. It's been a joy working with so many wonderful people, including Karen Clausen, Doria Turner, and Elizabeth Valway.

And finally, I want to thank you, my readers, for caring enough about your own practice to buy and read books that you trust will make you a better teacher. May this book do just that.

Introduction

We shape our self
to fit this world
and by the world
are shaped again.
The visible
and the invisible
working together
in common cause,
to produce
the miraculous . . .
DAVID WHYTE,
THE HOUSE OF BELONGING

They Learned to Read

In our first grade in 1965 I could usually expect that most kids would arrive in September knowing few or no letters of the alphabet. By the year's end, all but (maybe) a couple were fluent readers. By 1980, when I was teaching on the other side of the tracks, surprisingly many more of the twenty-six to twenty-eight first graders knew their letters *before* they walked through our door; however, I still always had about eight who knew few or none. Regardless, most of them—even the letterless—went "over the hump" by mid-November. Over the hump was what we called it when a student could read *Are You My Mother?* or *Hop on Pop* independently. The few who could not, always went "over" by spring. Always. Even those who were later identified as having an IQ below 75.

They came to us without socks in the Buffalo winter snows, but they learned to read. They had never been to Niagara Falls—just twenty minutes away—but they learned to read. Few had professional parents, but they all learned to read. Some of their parents could not read, but *they* learned to. My colleague, Linda Schott, and I just took it for granted that our first graders would learn to read. And they did.

No Easy Answer

It was during the early '80s that educators began visiting our school. The kids welcomed the company and took much of the responsibility for meeting our visitors' needs. The students could show them around, explain our day and its activities, and readily answer questions—with the exception of one. Oh, the students answered that one, too, but not with enough specificity for the visitors' inquiring minds, so they approached Linda or me and asked, "How did these kids get to this point in their reading?" or "How do they know how to read so well?" There was no easy answer to that question. I'd mention this or that, but eventually, I myself began to wonder what, exactly, the answer to their question *was*.

In the beginning, Linda and I spent considerable effort trying to answer it. We highlighted specific, obvious methodology that worked: shared reading, guided reading, sustained silent reading or independent reading, student read-alouds, journaling, writers' workshop, and so on. Our visitors, more often than not, said they, too, used most of the methodology we were using. They continued to wonder what magic we had cast on these kids, so we dug deeper for an answer.

Instruction in a first-grade classroom of twenty-eight kids is a pretty complex network of interactions. What, within all that complexity, made the difference?

On-the-Fly Teaching: A Covert Program

Eventually, it became clear that what was just as important as our overt program was the covert one, which could have been overlooked by visitors and even sideline researchers. An important facet of our reading instruction found us beside each child, helping him by providing specific feedback that would scaffold that reader to the next level on his own private reading ladder—the one that led to fluency. I called us *on-the-fly teachers*, after an article I had once read about on-the-fly mothers, who met the individual needs of each child in the family by tucking instruction, answers, and care in between the day's hectic routines. That's what we did, too, but in the classroom.

We shared this aspect of individual support with our visitors, but still I wondered just exactly what we *were* doing when we scaffolded readers on-the-fly. If someone asked me that question, what would I say? What kind of scaffolding *do* we teachers use with beginning readers? Specifically, what do we say to the kids? When we scoot up beside a novice reader, just what do we do? This wonder, this inquiry, became the inspiration that led me into a lengthy investigation in search of an answer.

Investigating Reading Relationships via Videotapes

After a while, I became so caught up in answering that question that I decided to videotape myself and others to investigate just exactly what we did to help a variety of readers up close. K–2 colleagues in my school and two other schools supported my obsession and volunteered to be videotaped. (Teachers are the kindest people I know.) That initial study revealed a good bit and inspired me to undertake a larger, more formal study with suburban and inner-city grade 1 teachers. The videos of one-to-one reading interactions between teachers and their students helped me to finally find some solid answers to that perplexing question: What exactly do teachers say and do to scaffold beginning readers?

It took many years to find the pieces and understand them and their part in the whole, but eventually some meaningful answers fell into place—answers that have now found their way onto the pages of this book.

Background Information

I was fortunate because my family was involved in video production, which allowed me access to a camcorder. Therefore, over a twenty-year period, I was able to capture pieces of classroom life on tape. I now have well over one hundred videos from my own room, some of whose footage has been transcribed and will be read in this book. It became a natural occurrence in our classroom—kind of like the mom or dad who's always dragging out the camera.

Some footage helped me begin my scaffolding study; that is, by observing myself I was able to work out initial glitches before taping others. I placed a camcorder on a tripod, focusing it on my own transactions with individual first graders. Later, a number of K–2 colleagues in our small-city school invited me to come into their classrooms on my planning period, so that I could videotape them, too. Additionally, a couple of

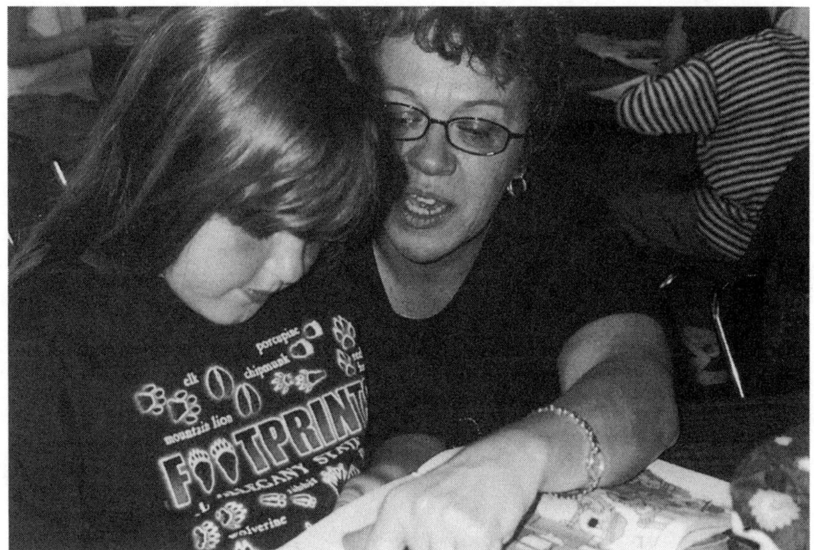
Linda Schott scaffolds a beginning reader on-the-fly.

reading-teacher friends who worked in rural districts became interested in my project, so they volunteered to videotape some K–2 one-on-one teacher scaffolding from their schools. Eventually, when I moved into an authentic, qualitative study, an inner-city group of first-grade teachers volunteered to be videotaped, and so did three first-grade teachers from a suburban district. In the end, I had over thirty different samples of novice to fluent readers being scaffolded through books by a grand variety of teachers. However, it is primarily those from the qualitative study whose transcripts are inside this book because they were more thoroughly analyzed.

Two of those teachers had a reading specialist degree, one had taught for thirty-two years and never taken a graduate class, a few had taught for over thirty years, and two had been in the classroom only one year. All were women. One man volunteered, but then backed out before the study began. Most of this book's examples come from first grade because those are the samples that contain the most specific information related to exactly what teachers do and say to scaffold novices into fluency. Nevertheless, I do mention the kindergarten and second-grade experiences occasionally. Furthermore, several years after collecting this data, I videotaped a few more examples from preschoolers (in home situations) being scaffolded into the reading act. These too are included.

Although I sometimes describe instances from all levels of proficiency, it is the scaffolding of novices that contains the richest information. It is those instances that allow us to peer closely into the process to see exactly how teachers support kids in ways that move them from preword readers into word reading and then fluency.

Occasionally, I mention Linda Schott, the first-grade teacher with whom I worked closely for many years; however, all other names of teachers and students exist only in pseudonym form. All transcriptions are actual data, transcribed from the videotapes. Furthermore, after each taping session, teachers watched the tapes with me to explain their actions and elaborate on their intentions. Those video-viewing conferences were audiotaped and also transcribed. All of this became the ground from which my understanding of reading relationships grew.

Interestingly, when all was said and done, it seemed that the scaffolding that most first-grade teachers demonstrated was far more alike than different. Yet, some of the differences are noteworthy. I hope that in the following you will learn, as I have, from the reading relationships of these generous professionals.

Chapter 1

Scaffolding: A Key to Reading Relationships

Making learning to read easy means ensuring cues at the time a child needs them, ensuring feedback of the kind required at the time it is required, providing encouragement when it is sought. Making learning to read easy requires an understanding of the reading process and of what the child is trying to do . . . Respond to what the child is trying to do. To my mind, this rule is basic.

FRANK SMITH,
ESSAYS INTO LITERACY

How many books have been written about relationships? Probably a ton. However, few have have focused on reading. Yet essentially, teacher-student reading relationships are secured by a similar ether as that which binds other lasting, caring, outside-school relationships.

Basically, teaching is a service profession. Those in a service generally serve, and in order to do that well we must be able to relate to others, in this case, our students. The teacher-student relationship is at the very core of teaching. It begins on the first day of school when our intentions lead the way. Sometimes, our main goal is to have our students pay attention during a period of instruction—one that finds us, their teachers, in front of the group entertaining, using a variety of media, varying our voice rhythms and tone, and targeting individual students for occasional response and accountability. Accordingly, after thirty years in front of every conceivable age group, I am a veteran in vaudeville. I know how to hook them, ignite them, and keep them paying attention—usually. However, entertaining is not real teaching.

Real teaching is an *elbow-to-elbow, eye-to-eye* thing. It's a transaction—as opposed to an interaction—and it finds me responding as a *guide by their side*. It involves specific *feedback*, *feedforward*, and *scaffolding*. Sometimes it's a scheduled meeting, but mostly it's done on-the-fly.

Learning Is a Negotiated Process

Although I feel like the ruler of the realm when I stand before my class, I can never know a student from that position. I can never know a child from the front of the room. Nor can I know children if I use scripted lessons. Knowing requires mindful, *individual* transactions. It requires relationship.

The essence of which I speak is the heart of all optimal teaching-learning events. When I was learning to do country painting, the instructor stood in the front of our group to model and explain every detail involved in constructing a pollywog, the fundamental stroke in that type of painting. She was comprehensive, organized, and articulate; and I paid attention. Honest! Yet, when I put the brush to the paper my polly didn't wog. We've all been in situations like that, and we have a pretty good idea of what it takes to get our pollies to wog—and it isn't any kind of scripted lesson or directions from a teacher's manual.

It takes what my painting instructor offered me: *sensitive, knowledge-driven scaffolding*. She observed exactly where I was in the process, then she leaned over me, put her hand over mine—finger to finger—and collaboratively holding the brush, she guided my journey into the process. We did a few pollywogs with her leading; then, she gradually released her grasp, and little by little, let me lead more . . . and more . . . and more. That instructor is a real teacher—one from whom we can all learn.

There are some politicians with little or no teaching experience who would like to have us believe that teaching is a series of steps that involve doing something to children—steps that can be assessed using a multiple-choice, standardized-teaching test. Yet, were those politicians to actually find themselves in the classroom, they would quickly realize that every child is different and that teaching and learning are negotiated processes. This means we fulfill our instructional intentions by *doing with, not to.* And it is when we are elbow to elbow with kids that a touch of magic energizes the entire reading relationship.

What Is Scaffolding?

Working one-on-one with readers is at the core of scaffolding. Anderson (Anderson, Armbruster, and Roe 1990) comprehensively explains this process for us. He says scaffolding

> consists of the support the coach provides as the students continue to practice. Scaffolding may be in the form of hints or suggestions. Or, the coach may perform part of the task students cannot yet manage on their own. Appropriate scaffolding requires accurate diagnosis of the students' skill levels and the ability to provide just the right amount of support to enable the students to perform the target task. (p. 192)

Anderson defined this term in the '90s, but Jerome Bruner (1973) actually coined it in the '70s. Nonetheless, theories related to scaffolding span the centuries.

The common tie that binds all definitions is *adult assistance*. However, there is an important difference between meanings. That difference seems to be rooted in *whose intentions are being honored*; or, as Searle (1984) puts it: "Who's Building Whose Building?" That is, essentially, whose task is it? Whose intentions are pulling the process forward? The teacher's? The student's? Both? Questions related to how, when, and how much scaffolding one should offer continually arise; and the answers lie somewhere between experience and wisdom.

Furthermore, scaffolding should continually change. It should be a gradual relinquishing of control of a specific behavior, a weaning off the expert. But when we're needed, we're there—elbow to elbow, sensitively offering the boost necessary to negotiate the difficulty, to move the learner forward—just as my painting instructor did for me.

From Complete Support to Learner Autonomy

Scaffolders support learners through many levels during their novice-to-expert journey. Literacy experiences can fuel this journey. Their absence

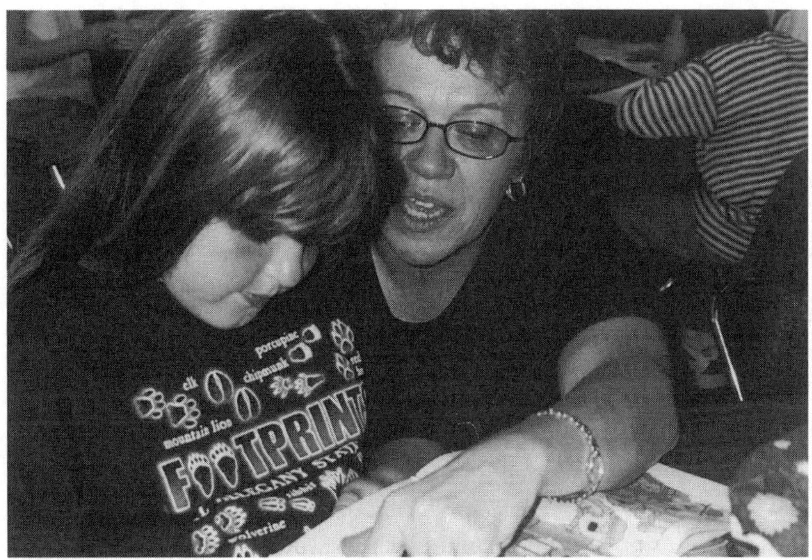

Early experiences with books and reading are stepping stones to success.

can deter it (Neuman 1999). A scaffolding adult or other plays an important part in this process.

Adults Demonstrate, but Invite Babies In

Adults facilitate the young child's learning through demonstrations of and immersion in the reading process while extending ongoing invitations to the learner to participate. Throughout this entire growth process adults revel in what the child can do, both with and without them. They give the young learners every possible chance to go it alone.

For instance, to involve infants in a triadic adult-child-book transaction, the little one may be invited to simply "read" the picture. Even before their first birthday, babies are invited and encouraged during book reading to "Look at the doggy." Then later, we invite a more specific response, "Find the doggy in the picture." Using a kind of *cloze* procedure, some moms invite their babies to fill in the blank the mother has just created. This often happens when books contain singsong patterns, animal sounds, rhymes, and other *predictables*. "Mother cat looked at her baby and the little kitten said, ______. What'd the kitty say? How's kitty go?" invited a mother to her eighteen-month-old, as she carried out most of the reading process for the child, yet invited the baby in here and there.

Perhaps, then, it is the prosodies of the text that first draw the child in and nurture prediction in what seems like an alluring flow-forward. Moreover, just as babies in their first year learn oral language, so, too, does the young "reader" fall into the rhythms and melodies of the text and is swept up by them. This is the time when we hear children reciting lines or pages from their favorite book. It's a time of melody and rhythm, a time of playing with language, a gentle scaffolding into books and reading.

Lap-Reading and Games Prepare Preschoolers for School Literacy

For many children, literacy experiences begin with lap-reading, a time when child and parent

Delanie investigates a board book that she and Mom are sharing.

share a book together. David Doake (1985) tells us that

> avid listening to stories in the secure and close proximity of a loved parent becomes a deeply rewarding, warm, human experience for the children and their parents. Through the sounds and rhythms of the rich and inviting language, through the interesting and colorful illustrations, through the constant stimulation of their receptive imaginations, and through the reliving of these experiences in anticipatory ways, the children soon begin to develop very high expectations for books and reading. (p. 85)

Indeed, it's a wonderful experience for the young preschooler, sitting on an adult's lap for a read-aloud. Research (Wells 1986; Holdaway 1979; Cambourne 1988) tells us that *lap-reading experiences* lay the foundation for later success in reading—later, when text's rhythmic flow is embedded and the child begins to realize the connection between that which comes out of our mouths and the squiggles on the page; that is, he makes the connection between *phonemic and orthographic patterns*, sounds and letters. It seems that this new stage would invite new mediation tactics—ones more directed toward the print itself.

Upping the Ante

Most schools now expect that a child will have had such early literacy experiences prior to the time they enter kindergarten. Thus, we see teachers consistently *upping the ante* by demonstrating the finer details related to how reading and writing work. Teachers use both speech or gesture as they show novices, "This is a model of what adults do when they read."

Scaffolding teachers invite novices to point to the words as the story is read. Or the teacher may ask them to provide a letter's sound. Teachers focus on the meanings inherent in the text by inviting, "What do you think is going to happen next?" or "What does that mean?" Indeed, by the time children reach school, scaffolders expect the youngster to make closer connections to print forms. Then, as the child develops, the teacher offers more and more autonomy, carefully weaning him off teacher support while taking the young learner further into the world of literacy. A process such as this involves significant amounts of individual feedforward and feedback.

Feedforward and Feedback

Two seemingly opposite terms, *feedforward* and *feedback*, often emanate from the same kind of intention; that is, they are acts that support the

Writing Reciprocity: Shared Ownerships

My four-year-old granddaughter, Delanie, began to make connections to print patterns in her environment. She noticed that most adults can write, and afterward, they can read that writing. Preschoolers notice that writing has letters—like the ones on the fridge, so they too try out this writing behavior. That's what Delanie was doing when she wrote *NMNT* and then asked, "What does this say?"

"It doesn't really say anything, Sweetie Pie," I responded.

"Why?" pressed Delanie.

"It needs some vowels in it, so I can say it," I explained.

"What's vowels?" Delanie asked.

I wrote the vowels across the top of the paper and told Delanie that one of them needed to go in the middle somewhere. So Delanie then wrote *NEM*, and asked, "What's it say now?"

And I responded, "Hey-ey! Now it says *NEM*." Delanie was satisfied, and didn't want to investigate the fact that the word had only sounds, but no meaning. Instead, she just scurried off to play with her dolls. Yet, we have to wonder how she might have responded had it been a real word.

Nevertheless, this preschooler was curious and was able to grow forward in her literacy because an adult provided the sound-symbol feedback she wanted. The child initiated the act; the adult merely responded. Such shared ownership in early literacy experiences is a very important aspect of scaffolding.

reader through the process. Sometimes that support comes *prior* to a troublesome section of text (feedforward), while at other times instruction comes *afterward* (feedback). Both offer aid to the learner, yet there are inherent differences between the two.

The Relationship Between Feedback and Errors

Feedback in the reading realm is an after-the-fact event that involves responding to errors made by the reader, ones that the teacher corrects. Yet, the teacher does not actually use the situation to teach. For example, Ann, a first grader, reads, "The doll is in bad," to which the teacher feeds back or corrects, "Bed, not bad."

Although feedback in a reading relationship is similar to that of the painting relationship I experienced, it is also very different. The tools, the texts, and the processes call for a distinct set of scaffolding maneuvers in each. In reading, some educators would call these scaffolding maneuvers *corrective feedback*; that is, responses made by the teacher to correct an error made by the student (Jenkins and Larson 1979). This kind of feedback has also been called a *terminal* intervention, because it involves a *brief*, one-way, teacher-to-student interaction (Anderson, Evertson, and Brophy 1979; Chinn et al. 1993). There is not an explanation, only a correction.

Researchers, to a lesser extent, have also studied *sustaining* or *process feedback*, which involves lengthier interactions between student and teacher, as opposed to those brief, corrective, right-answer responses (Anderson, Armbruster, and Roe 1990). Sustaining feedback occurs during reading when teachers offer a suggestion, provide a pathway to follow, ask a brief question, explain an uncommon term, or any number of other interventions. This lengthier response then differs from the previous corrective feedback.

When using sustaining feedback the teacher does not simply correct or tell unknown words, but instead, gives the reader a hint or strategy to help him discover pathways to meaning and fluency. The essence of this teacher-student interaction, then, models and teaches the use of strategies within the reading act. Research demonstrates "that children's year-to-year growth in reading is greater when oral reading errors are followed with 'sustaining feedback' rather than 'terminal feedback'" (Anderson, Armbruster, and Roe 1990, p. 171). Yet some researchers contend that sustaining feedback is seldom used (Meyer 1985; McCoy and Pany 1986; Anderson, Armbruster, and Roe 1990).

Most past research was not carried out in beginning-reader classrooms, such as kindergarten and first grade. Instead, researchers investigated older struggling students in other settings, such as reading clinics or special education classrooms. Maybe my observations produced different results because they occurred during the normal course of events in regular primary classrooms. As I videotaped over the shoulders of teacher-student dyads, I found there was plenty of sustaining feedback going on in first grade. As a matter of fact, the day was full of it!

Scaffolding: An All-Encompassing Term

Connotations around the term *feedback* do not seem to allow for all scaffolding possibilities. As we transact elbow-to-elbow with kids, we teachers open not only our minds, but also our hearts to the full picture of possibilities. Indeed, we emulate my painting instructor, assuming a sensitive, more proactive perspective; that is, we learn to dance with learners in a feedback-feedforward kind of cha-cha. In order to do this successfully, we have to possess an intimate knowledge of the reading process—a *mind perspective*; but we also have to know the whole child in order to develop an essential *heart sensitivity*. We should be aware of each reader's likes and dislikes, abilities and inabilities, background and lack thereof, as well as the text being used. This enables us to catch the beginner before he falls, to anticipate an error by feeling, by sensing, a slight nuance of change in the child's voice tone and tempo, gestures, and breathing, while at the same time responding with a scaffold that carries that young novice over the hump, free of scars and bruises.

It seems more reasonable, therefore, to use Bruner's term, *scaffold*, than to use feedback or feedforward, particularly because as we move into the nuts and bolts of this process, it is sometimes difficult to discern the two. However, another term that is synonymous with scaffolding is *mediating*; and, thus, that term will also be useful here.

Scaffolding Cues That Teachers Use

Actors are shown cue cards when they forget a line. Football players are cued by the coach to perform certain plays or maneuvers. And novice readers are cued by teachers to help them understand the reading process. In this text, I use the term *cueing* to signify teacher scaffolding acts—ones that give the reader a *sign*, a *cue*—that will hopefully move the learner forward, through and beyond a challenging section of text.

Two Cueing Channels

Teachers cue readers through primarily two channels. They cue through *gestural* behaviors, such as pointing, smiling, turning a page, patting a hand, or changing voice tone. They also cue through *spoken* scaffolds when they tell the child a word, offer him a beginning sound, read an entire sentence, or issue praise and affirmation. The myriad cues teachers use and their variety of purposes are thoroughly explained in later chapters.

Effective and Ineffective Cues

Some teacher cues are effective and should be readily used. Others are ineffective and should not be used—even though they sometimes are. Unfortunately, I myself repeatedly used some of those ineffective cues—until this investigation, that is. It is indeed fortunate that we can learn to put aside such ineffective response habits.

Teachers scaffolding in a regular classroom setting need to know what works. They also need to know what does not work, so they can discontinue its use. The following chapters, which describe this, gather their grist from observations within such regular classroom settings.

The Difference Between Preword Readers, Word Readers, and Fluent Readers

When a child first approaches the printed page, he may not even know that it is the print that carries the message. These are the children who announce, "I can read with my eyes closed!" That is, they open the book and repeat it in the manner in which they heard it read to them. They've memorized it! Such "reading-like behaviors" (Holdaway 1979) have been called *talking like a book* (Clay 1979), *pretend-reading* (Ehri and Sweet 1991), and *reenactment* (Holdaway 1979), and are often the first identifiable literacy behaviors. During this *preword* period, children do not even realize that the words issuing from the reader's mouth have something to do with the letters on the page. And even when they do make the connection between speech and the page's print, it is generally a tacit one.

Scaffolders lead preword readers toward a more explicit understanding of the page's microcosms of graphic symbols through pointing behaviors, ones that mark where the reader is looking. Yet even then it is quite some time before children understand *how* print works.

Pretend-Reading

Indeed, many preword readers know that the alphabet symbols on the page carry the message, but they have no understanding of how that print works, that is, how to *decode* print. For instance, when my grandson, Cameron, was twenty months old, he reenacted the book *Freight Train* (Crews 1978). He began by sliding his hand under the print in the title from right to left, not left to right. He knew where the title was, and he knew what the title was; however, he did not understand how print works. At that time, he appeared to have little awareness of English orthography's directionality. He had merely reproduced the behaviors of his mother, pretending to read by doing what he thought she was doing. But Cameron was still a preword reader at that time.

Fingerslide-Reading

When Cameron began to understand that reading has a quality of directionality he moved further into the process and began to use *fingerslide-reading* along with correct directionality; that is, he slid his finger under each line, just as he saw his mom do, from left to right. Yet, it was some time before Cameron was able to match each spoken word to its print partner on the page. For that, he had to have some understanding of *wordness*. That is, left-to-right fingerslide-readers must eventually also understand that their spoken words also have a *printmatch*. Scaffolders help them notice how those empty spaces, or *junctures*, between groups of letters mark the beginnings and endings of words. Once they begin to notice how the letters are word-grouped on a page, preword readers transition into a greater focus on words. Even so, their printmatch behaviors are usually inconsistent for quite some time. That is, transitioning novices tend to drop back into pretend-reading at times, especially when they become tired or pressured.

Fingerpoint-Reading

The next stage can be called *fingerpoint-reading* (Ehri and Sweet 1991), which requires a leap on the developmental ladder—one that can only happen after a novice notices that the letters on the page are indeed printed in groups set off by spaces. Even then, a child's exact understanding of the process is unpredictable because word units are not as noticeable in speech as in print; that is, we do not pause between words when we talk. Furthermore, in speech it's difficult to discern a syllable from a word, so transitioning novices may not understand that *once upon a time* is four words. Unable to connect concrete referents to the individual words in this abstract utterance, young children assume it is one word: "wunsaponatim" (which is exactly why novice writers in my classroom encoded it in a similar fashion in their journals year after year).

Phonemic Awareness and Printmatch

As *speech-to-print awareness* develops, transitioning readers come to understand the symbiotic relationship between writing and speech; that is, readers begin to learn where words are segmented in speech *at the same time* that they are learning about what words look like in print, and vice versa. As a matter of fact, Adams found that "training phonemic awareness produced little reading benefit unless children were also taught the printed letters by which each phoneme was represented" (1990, p. 54). Others have also researched this and agree that sounds should not be taught separately from letters (Krashen 2001b; Bus and van Ijzendoorn 1999; National Reading Panel 1999). It comes as no surprise, then, that research shows "explicit awareness of word in written language precede[s] explicit awareness of word in spoken language" (Roberts 1992, p. 135). Undoubtedly, the printed page itself scaffolds and grounds wordness. Thus, separating spoken words or sounds from their printmates by implementing phonemic awareness drills makes little sense because, in reading, *words and sounds are a package deal.*

This would indicate that reading scaffolding behaviors should involve exposure to print (Adams 1990; Lomax and McGee 1987; Ehri 1976). Kids need to be read to and to hang out with books in order to develop the underpinnings of the process (Krashen 1993; Neumann 1999). And they need scaffolders to answer their questions and guide their efforts. Otherwise, literacy takes longer.

A Package Deal: Sounds and Symbols

Even adults can experience childlike speech-to-print ambiguities when becoming literate in a foreign language. For they, too, find it difficult to understand where one word ends and another begins, unless they are shown it in print. Print helps clear up confusions—and in the thirty years that I spent teaching kids to read, I did not waste my time on oral exercises—that is, phonemic awareness that had young learners repeating my nonsense syllables. Why focus only on oral language when we have print to complement and support it? And it is actually quite amazing to see how quickly youngsters come to understand word junctures—especially considering how

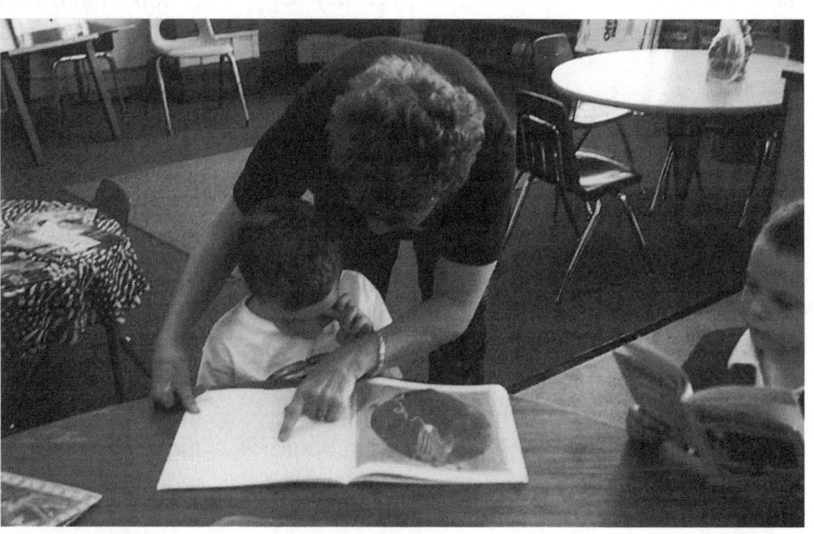

Linda points to the words to scaffold a novice.

rapidly we speak and also how we *in*articulately meld one spoken word to another.

Scaffolders need to show learners where to find a word's printmatch. Pointing to words helps clear up those confusions. Once learners begin to replicate their scaffolder's behaviors and can match speech with print, they have reached a new plateau. Yet some children who do give up fingerpoint-reading replace it with other, more novel pointing behaviors.

Voicepointing and Headpointing

Marie Clay (1979) talks about novices who exhibit a kind of reading she calls *voicepointing*. Some kids who are not ready to give up fingerpointing, replace it with voicepointing. As they focus on that one-to-one word match, they sound more like counters than readers, "1! 2! 3! 4!"

"The! boy! ran! to! his! mother!"

Each word is thrust out, like Krispee-Kremes popping from the donut machine into the boiling tub of oil below. The reading may be fast, but each word sounds the same. Identical inflection. Identical pacing. Mechanical. That's voicepointing.

Sometimes readers keep time with their heads, thereby substituting headpointing for fingerpointing. No kidding! Lots of novices try out headpointing for a while. Afraid of losing his place, a novice figuratively sits on his hands, but nods his head for each word. Headpointers, who have good word recognition and can therefore read very fast, resemble those nodding birds that drivers place in car windows—and some novices peck as though they are hungry woodpeckers! So indeed they are reading with speed, yet they certainly do not sound fluent!

Developing a Sight Vocabulary

As students begin to look more closely at individual words, they start to notice likenesses and differences between words. They realize that some words are long and some are short, some have tall letters and others have mostly short letters. They can find look-alike words. They begin to identify grouped letters, especially nouns, such as *zoo, dog*, and *mommy*.

Their environment helps scaffold them forward as they find high-frequency words in books, on word walls, and in myriad places at home and in school. The more they see the same words, the more rapidly they become theirs. Learners then begin to use this new vocabulary in their writing because they now remember how some words are composed. It is at that time that novices are on their way to accumulating a sound sight vocabulary that will eventually provide grist for letter-sound patterns.

The more children read, the faster they accrue vocabulary (Adams 1990), and the more comfortable they become with the process. Their knowledge of literacy expands and each reading experience becomes more predictable for them, more like others they've already had. Before long, the reader is sliding right into fluency.

Fluent Reading

Sometimes the journey from a mere awareness of words (being able to point to each word as the teacher reads aloud) to an accumulated sight vocabulary (an actual remembered visual image of particular words) and decoding (using cues to identify unknown words) and on into fluency (when word recognition is automatic) can take many months or even years. Readers transitioning into fluency learn to intone whole phrases at a time; they do not read haltingly or word by word, as novice readers do. And they do not have to point to the words. When reading text at their own instructional level, they slide along at an even pace because their sight vocabulary is large and they possess a number of strategies that help to keep them going. Unlike the word-by-word fingerpoint readers, fluent readers barely glance at most common words and, according to eye movement research, even skip highly predictable words (Paulson and Freeman 2003).

Students Take Ownership of Modeled Skills and Strategies

Of course, there are times when readers encounter a challenging section of text, but cannot receive specific instruction or support from a teacher. In such instances, readers will then need to independently use previously acquired skills and strategies to—correctly or incorrectly—move through troublesome spots. Novices can independently use decoding strategies when they have teachers who take a moment here or there to show them how it's done; that is, teachers who demonstrate how to jump the hurdles—teachers who use a variety of cues as models to emulate. Such teacher scaffolding is optimal when the text used is somewhat challenging, but just right for that particular child. Therefore, every reading relationship is unique, and will differ depending upon the text, the reader, and the scaffolder.

How Does Scaffolding Look and Sound for Beginners?

Preword readers may be able to slide through the words and reproduce a patterned text after someone has read it to them, but if they are unable to match spoken words with their print partners, they would still be considered preword readers. That is, they are unable to accurately read an *unrehearsed* text alone. These children do not discern the fundamental differences between and among words.

To support children having little or no experience with books, the mediator usually reads the text aloud while inviting the youngster to "read" the pictures, guess what might happen next, turn the pages, and such. These young reproducers can then indeed navigate that book autonomously; however, they will reenact the text from memory using its illustrations and language patterns for support, not the words.

Once preword readers begin to transition toward word reading, the scaffolding changes. And it continues to change as the reader changes. Let's visit a few scaffolders and see how each reading relationship differs.

Scaffolding Preword Reader, Cameron: Age Twenty Months

Earlier, I introduced preword reader Cameron, who was reenacting one of his then favorite books, *Freight Train*. Cameron's mom had read and reread that book many, many times to her son. She herself had it memorized! Again and again, she and Cameron had sat on the couch connected by the book, mom holding the left page and Cameron holding and turning the right. As Mom read, she used finger-sliding to show Cameron *where* she was reading and the *direction* in which print flows. She always read the title, along with the author and illustrator. Consequently, when Cameron reenacted the book, he also included the titles, authors, and illustrators of texts—on both the cover and the title page. And although Cameron slid his own finger backward through the lines of print, his mom honored those approximations.

When Cameron was able to remember a good bit of the book, Mom invited him to read it. And when this preword reader miscalled the train car's color, Mom gave corrective feedback. "Is that yellow? It's orange!" Mom corrected.

This dyad also asked questions of each other. Mom asked, "What color is that car?" Cameron asked, "What's this says?" pointing at the publishing company information that his mom had skipped. Together they danced through the pages, trading the reading and responding leads back and forth in a flowing relationship. In so doing, Cameron was becoming very familiar and confident with the world of print. It was a rewarding and comfortable time for both.

Scaffolding Preword Transition Reader, Sean: Age Six Years

Another child, who is more experienced in the process, may be ready for a greater focus on the print itself. Teachers do continue to demonstrate, reading for kids who are beginning to word-match; and, as a matter of fact, they invite them into many of the same responses that the less experienced Cameron had with his mom.

Teachers would, however, up the ante by expecting a transition reader to read using *both* the graphics or words on the page *and* the illustrations. In other words, unlike Cameron, this transition reader stands at the doorway of decoding. He may or may not associate sounds with letters, but he is beginning to understand wordness; that is, he notices word junctures and the way in which all words have a particular shape or structure.

Let's look at a scaffolding session I had with Sean, a novice six-year-old, who is beginning to match speech to print; in other words, he notices the junctures and also some of the ways in which words differ. As a school literacy specialist, I captured this experience on the pages of my classroom journal.

My Journal Entry: Scaffolding Sean

Students were meandering in after lunch, trying to find the books they would read during sustained silent reading (SSR), when I called to

Sean and invited, "Hey, Sean, want to read a book with me?" The tiny towhead, receiving my invitation in a positive light, ambled over and sat on my lap with his well-rehearsed book, *The Jigaree* (Cowley 1986). After he finished this personal, memorized favorite, I extended another invitation.

"Let's read a new one this time, Sean," I encouraged, as I rummaged through the stack of books I had carried with me. "How about this one?" I said, holding up another more challenging, yet patterned, text.

"I can't read that," objected the little blond cherub, as he shied away from me.

"Then, let me read it to you first," I invited, "It's about twins." Those few words seemed to have reestablished the reading relationship, because Sean then sauntered over my way, demonstrating more interest. He sidled up beside me as we settled into a comfortable position together on the corner carpet while the rest of the class finished their own book searches.

When I picked up that new book I had a good hunch that Sean could not yet read it. But I also knew that he now had speech-to-print, so I decided that if I first read this minimal-word, patterned text to him, pointing to the words, making it fun, he might catch the book's patterns and rhythms enough to join me on the second time through. And that is just what he did! However, as we broached the halfway point and I could feel his confidence developing, I began to fade in and out as needed. We traded off on the pointing, too. The third time through he played the part that I had played the second time through. That is, he did most of the reading and I came in only if he needed me. Throughout this process I applauded his efforts, celebrating, "Look at how you can read this now! That's probably because it's such a fun book!"

Scaffolding Considerations for Transitioning Readers

Sean was just getting used to the world of print, so I needed to first establish some kind of confident relationship between the child, the book, and myself. I knew I had to do the reading for him. But because we were using a just-right text for this reader, he modeled my reading and pointing within just a few minutes. In the days that followed, I would stop by Sean's table to repeat that process; but I would also keep tabs on his progress by inviting this transitioning reader, who was on the threshold of word-matching, to point to particular words. I needed to know if he was focusing on each word's distinctive features. I also asked him to tell me about the book, because I needed to know if he was making meaning. And I asked him to read his favorite page because I wanted to know if he was interested.

All of this is the scaffolding I would use with a child who is at the doorstep of decoding. When Sean becomes a confident novice reader, I will invite him into more autonomy in the reading process, just as Kara does with her novice reader in the example that follows.

Scaffolding Novice Reader, Serita: Age Seven

Serita is a novice reader. She can match speech to print and is becoming more independent. Yet she still needs help with cues and strategies.

In the following, first-grade teacher Kara mediates Serita through a patterned text called *My Messy Room*. The reader has stopped mid-sentence, attempting to sound through the word *socks*, but seems confused. Consider everything Kara does and says to support this novice through the sentence "I like socks on my chair."

Kara begins by offering an open strategy invitation:

TEACHER: If sounds aren't working, let's try something else. *(brings up her left hand, which is on the floor between the two, to grasp the corner of the book's page)* Let's jump right over it, *(at the same time makes a quick sign with her left hand that slices through the air, inferring a fast movement forward—a jump—then immediately moves her hand to the beginning of the sentence, pointing to the first word and then rereads)* "I like blank— *(skips right over the word* socks *and continues to point to each of the following words,* on my chair; *however, she does not use speech to accompany this pointing, but merely fingerslides to the end of the sentence)*

When this teacher said "blank," she used an upward pitch that signaled an invitation to participate. Therefore, without missing a beat, the reader took over, right after "blank," where the teacher had orally left off. The reader was then led (through teacher gesture only) to reread and supply the unknown word. That is, the teacher moved her finger from the end of the sentence, back to its beginning, knowing full well that as she slid forward she would pull the reader along with her. And she did.

When an adult scaffolds in mindful ways that consider a reader's specific needs, learning often takes place. Kara offered this child a variety of cues and strategies as she scaffolded the reader through the text using both gestural and spoken cues. Kara believed that if she mindfully guided her novice readers through text, showing them how the process works, they would soon be able to do it without her. And indeed, she was correct.

How Does Scaffolding Look and Sound for Fluent Readers?

That year, Kara led many of her students into fluency. Once they achieved that ability, she allowed them far more autonomy. As a matter of fact, the first thing she did when she sat down beside a fluent reader was to place her palm under her chin with her elbow resting on the table in a relaxed, somewhat nonparticipatory gesture.

When Kara's fluent reader hesitated on an unknown name, Kara did not gesture. First, she waited, allowing the reader to use decoding strategies. But after a few seconds, when the fluent reader demonstrated no evident strategy, Kara suggested one, such as "What if you broke it up?" The reader did then break it up, and as a consequence, decoded the word and read on. Kara did not use corrective feedback. She used sustaining feedback, which allowed the reader more autonomy.

For her fluent readers, Kara uses minimal cues, many of which are gestural or open-ended invitations that support a fluent, uninterrupted journey through text. On the other hand, Lani's fluent reader was so fluent that Lani focused primarily on comprehension strategies and only occasionally scaffolded fluency. Each scaffolding situation differs, because every reading relationship is different. It is of utmost importance that teachers know their students, their texts, and their craft.

Using a Text That Scaffolds Novice Readers

A significant part of a reading relationship involves the text being read. Text is what makes it a triadic transaction—a part that helps keep each transaction vital and unique. Any one text can present myriad variables that influence a reading relationship. From topic to readability to the kind of print on the page, as well as dozens of other variables, texts play an influential part in any reading relationship.

Books They Can Read with Their Eyes Shut

Teachers use highly predictable books with preword and transitioning students. They want to make certain that the text is as supportive as possible, so they select books that have lots of rhyme, rhythm, and consistent patterns—books that are so predictable they can easily be memorized. And that is just what happens. It is during this period that we receive notes from parents that say, "Dear Mrs. Cole, Mary brought her book home to read. She did not really read it. She has it memorized."

We still love to tell the story of the delightfully chatty little first grader from Linda's room who visited her older sister's teacher in early September. When the teacher asked if she had learned to read yet, the child responded, "Oh, yes! I can even read with my eyes shut! Wanta see?" She then began reciting the book—with eyes closed, of course.

It's quite obvious that this child's scaffolding support would be very different from that of a reader who possessed knowledge of wordness and a sight vocabulary. It's also obvious that the text we'd want to use would be different. It is easy-to-remember, minimal-print, patterned texts that we so often use with beginning readers, because they offer far more predictability than a text with no rhythm, rhyme, or repetition. In other words, sometimes *a text itself scaffolds* readers with its predictable structures. Yet this is what we want for beginners. We want them to feel as safe as possible, to enjoy the act, to feel in control. It is within that safe environment that they will learn, and it also offers the best circumstances for scaffolding.

Once novices begin to understand how print works, we need to up the text ante. We then move to texts whose patterns are not as predictable and ones that have more print on the page.

Just-Right Texts

A *just-right text* aligns with a reader's zone of proximal development (Vygotsky 1978); that is, it is just challenging enough to allow for scaffolding that will move that reader on to the next rung on the developmental ladder. This means that the book should contain some challenging aspects, such as vocabulary—tricky parts that could be made easier to circumnavigate with adult assistance. Optimally, the novice reader should encounter around five to ten challenging spots or words within a hundred-word section of text. Some call this the child's *instructional level* (Fountas and Pinnell 1996).

Sometimes, when I do not know a reader well, I must try two or three books before locating a just-right book. A too-difficult book would frustrate, while a too-easy book would provide no challenging or scaffolding opportunities. That is why the text used will definitely influence the reading relationship. Just right always depends on the individual child. Just right for one reader will not be just right for another. We know what is optimal by listening to a child read, and we will never know whether a book is just right for a particular child unless we listen to that child read that particular book. It always boils down to one child, one teacher, one book: the optimal reading relationship for a novice.

The Decodable Text Genre

Those who see phonics as the sine qua non of beginning reading, construct *decodable texts* and nonsense-word tests to accompany them and validate their use. Whereas real authors are inspired by ideas that they capture in writing, decodable texts are constructed using lists of words and a computer. The words precede the idea. Some of these books, therefore, sound very strange and contrived, which prompts us to wonder who would write something like that. And that is exactly what some of my first graders wondered when they came upon some decodable texts in the back recesses of our room. They became intrigued trying to understand the intention of the authors who wrote the Barnhart linguistic readers (the Nan-can-fan-Dan books). Yet because those kids saw the world as a meaningful place, they kept trying to attach meaning to that textual nonsense!

We had all kinds of old and donated books in our class library, and that small set of readers soon became grist for multiple wonders, as well as some tentative answers. For instance, one day during SSR, Shanasti motioned me over and, wondering about the page before him, whispered, "Mrs. Cole, do you think the author's trying to write a new kind of poetry?"

Kids continually reach to make sense of their worlds—whether or not they abide in nonsense. They, like Shanasti, will even make sense of our nonsense! But why would we ever want to start kids out on nonsense?

No Research Supports Use of Decodable Text

While we're on the topic of decodable text, I feel compelled to mention that although some profess it as the just-right recipe for beginning reading, there is absolutely *no research* that substantiates the use of this genre. Yet decodable text, along with all of its boring rules and regulations, seems to have become a favorite of publishing companies and mainstay for government mandates.

The entire fiasco is based on nonsense—even the supposed research. The National Reading Panel (1999) touted studies that measured reading ability through each student's decoding of nonsense words, that is, words without meanings (for example, *pim* and *gan*). But could those students actually read and comprehend authentic, unrehearsed text—real books? Again, we do not know. We only know that they could match sounds to letters. Trained parrots can also do this!

For more information on this, please see Elaine Garan's seminal work investigating the National Reading Panel's research, *Resisting Reading Mandates: How to Triumph with the Truth* (2002). Then ask districts and companies who are using decodable texts—and also the federal government: Where is the research supporting this? Will kids really enjoy a steady diet of these textual manipulations? Can kids even make sense of them? Are they fun? Interesting?

I have an idea. Rather than structuring texts by chopping them into those senseless decodable pieces, why don't we scaffolders simply *adjust our support, but keep the text meaningful*?

Grade-Level Mediation Differences

Viewing my first set of scaffolding videos, which were collected from grades K–2, I observed a remarkable difference in mediation tactics among grade levels. The most involved sustaining teacher mediation seemed to be offered primarily to younger or less capable students. When a kindergartner experienced some confusion within the reading process, the teacher would waltz right through with the child, sometimes interrupting after an error was made, but at other times saving the child before he even stumbled.

For example, when one little boy read, "Do you like animals?" instead of "Do you like elephants?" the teacher retroactively mediated, "Oh, does that look like *animals*?" (*pointing to the word*).

"It's a long word like *animals*, but it doesn't start the same way," she explained, trying to focus the kindergartner on the word's configuration and initial sound.

But then, as the child began again, "Do you like—" the teacher joined right in with the reader to cue in a proactive manner, "El—" to which the child responded, "Elephants!"

"Uh-huh," reinforced the teacher.

On the other hand, the second-grade students most often received only brief, *corrective feedback*, that is, their teachers corrected *after* an error. For instance, when a second grader read, "sticky" for "sickly" the teacher used retroactive feedback to supply the correct word. Another teacher of second grade allowed the youngster to finish the paragraph after a miscue. She then went back to correct the miscued part. Sustaining feedback was seldom used.

This reliance on corrective feedback seemed to be age specific, because it rarely occurred in kindergarten and first grade. Thus, it was during those first days of my initial study that I began to realize the differences between the ways in which teachers scaffold novices and the ways in which they scaffold more fluent readers.

Another noticeable difference was in the tone of each event. At the kindergarten level there seemed to be more celebration of success. The event was reminiscent of the way that babies learn oral language. These teachers seem to convey an abundance of reassurance, response, and lightheartedness. The children, in turn, mirrored their teachers' behaviors; that is, they were not as serious and appeared to be having fun (however, this was before No Child Left Behind with its higher levels of kindergarten accountability). On one delightful tape, a little girl stopped midsentence to say, "I'm a monkey, too!" I still have to smile just thinking about it.

So it is that teachers scaffold novices more often. They sometimes catch a reader before she falls, and sometimes come in afterward to help pick up the pieces and put them together again. Yet, the scaffolding usually occurs in one seamless flow—a dancing dyad with each partner intuitively accommodating and responding to the other. Not all reading relationships are smooth-flowing, but the ones that are trade leads like a seamless and sensitive ballet.

Reading Relationships, a Key to Learning

This chapter has described both the changes that occur in early literacy development as well as the evolving act of scaffolding that accompanies those changes. Responding to such change supports and nurtures a reading relationship. Teachers need to *read* their students' cues as well as the text being used. Students *read* the teacher's feedback and feedforward cues as well as the text they are using. Optimally, such reading relationships will ignite the flames of learning.

In this chapter I define teacher scaffolding, but to a great extent, I have circumvented the system of cues that readers themselves use to move through text. These are exceedingly important, because they are also related to the cues the teacher provides in her scaffolding. Therefore, in Chapter 2 we investigate those cues that all readers use as they navigate text.

Grist for Discussion

The following has happened to the majority of primary teachers: New student Marita was assigned to your room just three short weeks ago. It's been a busy time since she arrived, what with school pictures, snowstorm, and play practice. For no reason that you know of, Marita's mom makes an appointment to come in and "discuss something with you." This mom wears a look of concern as she enters the room and sits down across from you at a low table. After the usual amenities, Marita's mom says, "Marita is bringing books home. She seems to love them, but I don't think she's actually reading them. She has them all memorized. I'm worried she is going to fail because she *can't* read. She's faking."

What would you tell Marita's mom?

Chapter 2
The Cues Readers Use

A new way of looking, a new vantage point to look from, a new orientation in harmony with reality and suddenly we can see that the greatest significance is in things we never noticed that have been right there all the time.

KEN GOODMAN, QUOTED IN F. GOLLASCH, *LANGUAGE AND LITERACY*

What Are Cues?

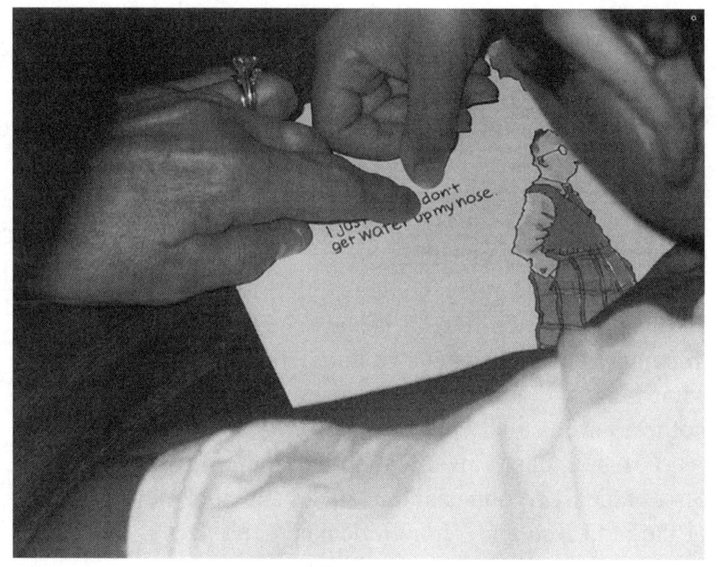

Cues are the signs that help us navigate our worlds. A stop sign is a cue. So is a school bell, the smell of hot bread, or the taste of lemon juice. Human beings make decisions and learn through a system of available signs or cues—visual, auditory, olfactory, kinesthetic, tactile, and gustable. Those signs and symbols in the world around us give meaning and direction to our thinking and actions. In a (rather large) nutshell, cues are everything, everybody, everywhere, and everywhen—all of which affect and evoke our emotions, and thus our intentions. Indeed, we are all cued by the world around us.

Time, place, tools, past experience, and the company in our midst make an enormous difference related to the way in which we read the world's cues. Take golf, for instance. Playing with a pessimist is far different from playing with an optimist. The cues presented from a wet and muddy terrain are far afield from those of a manicured, lush, just-right course. Tall grass cues some players to use a specific iron; whereas, they reach for a putter as they approach the smoother, flatter area surrounding the hole. The scream of a gull can be an unwelcome cue to a golfer; however, the gentle back pat of a supportive friend can evoke the kind of just-right emotion that breeds success.

Reading relationships have much in common with those of golf. Transacting with a pessimistic teacher along muddy text terrain in a noisy, confused environment provides myriad cues, all of which might deter a novice. Correspondingly, in reading relationships the entire classroom, including the attitudes within it, cue emotions and intentions—both those of the teacher and those of the learner.

What Are Miscues?

Sometimes we overlook cues, or we mistake a cue for something else. We think the ground before us is level; we overlook its lumps and bumps. As a consequence, our golf ball goes around the hole, rather than into it, and we log it as a stroke, for there are no second chances in golf.

Readers do the same thing. They overuse, underuse, and abuse cues. When they do this they sometimes *miscue*. This is the term that replaced *error* some decades ago, when Ken Goodman (1967, 1969, 1973) did extensive research on reader cues and the ways in which readers miscue or misread. Early in his career Goodman began using miscue analysis to help construct a valid reading model. He observed how readers, just as scientists, predict and then validate their hypotheses. They do this by collecting clues or cues. This is what drew Goodman (Gollasch 1982) to call reading a "psycholinguistic guessing game"; that is, readers make informed hypotheses as scientists do, drawing from their extensive understanding of what language is and how it works. These hypotheses are actually predictions.

For an in-depth investigation into these processes I highly recommend the articles and books of the both Ken and Yetta Goodman (see references). Miscue is an inseparable aspect of reading relationships, so this book will incorporate that concept. It is frequently such miscues that cue teachers to scaffold, and noticing the specific kind of miscue can more directly guide that response.

That's why miscues are not only important to the reader, they are also valuable information to the teacher who is cueing that reader. In other words, these signs provide direction for scaffolding and instruction, similar to the way in which a novice golfer's miscues would provide information to a golf instructor.

What are these cues that readers sometimes miscue? On what cues should we focus when scaffolding novices? What is the relationship among the cueing systems? How can teachers help kids follow important cues? Let's begin to answer those questions in this chapter by investigating some of the most important cues used by readers. Then, in later chapters, we'll investigate the cues used by the teachers as they scaffold (or support) readers into higher levels of performance.

Three Cueing Systems Plus One

It is common for reading textbooks to focus on three cueing systems: *semantic* or meaning cues, *syntactic* or grammar cues, and *graphophonic* or symbol-sound cues. All are linguistic cues, because each is a part of our language system. Peter Duckett (2003) and Paulson and Freeman (2003) studied the cueing systems through eye movement photography. Their work is fascinating and informs us quite clearly of the points of eye fixation (the cues) that all readers use as they move through the text.

The Validating Data from Eye Movement Research

This eye movement research also validates Marie Clay's (1985) work related to *cross-checking*. Clay explains that throughout the reading act, as readers construct a meaningful text, they are instantaneously cross-checking the various available cues from all systems. Mature readers do this proficiently, and we need to lead novices toward such behaviors.

Duckett (2002) and Paulson and Freeman (2003) explain how their myriad photographs provide reader cueing evidence, that is, where exactly readers' eyes travel and fixate during the process to find cues. Duckett (2003) describes it as follows:

> *Graphophonic*—readers' eye movements within individual words tell me that they are sampling graphophonically and that they are engaged in internal analysis.

Syntactic—readers' regressive and progressive eye movements across word boundaries (i.e., syntactic boundaries) tell me that they are using this cueing system.

Semantics—readers' eye movements primarily focused on content words and major meaning-carrying elements in pictures as well as movements between these major meaning-carriers tells me that they are using this cueing system.

Eye movement research should satisfy the incredulity of those who debate the concept of the cueing systems. By actually watching where an individual's eyes travel as reading occurs, we all can understand that graphophonics, syntax, and semantics play important parts in the reading act. It's right there on film!

An Overlooked Cue

After many long hours observing teacher-scaffolding videotapes, I watched one more very influential cueing system fall into the limelight. That frequently overlooked system of cues is called *pragmatics.* It can be less linguistic in nature, yet very relevant to the learning process. Pragmatic cues include all environmental, human relationship, and textual influences.

Although pragmatics has been investigated by many (Peirce [in Bernstein] 1965; Halliday 1975, 1978; Harste and Burke 1977; Harste, Woodward, and Burke 1984), this important area is most often shunned during cueing discussions and research. As a matter of fact, the federal government's National Reading Panel (1999) not only circumvented the influence of pragmatic cues, they also neglected the semantic and syntactic. Instead, they focused primarily on *alphabetics*, that is, *phonics* and its portended predecessor, *phonemic awareness*, devoting about half of the document's pages to only this part of a far greater whole. The *graphics* and the *phonics* (*graphophonics*) of the reading process are indeed obvious and important aspects. However, to neglect the other systems in the reading relationship is to eliminate the meaning of reading itself.

To focus only on sounding out words in beginning reading is analogous to focusing only on what it looks and sounds like when the club hits the golf ball, when a mountain climber's toe finds the right crevice, when a dancer concentrates only on steps without the accompanying music. In other words, although these pieces of the process are important, there is a lot more going on—a whole lot more!

Nevertheless, ability in phonics is easy to measure; whereas, many of the other cues that readers are using almost defy measurement. How do we measure the affect of an angry teacher, a noisy classroom, a meaningless text, a dull environment? Yet these cues also influence reading relationships—sometimes more than phonics. Indeed, cues are myriad and influential.

The box below offers some common cues that can influence a novice's progress.

Cueing in Action

Now let's observe the ways in which one teacher incorporates some of these cues into her scaffolding. Her novice is reading a Mercer Mayer Little Critter text when she stumbles on the sentence "Mom was too busy so I said I'll take her." The word *busy* with its irregular sounds was beyond this child's decoding abilities, so she stops dead in her tracks.

Wisely, the teacher offers a semantic-syntactic cue: "Why don't you skip it and go on and then we can come back to it?"

The novice implements the strategy to reread, "Mom was too *blank* so I said I'll take her." Throughout the reread-and-skip strategy the teacher continues to support this reader by silently pointing to each word as the child reads.

The Four Cueing Systems

Graphophonic (G)	**Syntactic (S)**	**Semantic (S)**	**Pragmatic (P)**
consonant sounds	fluency	meanings	environmental influences
vowel sounds	cohesion	sense	teacher relationship
word structure/parts	grammar/structure	prior knowledge	textual influences
	punctuation		

Then, just as the reader finishes, the teacher prompts with another semantic-syntactic (S-S) cue: "What do you think? Mom was too what?"

"Busy," correctly decodes the child.

"Excellent!" the teacher celebrates, and then she interjects one more semantic picture cue: "As you can see, Mom is working right there." The teacher points to Mom and then starts to turn the page as she adds, "You did a nice job figuring out that word." She then slips in a one-sentence summary-review, which becomes the introduction for the next page, "So Critter is going to take his sister because Mom is so busy." And the reader reads on.

It's obvious when kids are in a comfortable place.

Slipping these mini–strategy lessons in and around the oral reading of connected text is important for novice readers; they need a close and connected encounter. It's a view from the inside, a fundamental way in which they can learn how language works.

This teacher steered clear of graphophonic scaffolding related to this reader's miscue—probably because the letter sounds in the unknown word, *busy*, were quite irregular. Just as this teacher did, most scaffolders do readily implement all cueing systems. Yet the cueing system that weaves this entire novice scaffolding event into a smooth and successful whole is frequently overlooked. It is even neglected in most reading course-work and texts, so educators are far more familiar with these first three systems, yet it is the fourth, pragmatics, that actually sets the event in motion and then keeps it going. So let's investigate this important cueing system first.

The Pragmatic (P) Cueing System

Every reading relationship is rife with pragmatic cues emanating from three major domains: (1) the entire surrounding environment (field), (2) the emotional relationships involved (tenor), and (3) aspects of the particular reading medium (text) being used (mode) (Halliday 1975). It would be difficult for anyone—even the National Reading Panel—to argue that these three areas have no impact on learning to read—or learning in other areas, for that matter.

A Comfortable Relationship with the Place

First of all, just walking into a classroom gives one a sense of its invitation to learning. Is it brightly lit? Is it organized? Quiet? Crowded? Noisy? Is there an intrusion every few minutes? Is the work of children displayed with honor and respect? Is it a creative or one-right-answer, fill-in-the-blank place? All of these environmental elements shade and hue each student's emotions and intentions; but, so do the social interactions involved.

A Comfortable Relationship with the Teacher

Human relationships drive every transaction (Dewey 1949; Halliday 1975; Bruner 1986). Voice, gestures, touch, eye contact, and response patterns can enhance or hinder relationships. This prompts us to ask some relevant questions: Does a child feel comfortable with his peers? Is the relationship between the teacher and the student warm and friendly, strict and removed, apprehensive and guarded, interesting and motivating? It is a fact of life that our relationships impact everything we do, the spirit in which we respond, and the choices that we make. If students are disinterested, fearful,

Comfortable teacher-reader relationships are obvious, too!

unhappy, bored, or anxious, their emotions will limit their intentions, the reading relationships, and thus learning.

To ignore emotions is just plain foolish. For centuries philosophers and scientists (Dewey 1949; Buber 1970; Grinder and Bandler 1976; Csikszentmihaly 1990; Capra 1996) have told us that our emotions drive our intentions. This means that, for optimal learning, students need to feel comfortable and positive about their reading experiences, so that their intentions are focused and they are self-motivated. We've all been in situations with others in which we were uncomfortable, anxious, or even fretful. Most of the time in such situations, our responses are less than optimal. We shun involvement, begrudgingly respond, and often blunder. This happens in reading relationships, too. For this reason, it's important to consider the ways in which the human relationships in any learning situation affect a learner.

A Comfortable Relationship with the Book

The third pragmatics area, the relationship between the textual medium and the reader, is a rather obvious part of the reading process and one we've already mentioned. That is, whether we hand a beginning reader *Brown Bear, Brown Bear* or *Charlie and the Chocolate Factory* will make a considerable difference in that child's response. It's quite obvious that putting everyone in the same book reading the same story, regardless of individual interests and abilities, would no doubt disrupt many reading relationships.

There are obvious aspects of text that contribute to textual differences (Routman 2003; Cole 1998). When scaffolding novices, it's important to consider these carefully.

When I was scaffolding four-year-old Odette, so that Patrick, her dad, could capture a cover photo for this book, I invited her to share a couple of her own books first. Odette could not match speech to print yet, so she wanted me to read for us. Later I shared *My Home*, a repetitive, one-sentence-per-page Wright Group book, gradually inviting Odette into the process. Eventually, I invited her to point, and not suprisingly, she fell into wordness. Some of Patrick's photos capture that *aha*—her joy.

Elements That Influence Text Difficulty

- genre,
- topic,
- content and characters,
- author familiarity,
- vocabulary,
- white space,
- font style and size,
- sentence length,
- sentence juncture placement,
- illustration support
- book length,
- book size,
- title,
- cover,
- and even popularity of the book.

Textual relationships shine through loud and clear.

Two weeks later, Odette is still reading the two little repetitive books I shared with her. Alison, her mom, said, "But she still only reads those two books. She won't try any of ours." I responded, "She will, she will. But until then, let me get her some more really easy ones." Text makes the difference.

They even affect adult reading relationships. For example, before taking a lengthy plane trip I sometimes select a book with fewer pages, fairly large print, and lots of white space. Of course, the title precludes those intentions in importance. Many individuals primarily enjoy magazines with lots of white space, pictures, and less print on a page. We all have textual relationships that are driven by our tastes and intentions. When I say, "I like Ann Lamott's, Margaret Wheatley's, or Wallie Lamb's books," it means those authors' books evoke an emotion of pleasure in me. I choose their books because I am captured by their style or wit or mindfulness. My emotions drive my intentions, which in turn direct my text selection and also help scaffold the reading process. Thus, I zip right through them, almost obsessed.

We all have our likes and dislikes. And as my mom always said, "You can catch more bees with honey than with vinegar!" A honey of a text would therefore be a positive relationship influence.

In the preceding, I have offered but a smattering of the pragmatics realm; however, Chapters 4 and 7 share far more. Its impact will be most obvious when we investigate how, specifically, teachers use pragmatic relationship cues. However, at this early point in the book, it is just important to understand that environmental, human relationship, and text cues are ever-present variables that every good teacher considers, but that seldom get measured by researchers—sometimes aspects that count the most are the ones that defy being counted. Quantifiable or not, the pragmatic cueing system remains an integral part of the entire system.

It's now time to investigate the other three cueing systems. However, we will do this from two perspectives, a micro or local and a macro or global.

Micro and Macro Processing: The Short and Long Drive for Meaning

Although preword readers might not even look at the words in a book, transitioning novices begin to notice them. It's all about noticing. So as novices learn to notice more, they begin to focus on those units of letters that we call words. Sooner or later, word-by-word reading begins, just as it did for Odette. This focus on each *word unit* in its *micro context* can be called *micro processing,* a decoding act that is driven by *semantic, syntactic*, and *graphophonic cues*.

On the other hand, fluent readers focus on the *macro level* using *macro processing*, an act that takes in phrases, sentences, and paragraphs, the substance from which global understandings are constructed (Irwin 1991). They only get caught up in micro processing when they encounter an inconsistency at the macro level. Whereas proficient micro processing is driven by micro strategies, proficient macro processing is driven by *comprehension strategies*. These global understandings that unfold via the macro level can be thwarted by too much emphasis on pieces and parts at the micro level. Let's see why.

Micro Processing: How Novices Use Graphophonics to Decode

Graphophonic cues are part of the micro content of text. They are local cues within words themselves. These letter-sound cues function far from the macro context, yet they still maintain an influential relationship to the whole.

What Is Graphophonics (G)?

Graphophonics is a sign system that helps readers decode sounds through their letter relationships (that is, graphics and phonics). Our English orthography uses an alphabetic writing system whose symbols we learn to read. And merely recognizing those alphabet letters appears to have a strong correlation with beginning reading success (National Reading Panel 1999; Adams 1990; Anderson et al. 1984); however, knowing the names of tennis maneuvers does not a tennis player make. Likewise, knowing the alphabet does not a reader make. Letter knowledge is but one graphic cue; there are many more that influence the act of reading.

Our English orthography attaches sound cues to alphabet letter patterns (for example, st-, -oy, -ing). Along with the applications of these graphophonic patterns, novices must learn to construct micro-contextual syntactic congruent understandings (semantics), which, as the text unfolds, must align with its more macro-contextual, wholistic meanings. That is, youngsters must learn to look at the particularities of words, apply sound patterns, and construct an appropriate semantic connection, which must also align with syntax, as well as the greater context of that text.

Whew! That's one complex process, isn't it? Yet, most all of the first graders whom Linda and I taught to read caught on within about three months. So as I wander through graphophonics and the rest of the micro processess, I beg that you remember, *there is definitely a magical side to this complex process.*

Configuration-Reading

We know that English orthography has a relationship with sounds, yet it's important to understand that there are indeed some written language systems in this world where readers use *only* the graphics; that is, such systems have no sound-symbol relationship. Chinese and Japanese are examples of such ideographic (picture-symbol) systems. Nevertheless, kids learn to read the thousands of nonphonetic graphics of these literate countries. But perhaps the English are a bit more cue fortunate, in that we have an extra cue to use—sounds.

Similar to students in Japan, preword readers sometimes know a word by its looks, its graphic form, rather than by its sounds. They may even learn quite a few words by their *configuration* (word shape and and length). Research demonstrates that preword readers first cue into word length (Adams 1990; Rozen, Bressman, and Taft 1974) and the context into which these groups of letters are embedded (Masonheimer, Drum, and Ehri 1984), which is probably what Odette was doing. When they do begin to notice particular letter composites; it is still some time before graphophonics is operationalized.

Moreover, the more kids concentrate on letters, the less they concentrate on words; and the more they concentrate on individual words, the less they concentrate on phrases and sentences. Our intention is always to move them toward the meaning that is captured not in individual letters or individual words, but in the unfolding macro meanings packaged in larger chunks of text.

Reciprocol Writing: Scaffolding Speech-to-Print

Scaffolders use writing opportunities to nudge preword writers toward word writing. At first, these preword writers use pictures to get their messages across. To pull these young illustrators into the message system of written words, scaffolders invite, "Tell me about your picture," and later, "What do you want me to write for your picture?" Only a few written words are best scribed at first—no more than two or three.

All it takes is this gentle invitation with its follow-up scribing to scaffold preword writers toward words. Sooner or later, that preword writer will begin to ask the scaffolder to write transcriptions for new pictures. At first, this preword writer will not understand the speech-to-print match. Yet, as the scaffolder continues to say each (complete, not segmented) word as it's written, the preword writer/reader comes to understand the connection between spoken and written speech, that is, wordness, and thus moves closer to word writing and word reading.

Accumulating an Initial Sight Vocabulary

As these preword readers transition into a greater awareness of the particularities in individual words, they begin to develop an *initial sight vocabulary.* This recognized list of words is of utmost importance, because "being able to read even a few preprimer words enables beginners to remember how to read individual words in the text" (Ehri and Sweet 1991, p. 456). Furthermore, "phonemic awareness seems to develop alongside [readers'] word recognition skills" (Adams 1990). A hefty automatic sight vocabulary will support the generalization of sound patterns. That is, as novices collect whole words they begin to make analogic connections among their parts—to notice that *zoo*, *bathroom*, and *boo* all possess the same sound for double *O*.

Ultimately, novices do begin to use our English sound-symbol relationships—a realization that, for a brief time, seems to focus readers into painstakingly attending to the print, pointing carefully and meticulously focusing on each word. Thus, these transitioning preword readers no longer "read with their eyes closed."

As they become more familiar with the process, the more spontaneous it becomes—so much so that a mere glance may provide all the cues a reader needs to flow easily through the text. And someday, those novices will be fluent readers, able to read one hundred to two hundred words per minute. But not at first.

Using Graphophonic Cues

There are many kinds of graphophonic cues—*sound-symbol relationships*—that support both adult and novice readers. For instance, when adults encounter a strange term, they slow down and look for parts of that word that match known word chunks and then they transfer that to the new word. Thus, if a skilled reader (such as yourself) comes across the term "beglough," she might first focus on the prefix "be." (What did *you* focus on?) Observing the remainder of the sound-letter relationships, she may decide that maybe the second syllable rhymes with "tough." (Is that what you did?) Knowing this, she slides through both syllables accenting maybe the second. However, with no conception of that word's meaning, she may never know if her phonic assumptions matched appropriately. (And neither will you because I invented the word!)

Novices attempt unknown words in a similar, but less mature fashion. That is, they often focus only on the initial consonant cue. And don't be surprised if they omit the medial sounds, especially in multisyllable words. On the other hand, many novices, who may have overexperienced the "Sound it out!" cue, sometimes sound through each and every letter individually, using a kind of "tunnel vision" (Smith 1994, p. 80), which then distorts the word into a lengthy series of grunts and barks. They say, "I-m-p-o-r-t-a-n-t," and by the time that they get to the end they have no clue what all that noise was about.

Just as in learning any new skill, novice readers rarely get it right without lots of experience. But by applying new strategies to a variety of texts novices begin to understand more about how the process works at the same time that they acquire an ever-increasing automatic vocabulary. All of this provides grist for more sophisticated graphophonic pattern recognition.

Graphophonic Patterns: Micro Cues That Readers Use

Earlier in this chapter, a condensed list of influences was presented as The Four Cueing Systems. Under graphophonics three major categories were listed: consonant sounds, vowel sounds, and word parts/chunks/structures. The graphophonic categories can be further defined in subcategory lists, each of which demonstrates particular sound-symbol patterns.

The box on page 23 provides a kind of overview for some of the English sound patterns. Their utility will be discussed after the list and will include those that warrant the most attention.

I love lists! Most teachers do. But don't let this one fool you! Before you take out your plan book or lay this page on the copying machine let me share a bit of research related to the utility of these different cues. Then we can decide which ones should be pulled out and used during scaffolding and which should just be left in the list.

It is important to know that "out of the 150 most frequent words in English, only 14 follow the sound-symbol generalizations that might be taught during first grade" (Adams 1990, p. 108). Therefore, for the grand majority of words, which might include *there*, *could*, *little*, and *one*, it is best for novices to focus on consonants, which are far more reliable than vowels (Adams 1990).

Graphophonic Cue Patterns

Sound Patterns	Type	Examples
Consonant Patterns	• initial (onset) consonant sounds	b-, t-, m-, f-
	• final consonant sounds	-d, -m, -p, -x
	• medial consonants	-c-, -g-, -l-, -n-
	• blended consonant sounds	pl-, str-, -nd, -lt
	• consonant digraphs	-ch-, -th-, -sh-, -ph-
	• silent consonants	know, night, gnaw
Vowel Patterns	• short vowel sounds, one-syllable words (CVC))(VC)	pan, in
	• long vowel sounds, one-syllable words (CVVC) (CVCe)	feed, bike
	• r-controlled vowels (__r)	bird, hurt, car, for, her,
	• vowel digraphs	rain, blue
	• vowel diphthongs	boy, cow, out
	• schwa (unaccented vowel)	again, conceal, apple
Blended and Unblended Patterns	• silent vowels (or markers)	made, see, road
	• irregular vowels	look, all, my
	• consecutive unblended sounds	i-m-p-or-t-a-n-t
	• consecutive blended sounds	important
Word Chunks or Structures	• rimes (phonograms; families)	-ill, -an, -op, -ed, -un
	• little words inside big words	yesterday
	• inflectional endings (-ed, -ing, -s)	going, walked, sits
	• compound words	dog/house, down/town
	• prefixes and suffixes (pre-, -ful)	untie, hopeless
	• roots/morphologic structures (bio-, -port)	bicycle, importation
	• open syllables (end in vowel) and closed syllables (end in consonant) in multisyllabic words	pro-tect, in-stead

Consonants Hold a Scaffolding (G) Priority

Yes, readers rely primarily on consonants. This is no doubt because "the mapping from single consonants to phonemes tends to be one-to-one . . . [whereas] vowels are rampantly irregular in the English writing system" (Adams 1990, p. 76). And short vowels are especially difficult to learn (Carnine and Silbert 1979). As a matter of fact, phonics so seldom works the same way in different words that many now call phonics rules *generalizations*. For instance, the popular "two vowels go walking" generalization was found to work only 45 percent of the time (Clymer 1963). We'll discuss this more in Chapter 8.

Yet, the consonants are fairly dependable in their sound relationships. Perhaps that is why consonants help to graphophonically guide us as readers—primarily the first and last consonant in words, that is. Reading "What's Important for Reading?" on page 24 will help demonstrate this to you.

Obviously, this could have been made much more difficult by including fewer high-frequency, as well as more multisyllable words. Nevertheless, this little example demonstrates the importance of consonants, especially initial and final ones. We can do almost anything we want with internal vowels, and still be able to read most common words. This makes consonants, especially in the initial and final positions, a high scaffolding priority.

Rimes Hold a Scaffolding (G) Priority

Fluent readers use primarily onsets and rimes to decode unknown words (Adams 1990). You do. I do. We search for known chunks in unknown words, and those chunks are usually onsets and

What's Important for Reading?

I hread a rperot taht siad it deons't mttaer waht odrer a wrdo's ltetres are in,
but as lnog as the frsit and lsat ltetres of wrdos are lfet in the rghit sopt,
you wlil sitll be albe to raed the sntecne.
Taht is, deirvn by mnaineg, we tkae in wlohe wrdos,
and pay aettneison to the bgeninnig and end.

rimes. No doubt that is how you decoded *beglough* earlier in this chapter.

There are hundreds of common rimes or phonograms, but five hundred primary-grade words can be derived from just thirty-five of the most common (Durrell and Wylie 1963). It seems profitable, then, to focus particularly on these, especially during scaffolding (see list below).

These rimes are of high utility because of their generalizability—especially in primary books. This means that almost every time a novice runs into one of these, he can count on its sound remaining stable. This, therefore, makes them a high scaffolding priority.

So there you have the graphophonic priorities. Obviously, scaffolders will from time to time mention little words in big words, compound words (which are actually little words in a big word), inflectional endings and affixes; however, the main priorities with novices are consonants (especially onset consonants) and rimes.

Cueing Conservation: Readers Use Only What's Needed

However, we use these graphophonic elements *just* to the extent that meaning is satisfied. That is, we may only decode one chunk of a multisyllable word when we realize what the word is, because we received cues from the other cueing systems, which were working in harmony supporting the graphophonic system. That is, as science demonstrates, we use only that which is needed to make meaning (Paulson and Freeman 2003; Duckett 2003).

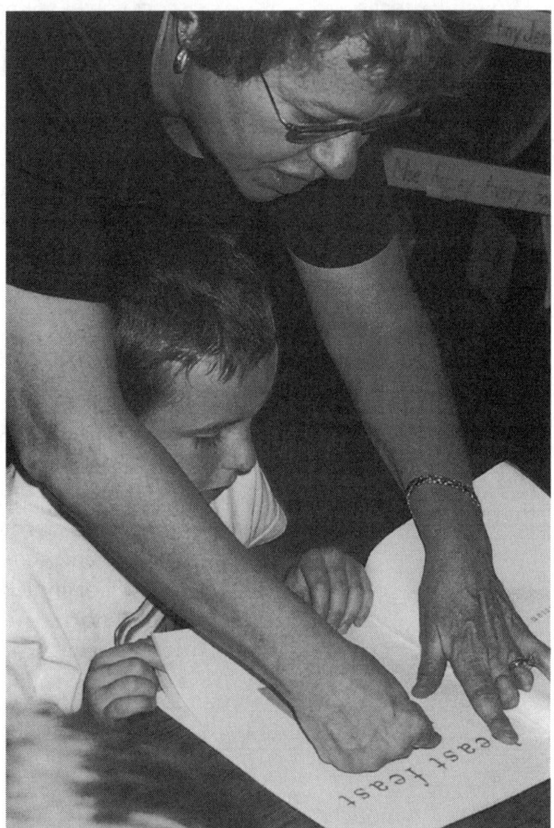

Linda masks the onset to scaffold the rime for her novice.

Furthermore, we want readers to use graphophonic cues with sense and synchronicity. I use the term *synchronicity* here because readers need to have several *cross-checking* (Clay 1993) intentions at the same time: to make meaning, to stay in flow

High Priority Rimes

-ack	-all	-ain	-ake	-ale	-ame	-an
-ank	-ap	-ash	-at	-ate	-aw	-ay
-eat	-ell	-est	-ice	-ick	-ide	-ight
-ill	-in	-ine	-ing	-ink	-ip	-ir
-ock	-oke	-op	-ore	-or	-uck	-ug
-ump	-unk					

with English grammar, as well as to follow the word's graphophonic clues. They need to synchronistically move from one to the other, cross-checking. Again, we have to admit that such a complex process seems pretty magical!

Micro Processing: How Novices Use Semantics and Syntax to Decode

When a novice reader is first attempting to decode unrehearsed text, his focus is at the word or even letter level because his reading is not proficient enough to capture larger textual *chunks*; that is, phrases or sentences. These young novices consciously fixate on each and every word as they grow out of the preword stage. Throughout this early act of decoding, their body and head movements, as well as their pointing behaviors, demonstrate word-by-word fixations.

What Are Semantic-Syntactic (S-S) Cues?

I am going to combine meaning (semantics) and grammar (syntax), because they are so interdependent that one affects the other. For example, let's consider the sentence *The boy ran up the* ____, using a cloze (completion) technique. Years of experience in listening to and speaking English cues us to predict that either an adjective or a noun would fit nicely into the blank. Thus, if a reader decodes the final word as *hill*, it makes sense to him, both syntactically and semantically. However, if the reader decodes the final word as *hoping*, it should not make sense to him. That is, it should disturb his internalized sense of grammar and meaning, because grammar influences meaning. That is, confuse the syntactic order in a sentence and it often will not make sense. With semantic and syntactic cues so closely related, it's just easier to combine them.

Yet there are also times when the syntax vested in the miscue is acceptable, but yet the word's meaning cues that it is incorrect. That is, if a reader read *The boy ran up the home*, his sense of semantics tells him, "That sentence did not make sense!" And that sense of meaning drives everything we do. It evokes a feeling of security and confidence. It tells us that we can keep going because there is nothing to question—as long as it all makes sense.

The Impact of Meaning on Sounds: An Interdependent Relationship

All reading relationships begin with meaning. A reader may know the meaning of a word, yet be unable to decode it. For example, sometimes novice readers substitute a meaningful word for the one in question, that is, if the word is *puppy*, the child may substitute *dog*. We all substitute to some degree when we read, but basically, reading means accurately identifying words while at the same time constructing textual meanings. These are the inseparable attributes of the act of reading, that is, *we decode for meaning*.

Let's again use foreign language to understand this idea. Visitors to Spain or Mexico may predict meaning through other cues (pictures, objects, and so on); for instance, what a store might be selling. Yet, because the sign above the store's door is in Spanish, they cannot read it. They might be able to sound out the letters correctly and guess that it says "ice cream shop" and although that may be an admirable guess, in actuality the sign says "frozen yogurt cafe." Constructing meaning and decoding are inseparable properties of the act of reading. Their relationship synergistically supports the entire process. Neither stands alone.

Novices must therefore learn to cross-check cues, that is, to make certain that the decoded word demonstrates a semantic match. Readers must internalize this checking system that repeatedly asks, "Does this decoded word fit with the meaning of what I am reading?" and "Does this decoded word fit with the graphics I see on the page?"

Word-Level Semantic Strategies

As novices process locally, that is, one word at a time, they come to understand that the letters and their sounds are not the only thing involved in reading. Even more important is whether each word makes sense within its local context of phrase, sentence, or picture. They therefore learn to use semantic-syntactic strategies within that context that will provide a semantic match for their graphophonic cues. The following demonstrates some of the semantic micro processes that readers use:

Micro-Contextual Semantic Strategies

- Check the picture.
- Reread for a running start.
- Skip, read on, and then reread the sentence.

Word-by-word readers need these micro cues to make immediate semantic matches—ones that help carry word readers more efficiently through text. It is obvious that, for word-by-word readers, there is much going on at the micro level—too much to be able to simultaneously incorporate the macro context. For the further they travel into the micro context, the further away from the macro they move. Thus, a focus on letter-by-letter decoding takes novices far, far away from the macro meanings of the text!

On the other hand, word-level strategies do *not* completely ignore the macro context. Yet during this early period, meaning can get anchored at the local level. This taxes short-term memory, which can only hold around seven pieces of information at one time (Miller 1956), and when these information units are only word chunks, rather than larger phrase or sentence chunks, text comprehension is challenged (Schreiber 1980). It is little wonder, then, that scientific eye movement photography shows that novices who are striving to make fast semantic matches lean heavily upon picture cues (Paulson and Freeman 2003; Duckett 2002), a speedy way to grasp the word's context *before* reading the entire phrase or sentence.

Leading Novices Toward Chunking

During the micro process, word-by-word decoders quickly use up chunks of space in short-term memory, and a seven-word store is very different from the more rich and robust phrase and sentence stores of fluent readers. Scaffolders therefore lead word-by-word readers toward *chunking*, that is, sliding through several words at a glance, because until they learn to chunk, macro processing will be difficult. In fact, Irwin (1991) suggests that "To comprehend, readers must be able to *chunk* words into meaningful syntactic units" (p. 32 [italics are mine]).

All of this points to the fact that accurate semantic matches at the word level will *not* necessarily lead to comprehension, because some readers remain planted in the micro context hampered in considering macro meanings. Nevertheless, proficient word-level decoding ultimately relates to chunking and to the mindful processing of lengthier portions of the text—all of which are held in a relationship. Thus, micro-level skill is integral to macro-level processing. Likewise, understanding the whole helps readers decode its parts. It's an *interdependent* relationship.

In this book you will see the ways in which teachers consistently draw readers forward beyond individual words. They seem to have an internal compass that points toward chunking strategies, so that by the end of first grade, we find kids reading in lengthier, meaningful syntactic units instead of individual words. Peter Duckett's (2002) eye movement research of first graders' reading demonstrates this shift away from word-by-word fixations.

Macro Processing: How Novices Use Macro Strategies to Comprehend

As novices continue to reach forward, beyond just word level, eye fixations show that their *perceptual span* increases (Paulson and Freeman 2003), thus enabling macro processing. This process itself ushers readers into fluency. As a matter of scientific fact, Freeman (2001) found that by fourth grade even *fluent bilingual* readers fixate on only 56 percent of the words in their English texts.

Paulsen and Freeman (2003) explain that

> eye movement research clearly shows readers *never* look at every word in a text . . . because they don't *need to* in order to read. And since the brain is concerned with efficiency, it's not about to direct the eyes to look at every word when it's getting the information it needs by actively sampling the text. (p. 3)

When readers do move into this *sampling process* that chunks text into larger pieces, they reduce the number of ideas to be remembered (Irwin 1991). As they mindfully process lengthier units in a more meaningful manner, each short-term-memory information unit becomes more robust so that larger quantities of general information can be held at bay. Readers are therefore not only increasing their perceptual spans, but also paving a more fluent road to comprehending.

Comprehension: A Macro Process

Semantic (micro) matches support macro-level processes, which lead to comprehension, yet they do *not* guarantee it. On the other hand, comprehending unrehearsed text at a macro level almost

> **How Teachers Scaffold Comprehension Strategies**
>
> Comprehension strategies are used at the macro level of text. Such strategies are more apt to involve a paragraph, a page, a section, a chapter, or even an entire story. For optimal comprehension students need to learn how to:
>
> - ask questions of the text and its author,
> - make connections to events, characters, etc.,
> - visualize, image, or reenact parts of text,
> - siphon out the important ideas,
> - make inferences backed by evidence,
> - summarize and synthesize sections of text.
>
> (Pressley 2000; Pinnell 2002; Harvey and Goudvis 2000; Keene and Zimmerman 1997; Pearson et al. 1992; Irwin 1991)

certainly guarantees that the semantic matches were in place at the micro level. This means that most words need to make sense at the micro level in order for sentences and paragraphs to make sense at the macro level.

Accordingly, Pinnell (2002) suggests there are some strategies that *sustain meaning* and others that *expand meaning*. Those that expand meaning fall in step with macro processing. They are the *comprehension strategies* that will help readers expand meanings and process at that macro-context level. That is why teachers scaffold readers toward such strategies.

Macro Processing: A High Priority

Although micro processing undergirds macro meanings and comprehension, it is only at the macro level that readers come to understand the author's message. For this reason, it is mandatory that, from day one, scaffolders lead novices toward those macro contexts, because the further into the micro we take a novice, the further away from the macro he will be. How do teachers lead readers to the macro and help them comprehend? The remainder of this book helps answer that question.

Metacognitive Behaviors

Most macro processing is driven by reader *metacognition*, that is, "conscious awareness and control of one's own cognitive processes, [which] involves knowing when one does or does not understand something and knowing how to go about achieving a cognitive goal, such as successful comprehension . . ." (Irwin 1991, p. 4). Yet it's fairly obvious that the reader needs to also have a grasp of the micro processes in order to successfully operationalize the macro.

Readers must learn to instantaneously use available cues and strategies to keep meaning intact in both contexts. But when meaning breaks down, metacognitive strategies will help readers recover that meaning.

Self-Correction: An Early Metacognitive Behavior

Some of the first metacognitive behaviors that we observe in novice readers are those related to the *self-correction* of a miscue. This occurs when readers realize that something is not right with their reading, that is, when the text is not unfolding in a meaningful manner. There is, consequently, a causal relationship between meaning and self-correction. When meaning starts to break down, we readers experience a kind of "What-huh!?" Sometimes we push on a little further, but often, rather than continue on, we go back to locate the problem and fix it. We strive to keep meaning intact. When readers do reread, fix the problem, and restore meaning, we say that they have self-corrected. Thus, self-correcting is a laudable behavior. It is something all good readers do. And it is a metacognitive strategy because the reader had to know, first, that something was wrong, and second, how to fix it.

As a matter of fact, for fluent readers like you and I, this self-correction process is so woven into the fabric of our reading that it is barely evident. When we come to an unfamiliar word we usually make a tentative attempt, but then we keep going—unless the meaning starts to suffer. When that happens, a red flag goes up, and we meaning makers realize that our tentative hypothesis needs to be revised. So we either return, reread the sentence correctly, and go on or, while not overtly regressing to revise, revise intuitively as we read on.

When children read, we always want them to understand that a red flag should go up:

- when reading no longer makes sense;
- when reading doesn't sound like language.

And that flag should go up anytime meaning breaks down, in either the micro or the macro context. It is then that a range of strategies can lead novices back to meaning. And it is those strategies that teachers scaffold.

Point-of-Miscue Corrections and Quagmires

For novice, word-by-word readers, the process has a somewhat different slant at first; that is, until novices take ownership of that read-on-and-return strategy, they tend to get mired in the microcosm of point-of-miscue behaviors. Their early decoding of unknown words relies more on the picture and some of the graphophonics; consequently, they may try out a few sounds, or they may test a few words in the slot, or sometimes they just stop dead in their tracks. Novices do not always move on into the macro context, as we do, because they are still too absorbed in the micro. This helps us understand why it's important for teachers to scaffold novices beyond that point-of-miscue quagmire and into a sense of macro meaning, for it is beyond the miscue that the novice can construct enough meaning to make the prior semantic match, that is, to self-correct his miscue.

When Meaning Breaks Down at Point-of-Miscue

Readers who get stuck in point-of-miscue quagmires can be shown how to get themselves out. That's our job as scaffolders. If novices have indeed sought a semantic match for their graphophonic cues, but their cross-checking proves to be unsuccessful, they often realize there is a glitch, but they don't know what to do about it. At times like this, when readers use up all their cross-checking fuel and still end up with a semantic mismatch, they need to be shown how to move beyond that point-of-miscue, to read on. This is a perfect scaffolding opportunity because we can show these novices that, if they read further into the text to gather more meaning they create the potential for a self-correction of that mismatch. In the following chapters scaffolders nudge novices forward by using gesture and voice to lead learners down a self-correction path.

When Meaning Breaks Down Post-Point-of-Miscue

Sometimes, novices have grown beyond becoming mired in the micro. Such readers may be reading along just fine when, suddenly, a "What-huh?!?" occurs. Up pops a red flag, and they say to themselves, "Hey! That part didn't make sense!" For some novices that red flag may be waving vibrantly, but they think reading is just identifying words, an act they feel they've accomplished. Thus, they keep going—with or without meaning. It is then that scaffolders need to step forward and explain that reading is really about making meaning. They can show these novices that retroactive behaviors are indeed part of the process.

Kids need us to demonstrate that reading does not always move forward in a linear manner. Macro-process "what-huhs," along with their accompanying self-correction behaviors, draw us back to the micro context. And that's okay! It's a symbiotic relationship that, at times, makes the reading process *bidirectional* (or actually, multidirectional, if we consider picture cues). Even adults regress to keep meaning intact. Kids need to know this. And to make such a covert process more overt, these self-correction behaviors need to be explicitly demonstrated for novices. Upcoming chapters investigate these scaffolding processes.

A Micro and Macro Summary

Novice readers need all those micro-level semantic matches to build syntactic units leading to macro processing, comprehension, and eventually, the metacognitive behaviors that will make them independent readers. But micro-level semantic matches are not synonymous with comprehension. Both micro and macro processing involve meaning; however, the strategies used for each are different. Scaffolding strategies are defined in Chapter 4 and then play out in the remainder of this book. Teachers who understand these micro-macro strategies are more apt to effectively and efficiently scaffold their novice readers.

A Synergistic Relationship: Keeping the Whole in Harmony

In a nutshell, these are the cues that drive the micro and macro processes—pragmatic, graphophonic, semantic, and syntactic. They maintain a kind of synergistic, dynamic, interdependent relationship wherein each affects the others. What confuses some educators is the fact that 99.9 percent of the miscues made are graphophonic, because—let's face it—if the reader utters the wrong word, *it is not the right word*. It is therefore not an appropriate graphophonic match.

However, that is not the point. The point is that we teachers do not want readers hobbling along on one cueing system when there are others that, when used in tandem and in harmony with graphophonics, can take the novice more rapidly into chunking and fluency.

When we focus on graphophonics to the exclusion of the other cueing systems, we are like an inept foreign traveler who refuses to use gesture when it could help him move his ineffectual grasp of the language toward meaning. Meaning is always our most important goal in any communication, be it written, spoken, read, viewed, or signed. Readers need to make use of every possible sign to construct meaning. Cross-checking that rapidly incorporates all cueing systems leads novices into fluency, but this only occurs when readers are offered daily, sustained reading opportunities using authentic texts.

Successful scaffolders consider the atmosphere in the room, their own relationship with the reader, the text that child is reading, the letters and their sounds in the story, how the reading relates to the structure of our language, and, very important, the way in which meaning unfolds. This means we teachers have to be a kind of one-person jazz band, learning how to fade in and out when needed, but also using the appropriate instrument each time. Sometimes, we come in with a graphophonic toot, sometimes a semantic-syntactic melody, while other times a small word of praise keeps the flow going. But our main goal is always to maintain harmony in all reading relationships, for where there is harmony, there is usually meaning.

I've been discussing several kinds of cues, but there are important questions left to be answered. How do teachers teach these cues? What does this teaching look like? Sound like? And when on earth do they get a chance to scaffold *individual* readers? The following chapters describe in detail when, where, and how teachers incorporate these cueing systems into their reading instruction.

Grist for Discussion

Find the miscues and name each one in the following in which a reader was reading the nursery rhyme "Jack and Jill."

Actual text:

> Jack and Jill went up the hill,
> To fetch a pail of water.
> Jack fell down and broke his crown,
> And Jill came tumbling after.

Child's oral reading of (above) Jack and Jill text:

- Jack and Jane went up the hill,
- To catch a pail of water.
- Jack falled down and breaked his head,
- And Jane come tumble afterwards.

Chapter 3

When and Where Teachers Scaffold

Relationships are all there is. Everything in the universe only exists because it is in relationship to everything else. Nothing exists in isolation . . . Today, we live in an unnatural state—separating ourselves rather than being together.

MARGARET J. WHEATLEY,
TURNING TO ONE ANOTHER

One-on-One Reading Relationships?

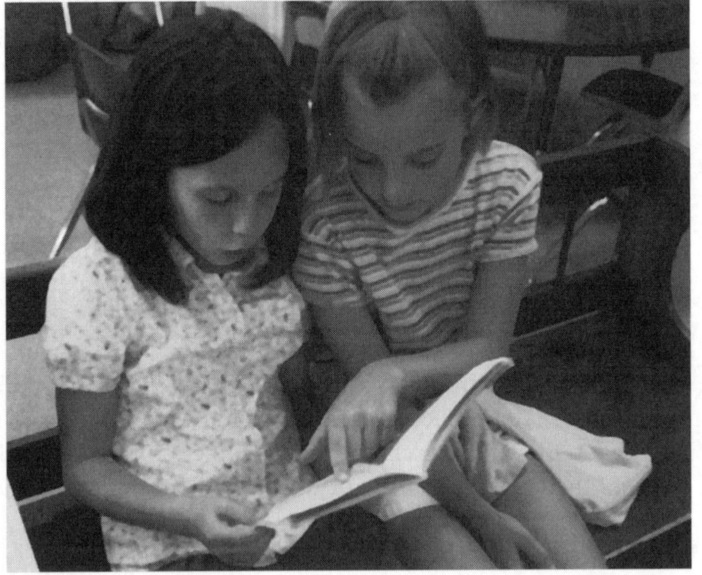

"Are you kidding!" you say. "You want *me*, with no time to fit in all my current curricular needs, to spend one-on-one time with the kids in my class! You gotta be kidding!"

I'm not kidding. But it's not exactly what you think, either. It's not something you write in your plan book. It's just something you do—on-the-fly. Furthermore, it doesn't have to be something that only *you* do, because scaffolding behaviors can be modeled so *others* can scaffold, too. Even kids! No kidding!

Teachers develop reading relationships every time they scaffold a child in reading. All day long we help individual kids when we meet them eye to eye and elbow to elbow. Individual assistance is the core of good teaching.

On-the-Fly Cueing

There are many times during the day when kids are reading that every teacher already individually scaffolds. Sometimes we're walking around the room checking on progress, and we stoop down to facilitate here or there. Other times, we scaffold during a small guided or shared reading group. It's easy to

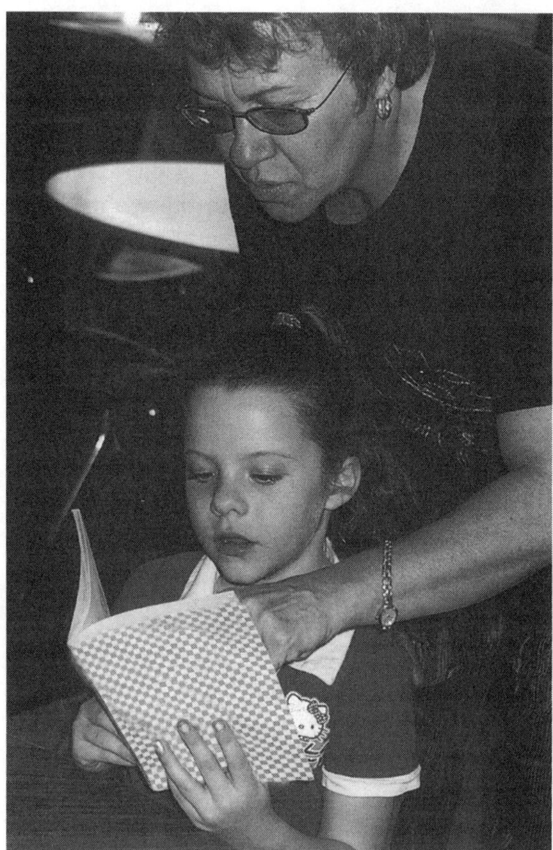

Linda stops to quickly scaffold a reader.

scaffold individuals in small-group settings. Teachers do it unconsciously all the time. Reading and writing are so codependent that when we are conferring with kids about their writing, we are also facilitating reading needs. Throughout the day, there are a multitude of times when every primary teacher already scaffolds readers. Actually, the day is like one long teach-a-thon in which we are continually catering to individual children.

So please do not think scaffolding individuals is like a tutoring pullout program, because it is not. We are not pulling kids aside. We are not writing individual lesson plans. But teachers are doing some of what goes on during programs like reading recovery, even though they may not currently realize it.

Who Sits Down Anyway!?

I had (environmental print) signs all over my room. The one above my desk read, "Mrs. Cole sits here." One day Linda crept into my room and revised it. She put a caret between *sits* and *here* and inserted the word *doesn't*. When I saw it, I knew who the editing culprit was, and when I laughingly asked her about it, she responded, "Well, when do *you* ever sit there?!"

Most teachers do not sit at their desks. We're too busy scaffolding; from the time the kids walk in until the time they leave, we are teaching, teaching, teaching. And most of that teaching is focused on small groups and individuals. That is when we scaffold.

Read-Alouds: A Rich Resource for Scaffolding

There is a great deal of unconscious scaffolding that occurs during every read-aloud. Most is not one-on-one, but is still highly effective. That is why research shows that children who have been read to during their preschool years come better prepared for school reading (Neumann 1999; Adams 1990; Anderson et al. 1984). Quite often we adults do not even realize the impact of our modeling on young learners.

During read-alouds teachers scaffold by demonstrating a variety of behaviors related to the reading act. They are steeping children in the world of books and reading. They demonstrate interest, excitement, questioning the text, book behaviors (such as turning pages), reading behaviors (such as pointing to the words), graphics that contain the message, illustrations that complement and supplement text, as well as many other facets of reading. Expert teachers plan ahead for each day's read-alouds, attempting to weave in specific behaviors that can later be handed over to the listeners. Cunningham and Allington (1994) demonstrate such teacher behaviors in a book related to their expert-teacher study. Its title is apt: *Classrooms That Work*.

In my own work, I have seen a teacher model how to reread to self-correct a miscue when she herself confused some words during a read-aloud. Another teacher used a cloze technique (stopping to let kids fill in the blank), which demonstrated how prediction works.

No wonder almost every notable reading educator advocates daily read-alouds! They are essential scaffolds—especially for those children who do not have such privileges at home.

One-on-One Scaffolding During Reading Groups

Most teachers plan for some kind of small-group instruction, because trying to teach reading to the entire class from the front of the room is somewhat ridiculous—especially for preword readers. The scaffolding that takes place during these small clusters differs between groups and throughout the year. That is, when a teacher scaffolds within the context of a Shared Book Experience (SBE), it looks and sounds different than the way in which she scaffolds within a guided reading context. Let's see why that is.

Scaffolding Preword-Transitioning Readers During Shared Book Experiences

The (SBE) developed by Don Holdaway (1979), presents a method through which readers interact with an adult who, first, model-reads an easy text for them. Once preword and novice readers experience an easy text in this manner, they gravitate toward *reproducing* the act. That is, knowing what the text sounds like, they merely try to reenact what they watched and heard the teacher do. This is a good introduction to the reading act, but it is only that—an introduction.

Most of the initial SBE texts used with preword readers should be very patterned and repetitive like *Brown Bear, Brown Bear* (Martin and Carie 1996)—ones that are easy to remember (Adams 1990). As the teacher initially scaffolds toward the tones, tempos, and meanings of the book, young readers just sing the text aloud without paying much mind to the words. It's a wonderful way to begin a reading relationship with preword readers, for they love mimicking the flow and tempo of the text.

This transition period is always one that is fairly hectic, but I know that unless these preword readers actually focus on the words, they will never learn to read. It's the words that hold the message and to be scaffolded toward such understandings, I want kids to point to the words as we reread SBE books. I work with one small group at a time. The group sits in circle, each child ready to point through a copy of the SBE text, and although we all begin on the same word, it is not long before I am flitting from child to child to scaffold by redirecting the pointing of those who are missing the mark. Exacerbating the confusion is the fact that attention wanes more easily when kids do not understand the task—and at the beginning, preworders certainly do not. This is indeed a period requiring persistence, patience, and very short stories.

Usually we are on the floor, so it's probably pretty comical to watch me crawling around the circle like Road Runner—pointing here, pointing there, redirecting everywhere! Believe me, if there were another way to make certain everyone was focusing on the correct printmatch, I would surely use it. Yet every year, you can find first-grade teachers playing Road Runner for the first few weeks of school. This one-on-one scaffolding experience takes the honors in the Most Hectic category. Perhaps we could try roller skates?

Here I am! The fingerpointing Road Runner!

But these early scaffolding behaviors offered to preword readers who are transitioning into a greater focus on the graphics are often omitted from preservice reading education courses and are, therefore, one of the most difficult imperatives to impress upon student teachers, most of whom just *tell* the kids to point. However, learning the printmatch process takes more than telling; it takes individual scaffolding by showing. Yes, it's hectic, but the results are incredible. Luckily for us, the SBE includes follow-up partnered reading. It's a perfect period for partners to help each other point.

Sometimes, Linda and I have one child point as the other reads. It's fun and the in-tandem pair stay glued to the text. At other times, we invite the reader on the left to point and read the left page, and vice versa for the reader on the right. There are a variety of SBE options that encourage pointing—from the very beginning when the teacher herself models it.

Once kids understand that the print carries the message, they consistently point and look at the words and no longer need much scaffolding in that area. This means that not only will teacher-scaffolding behaviors take on different shades and hues, but the method used for instruction should offer these budding readers more autonomy. That's why it is time to move into a guided reading protocol. (For more background on this protocol see *Guided Reading* by Fountas and Pinnell [1996].)

Scaffolding Novice Readers During Guided Reading

We know that a guided reading protocol offers more student autonomy because after teachers prepare novices for reading the story, readers are expected to process the text independently. Some suggest the readers can leave the group to do their independent reading, but I usually keep those budding readers right there in group with me for a month or two while they are reading a page or pages alone—even if not-so-independently or silently at first. That way, their subvocalizations sometime provide grist for our scaffolding mill, a time that finds us reaching forward to cover the first letter of *Bill* with our finger, hoping the child is scaffolded into its rhyming familiar *hill*, or its *-ill* rime, trusting that with our strategy scaffolds each reader will move further toward fluency and independence.

Frequently during guided reading, a novice reader has trouble with a word, so he raises a hand and points in a questioning manner. Scaffolding teachers of novices do not usually tell the children unknown words, but instead move him toward a strategy that he can use to unlock unknowns himself.

The remainder of this book describes myriad strategies for scaffolding. At this point, I merely draw attention to the fact that all of us teachers scaffold kids one-on-one during reading groups every day.

One-on-One Scaffolding During Read-a-Book Time

Practically every professional book on reading tells us we should incorporate reading to, with, and by kids into our daily schedules. During shared and guided reading we are reading *with* kids. And we already know how important it is to read *to* children, but reading *by* children using self-selected texts is just as important, so we'll assume that most teachers already include all of these into each day's plans. But I can honestly say that if I had to omit any of them on a busy day, it was seldom Read-a-Book time.

Read-a-Book Time: A Key Structure for Scaffolding

Read-a-Book was our half-hour period each day for independent reading in first grade. At first, I called it Sustained Silent Reading (SSR), but after having beginning-of-year visitors, such as parents, ask me what SSR stood for, I decided to change the name to Read-a-Book time. Let's face it, to suggest that a roomful of beginning first graders, who are all reading *aloud*, are engaged in sustained *silent* reading is pretty ridiculous. Besides, Read-a-Book was far more comprehensible to the kids.

Beginning with a Secure Management Structure

From the first week of school, kids came in after lunch and found a few books they could read. During those initial weeks we made sure we modeled tons of easy selections just before Read-a-Book—some with only a word under each page's picture. Once the kids selected their books, we asked them to please stay put. In other words, if they needed another book, they could raise a hand and we would give them a new one—which we first quickly and quietly modeled. It didn't take long for the class to get the idea that it was best to be prepared for Read-a-Book time.

Many teachers place baskets of books in the middle of each table, a place where kids can reach for another selection when the need arises. This works well unless the children are at desks. But it's probably pretty important to again mention that the kids are expected to stay put once they get their books. Many teachers who observed our classrooms commented on that facet of Read-a-Book time. They noticed that it was *not* a time for kids to mill around; but like the name we gave it, *it was a time to read*—even in first grade.

One time I tried inviting the kids to find a comfortable spot to read anywhere in the room, but that did not work, because I could not so easily scaffold. Moving from desk to desk or table to table is much easier than crawling under tables and behind bookcases. So I quickly revised that plan.

Thus, our Read-a-Book time differs from the original concept of Uninterrupted Sustained Silent Reading or even Sustained Silent Reading, which suggest that, to model, the teacher should sit and read silently while the children are reading; however, when the classroom is full of preword and novice readers, those beginners need us there with them, scaffolding. Modeling adult reading behaviors at my desk for a half-hour may be well and good for classrooms full of fluent readers, but teachers will eliminate their major one-on-one scaffolding period, if they do that in classrooms full of novices.

Tending to Needs

At first, when the kids are independently pretend-reading or real-reading I walk around the room listening, because they all read aloud. Even so, I encourage *whisper reading*. Often, especially in the beginning of the year, kids will quickly deplete their pile of minimal-print books, so I tote a broad assortment with me. (But book baskets can facilitate this need, as well.) I quickly read aloud a few pages of a new book to demonstrate the inherent pattern and then invite the child into the act.

Basically, Linda and I both walked around and helped those who got stuck, stooped down to receive or offer a comment, or helped in any way that seemed necessary. In other words, we spent that period walking around scaffolding individual kids. We did not sit at our desks, but after listening long enough to scaffold a few times, on we'd go to the next student. The following chapters explicitly discuss how this looks and sounds, but there are a few overarching suggestions for entering the act.

How Teachers Enter the Act to Scaffold

Occasionally, I'll sidle up beside Nathan or Natalia to enter their reading world. There are a variety of ways in which I approach readers during this independent time. I stoop down and quietly enter the reader's world with a question (see page 35).

Yet, more often than not during the first few months of Read-a-Book, hands are popping up all over the room, so I'm flying here and there to scaffold. Those one-on-one meetings are like mini–reading lessons, a time when we could help a preword reader or a novice move up to the next step on the reading ladder. Most hands go up for an unknown word, but rarely do I just tell the word. Instead, I show novices how to use the cueing systems. *I help these readers help themselves*. In other words, once each novice has internalized strategies, *I've worked myself right out of a scaffolding job*.

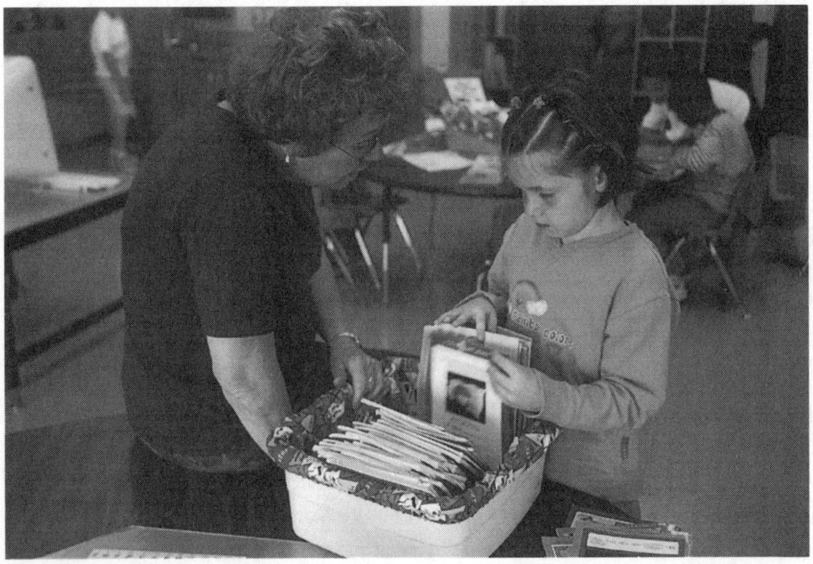

Linda supports a novice who is searching for a book in her table tub.

Entering a Reader's World for Possible Scaffolding

- What would you like to share with me?
- How's it going?
- What's your book about?
- Isn't this a good book? What's your favorite part so far?
- May I read a little? (After reading a little bit, I invite the child in.)
- Would you like a different book now?
- I love this book! Didn't you like the part where . . . ?

Rich Scaffolding Opportunities During Read-a-Book

Students love Read-a-Book time because of the autonomy involved. And what child doesn't enjoy individual attention! Sometimes, I'll feel a tug at my pantleg or skirt when a reader has something to ask or share. "Mrs. Cole, look at this huge whale!" Eric would exclaim.

To my way of thinking, such qualitative data is important, so sometimes I carry a clipboard with me and make assessment notes. Occasionally, I even carry a tape recorder and say good things into it, or I'll invite readers to read a page or so aloud to the recorder. The kids love this and can't wait until I listen to them. They motion me over and invite, "Say good things about me, too, Mrs. Cole!"

Linda stops to scaffold a reader during Read-a-Book time.

But most of the time I just simply scaffold, because Read-a-Book presents such a wonderful opportunity to do just that.

One-on-One Scaffolding During Share-a-Book

Following Read-a-Book time, Share-a-Book has merits of its own. This is a fifteen-minute period when kids have an opportunity to read aloud for an audience something they've read during Read-a-Book time. During the first few months of school, in order to lay the groundwork for what sharing looks and sounds like, the class participates in a whole-group share. That is, one child at a time goes forward to sit before the group and share a book that he or she read during Read-a-Book time. In the weeks that follow, when the kids start consuming lengthier texts, I gently stop each reader after about three minutes, call for a few responses to the reading and move on to another reader.

This whole-group period is one of the best times to demonstrate how to help a reader who is experiencing difficulty with a section of text. That is, I can show the kids how to scaffold a reader over a variety of humps. Again and again, I suggest, "Just give the reader a hint."

I offer, "Check the picture," or "How does it begin?" or "Back up and read that part again."

However, when a reader becomes stumped, the class and I often make guesses as to what the word in question might be—guesses which may or may not actually be correct.

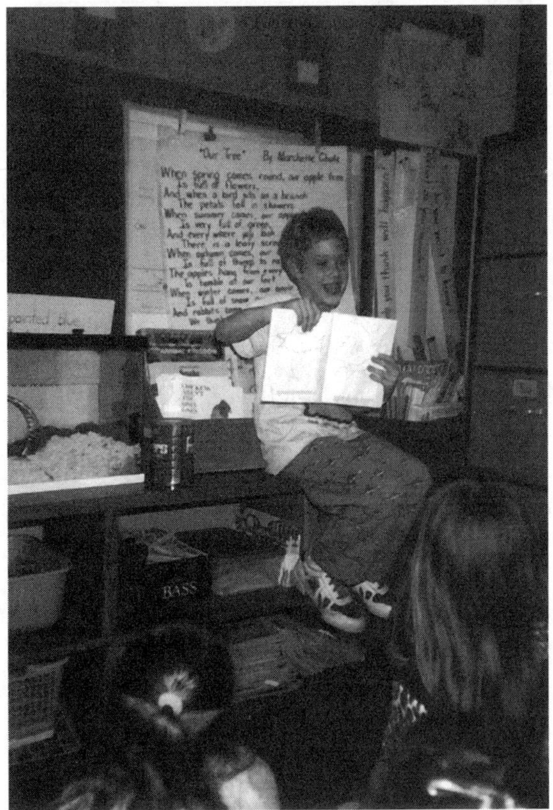

Author Eric shares one of his own books during Share-a-Book time.

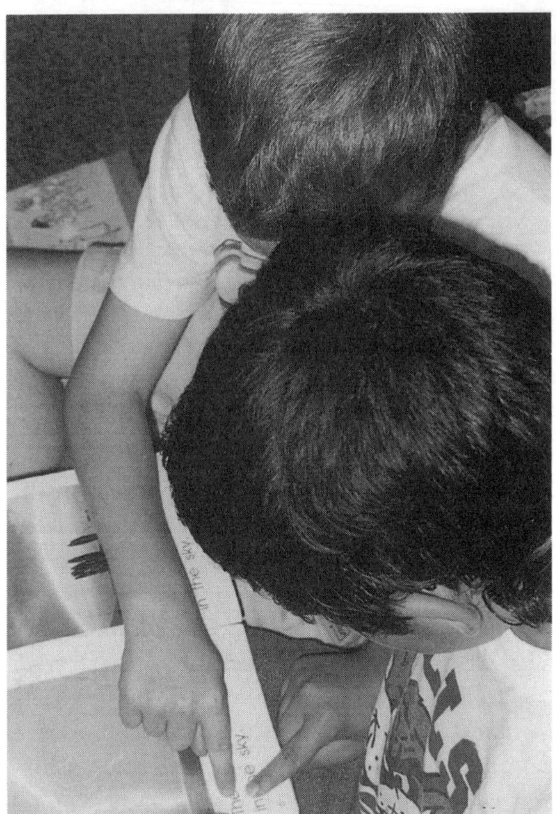

A partner fingerpoints to help his friend over a hump.

A novice reads, "The girl ran into her—" and she stops, silent.

"*House*!" someone offers.

"No, it doesn't start with an *H*," responds the reader.

"What does it start with?" I ask.

"An *R*," the reader answers.

"Back up and reread, but this time put an *r*-sound there," I suggest.

"It's *road*! It's *road*!" a listener interjects.

"Hang on, let's let the reader decide," and the ownership goes back to the reader again.

With such strategy scaffolding, the kids learn how to help a reader without actually telling the word. They learn to use hints—cues. Thus, when readers go on to partner *without* teacher guidance, we hear them scaffolding each other in the same manner. We also see partners fingerpointing to help a friend. Our standing rule remains: Do not give the reader a word, if there is a hint you can give instead.

Thus, the reading relationship can include a scaffolding friend, one who knows to give only as much of a hint as the reader needs. This then becomes a different kind of one-on-one scaffolding, because a partner replaces the teacher as a scaffolder.

One-on-One Scaffolding During Writing

Whether novice readers are involved in journal writing, writing workshop, or any other venue that involves composing, we teachers are usually there with them scaffolding one-on-one. Yet because writing is meant to be read, reading is also going on. Thus, we just naturally scaffold reading during writing. It's a symbiotic literacy relationship.

Graphophonic Scaffolding During Journal Writing

While the kids are involved in journal writing first thing in the morning, I might stoop down beside Sim, who is writing about his new bike, and invite, "Read what you've written so far, please."

As Sim reads I have the opportunity to scaffold in a variety of ways. I might ask him about the new bike he just got for his birthday, suggesting that good writers describe things for their audience so that readers can picture it in their minds. In so doing, I am showing Sim that readers visualize and authors describe for that very purpose.

More often than not, a writer will raise his hand to inquire about a word. "Mrs. Cole, how do you spell *marrow*?"

"Marrow, hm-m," I ponder. "Why don't you read what you have so far so I can get the feel for what you need?"

Lonny reads, "My dad is taking me to the game to marrow."

This becomes a perfect way in which to teach another lesson in wordness. For the young child, compound words, words containing whole words within them and even syllables are heard as separate entities. I usually teach *today* and *tomorrow* together to show how a word can contain the whole word, *to*, within its broader borders. Novices love to investigate for the possibility of compoundness and what makes multisyllable words tick—that is, they do as long as they are taught in an atmosphere of open and expected inquiry.

Semantic-Syntactic Scaffolding During Writing

Meanings were often scaffolded during the sharing of a writer's work. When first grader Samantha was sharing her own thirty-one-page retelling of *Hansel and Gretel* during Share-a-Book time, Joey asked her, "Did you say it was retold?"

Sure enough! Sam told us she had done that. But then Joey scaffolded the group by interjecting, "Just like Steven Kellogg!" and he held up the *Little Red Hen* book he himself hoped to share. "Look! It says 'Illustrated and retold by Steven Kellogg!'"

At this point, Samantha proudly displayed her title with authorship below it and read: "Retold and illustrated by Samantha."

"Well, why do you think authors say 'retold'?" I asked.

"Because Steven Kellogg and Kelly told their stories, but people keep telling them over and over and over, so ya gotta say, 'retold,'" Joey explained.

Here, we were in a group, but individuals were scaffolding each other and the group into textual connections—that is, retold stories. And they were using both writing and reading to do that during Share-a-Book.

Writing makes it so much easier to teach reading. How strange that when I began my career some educators believed that children should not receive a pencil until the second semester of first grade! Holding kids back from writing makes the teaching of reading a far more difficult task (Adams 1990). Furthermore, it eliminates a period of rich, one-on-one scaffolding.

Scaffolding On-the-Fly All Day Long

I guess it is easier now to understand what I mean when I say that we scaffold on-the-fly all day long. Every time a child raises a hand, tugs on our pantleg, walks forward with his writing, shows us a new book, or sits with another child to read becomes an opportunity to scaffold. Knowledgeable teachers scaffold mindfully. That is, they have a solid background in the teaching of reading, a sound knowledge of the children in their keep, and they have internalized facets of the process to the point where they can scaffold at a second's notice.

This goes on all day long in every classroom where teachers know how to teach reading. It *cannot* be done through a scripted approach, because it requires thinking on one's feet, in-process responses. Yet, although no script can instantly adjust to different children's minute-by-minute needs, people can—and moreover, those people do not all have to be the teacher. I've already mentioned how partners can scaffold each other. Yet, there are other structured situations that will allow for one-on-one scaffolding of preword and novice readers. Let's look at a few.

Pay-It-Forward: Kids Scaffolding Kids

We've already seen how kids can learn scaffolding techniques during Share-a-Book time. However, let's investigate a variety of structures in which student scaffolding might take place.

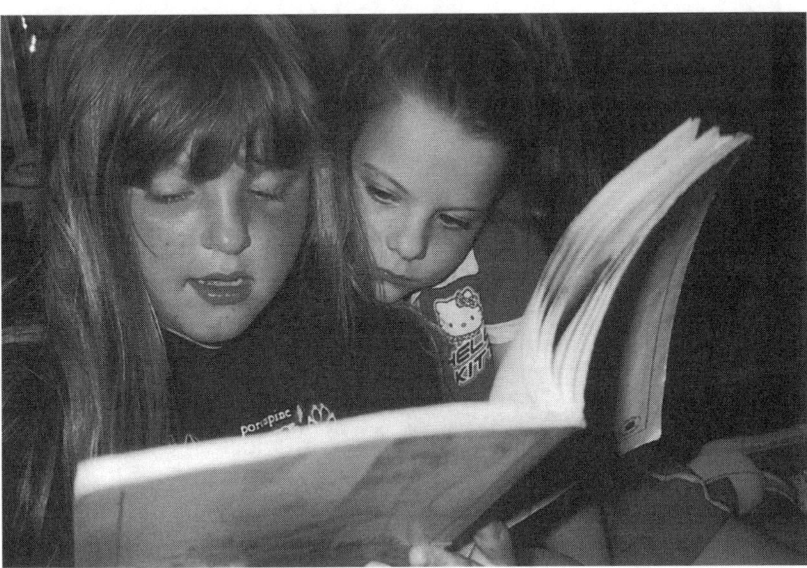

Reading flourishes during partner relationships.

Although the students had free reign on choice of partners during this Share-a-Book period, which lasted around fifteen to twenty minutes, they had already been steeped in scaffolding techniques through the large-group shared venue. Readers learned how to help another student during a read. They learned to allow time, to give an appropriate hint, to mask part of the word, and many other tricks of the scaffolding trade. In the following, Mohammed, who was transitioning into word reading, wisely chose his own partner, Sonya. There is no doubt that Mohammed knew Sonya was a compassionate individual who could read his beloved book almost fluently, and thus she would oblige him. And indeed she did.

Consequently, Sonya, an average first-grade reader, scaffolded Mohammed, a novice who desperately wanted to read *Where the Wild Things Are* (Sendak 1988) in February of first grade. Mohammed was quite determined, and Sonya was just as determined to scaffold him through this classic text.

In this video transcription, we discover that the two have decided to take turns reading the pages, but when Mohammed experiences difficulty Sonya slides right in. Let's see how she does it.

MOHAMMED: *(reading and pointing)* "And when he came to the *(omits* place where the*)* wild things—"

SONYA: "place where—" *(takes reader back to reread, pointing to the omission and then to the beginning of the sentence)*

MOHAMMED: *(rereading from the beginning to self-correct)* "And when he came to the place where the wild things are, they roared their terrible roar and they . . ." *(stuck on the word* gnashed, *so his partner scaffolds gesturally)*

SONYA: *(covers the* G *in* gnashed *with her finger to indicate a silent letter and then runs her finger under the rest of the word as an invitation to try it, so her partner reads)*

I use the analogy of the pay-it-forward approach from a recent movie that demonstrated how acts of support and kindness can grow once someone sets them into motion. That is exactly what happens in all of the following structures. And it can happen in your classroom, too.

Paired Partnering

Both planned and unplanned social groupings will support the scaffolding of novices, if the seeds are planted prior to the pairing. When we pair two kids, researchers (Johnson 1978; Topping 1989) tell us to structure the pairs so that one partner is more advanced than the other. It might then seem that only the one with the lesser ability would profit. Not so, because the more advanced student must actually use metacognition to make effective decisions, to explain, and to predict, and in doing so, he too becomes more literate.

Unplanned Partners

As I explain above, during the first few months of the school year, we always enjoyed a large-group sharing after Read-a-Book time. However, later in the year, I invited partners and, eventually, small conversation groups to share books. Partners usually shared different books, while conversation groups planned for and then discussed the same book (for more on this see *Knee to Knee, Eye to Eye* [Cole 2003]).

MOHAMMED: "N- n- na- nashed their—nashed their terrible teeth—"

SONYA: *(and it's Sonya's turn on the new page)* "And rolled their terrible eyes and showed their terrible claws."

Sonya had internalized many helpful cues, such as pointing to the words for a transitioning reader, covering parts of words, and pulling the reader forward. She used these behaviors fluently inside the process to scaffold Mohammed through a self-selected book that was considerably challenging for him at that time. Sonya did this because that's what I had modeled for her.

I may have wished Mohammed had selected an easier text. Yet I, no doubt, would have scaffolded him in a similar fashion had I been doing it myself. When kids select their own books during Read-a-Book time, and when kids scaffold kids, we teachers cannot expect perfect situations. Yet, the good that unfolds continues to surprise me and warm my heart.

Pay-It-Forward: Volunteer Read-with-Me Programs for One-on-One Scaffolding

When I was Maplemere Elementary School's literacy specialist for nine years, I had the opportunity to work alongside teachers to create new programs and ways to help all kids move forward in their literacy growth. Thus, I had the privilege of working with Angie, Bev, Karin, and Tammy, four wonderful kindergarten teachers. For several years we developed some wonderful support structures for reading, many of which involved volunteers.

One by one we created settings where the kids could gain more experience with books. Each setting found the preword reader sharing a book with a more capable other, and that is why we called it our Read-with-Me program.

Older Buddy Scaffolding

One year we had quite a few fourth graders who were not very confident in reading, so it seemed like a match made in heaven when the majority of the fourth graders joined our *buddy reading program*. It was a way that we could give every single kindergarten student one-on-one scaffolding for a twenty-minute period twice a week—while at the same time helping some fourth graders develop confidence through the reading of easy texts.

Classroom instructional time of fourth graders is quite precious, so we decided to ask for volunteers who would relinquish part of their lunch period to meet with a kindergarten buddy. We had a ton of volunteers, so permission slips went home to make certain parents did not object. Afterward, I went into each fourth grade to teach the basics of scaffolding. We set it up so that the older students would read to the younger, but afterward, the younger would have a book that they would read to the older student. Some fourth graders had two kindergarten students, which worked out fine. Several more volunteered once they saw how much fun it was.

The results were amazing. And one of the most rewarding was when we'd hear a fourth grader at the end of the school year singing the praises of his little kindergarten reader. They'd celebrate, "Mrs. Cole, did you know Georgio can read now?!" And sometimes I wonder if maybe the seeds of altruism that were planted might have been the most important facet of the entire program.

Parent Volunteer Scaffolding

In October the kindergarten teachers and I carefully assessed each student's literacy development. For those students who seemed to lack experience in text, we asked the parents to come in for a conference in which I could demonstrate scaffolding maneuvers.

I explained via letter that I would share some ways that parents could help, and we never had one parent who was anything but cooperative. I also invited the child in for the conference, which added an authentic flavor to the scaffolding.

I began by explaining the difference between (1) books whose pages are full of print and rich with a story that lends itself to parent and child book chats, and (2) books with very little print, large font, and a high level of predictability, making it easier to draw attention to the graphics and their sounds.

I scaffolded parents toward an understanding by explaining how a novice hiker might look around a forest and notice some big trees and pretty flowers, but if that hiker was with a botanist, the scientist would see far more than just trees and flowers. She would see specificity and be able to name that specificity. Botanists see more than we novices do—unless they show us, that is.

"It's about noticing," I told them. Skilled readers perceive the page differently than preword readers. Preword readers do not notice words. They have not yet been introduced to that level of book specificity. Thus, I demonstrate with the child how to draw attention by pointing and later finding particular words, but we also chat about the book. I usually chose a Dr. Seuss book, such as *The Foot Book*, because parents are more familiar with Dr. Seuss. Then, every week, with the help of Heidi, the librarian, we'd send home the two kinds of books in Read-with-Me logoed bookbags (which we obtained through a grant). Parents then understood how they could help lead preword readers into a forest of letters, showing them how to discern each clump that matches a spoken word. With their assistance we took preword readers into reading.

Parents can be a wonderful asset in one-on-one scaffolding. They want to help, yet often they are not sure how to go about doing that. Therefore, most parents were exceedingly grateful for these services our school provided. And we were grateful to have more caring scaffolders.

Senior Citizen Volunteer Scaffolding

I had begun a senior citizen volunteer program when I was teaching first grade and multiage; however, let me continue with our kindergarten program and the way in which the seniors helped provide one-on-one scaffolding, while at the same time enriching the reading relationship.

First I visited a nearby senior citizen center, and later we put an ad in the local paper searching for volunteers who could come in one morning per week to read with kindergartners. We accrued enough volunteers so that each kindergartner in need of literacy support could meet twice a week for fifteen minutes with a senior scaffolder.

The seniors met with me first, just as the parents had. I explained the two kinds of books, letting them know that they could collect the texts from my library prior to meeting with a child. The teacher would make certain the child had a minimal-print book to share as well.

We were well aware that there were and are many tutoring books and programs. However, our intent was simply to offer these kids a similar background as others in their class have had in their homes. We tried to replicate the experience as much as possible, and side-by-side reading seemed to do just that. After all, if it worked for the other kids, why wouldn't it work if we set up similar situations? And it did!

Almost any day, if you walked down our hallway past the kindergartens, you could find a smiling senior sitting on the couch at the end of the hall connected to his young friend by an open book. I'm not certain who enjoyed the experience more, the kids or the seniors. I do know that the seniors loved to stop and tell me about their scaffolding tactics and their child's progress. It was a beautiful one-on-one relationship!

We believe that all those reading relationships had to have had some influence on our kindergartners' literacy success. As a matter of fact, within two years we only had eight kids in the kindergartens who moved into first grade *not* able to read.

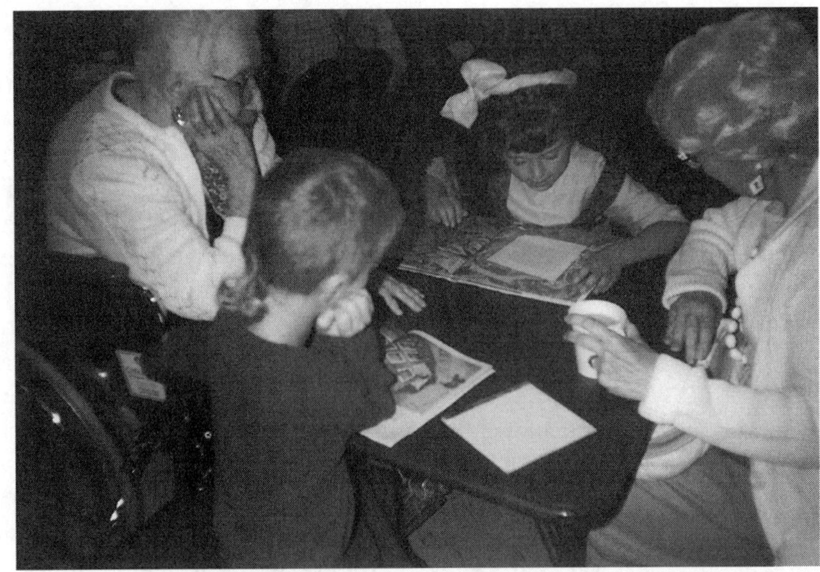

My first graders loved their bimonthly sharing at the Senior Center, a ten-block walk from our school.

Constructing an Environment That Cues

Earlier I discussed how the entire environment can scaffold a reader toward success. Large open walls can hold lists of *high-frequency words*, that is, words that frequently occur in both reading and writing. Their mere presence becomes an anchor for identification.

Meaningful signs around the room help direct children and invite easy reading. Some of these may indicate "Please turn the lights off," "Please wash your hands," "Please put your coat on a hook," or any number of other suggestions. Labels might indicate "tape recorder," "Line forms here," or "Animal Books." Indeed, our outside world is brimful with print, so why shouldn't the place where children learn to read also exhibit a bountiful array?

Rooms should have a library of plentiful books from a variety of levels—at least 1,000, but 2,000 would be more appropriate for early primary, where children read through one book in a few minutes. Rooms should have an audio library of read-alouds, as well as song tapes accompanied by booklets containing the songs' words.

Other important resources for early primary classrooms are dictionaries and pictionaries. For preword and novice readers pictionaries provide a key to writing. Labeled pictures are grouped by categories, so that if a child wants to find family words, such as brother, sister, or aunt, he can find that section of the pictionary. There were more choices years ago, but now it seems that only Scott Foresman carries a quality *categorized* pictionary for beginners. Kids love to just sit and read through all the categories—animals, colors, plants, helpers, and so on. I've even had first graders try to hide a pictionary inside their journals, just to make sure they'd have it for the next day's write!

Just-Right Texts That Scaffold Readers

The topic of just-right texts has already been discussed earlier, but because of its importance, I feel I must also mention it here. This topic pops up again and again throughout this book because, let's face it, the text is a major part of any reading relationship. Just as a scaffolder, a text can make the relationship or it can break it. Therefore, merely using a text because some company says to "use these stories" is going to challenge any reading relationship. For one thing, big, old, thick texts do not appeal to most little kids. Plus, they're too heavy to lug home all the time for sharing. Kids love books they can embrace. They love to locate their favorite, to try and get a friend to read it, too. And when there are only a few of one book, they like to be the one who gets there first. That's what happens in a literate community!

Recent research done by the National Association of Educational Progress (2002) indicates that districts who use multiple texts in a literature-based curriculum outscore basal (or reading series) districts. A grand variety of books provides a grand variety of experience. Plus, small,

Writing Reciprocity

Using Word Walls to Scaffold High-Frequency Words

Some words in our language are used frequently, so we call them high-frequency words. The trouble is, most of these words possess irregular sounds; thus, sounding them out is of little or no use. For instance, look at the following: the (thu?), is (iz?), of (uv?), to (tu?).

Making a word wall of these words and listing them in alphabetical columns in a place where they can be readily accessed or noticed seems to serve as an easy reference resource that scaffolds novices in their writing. But it also helps kids read, too. After all, they must read them in order to write them! Furthermore, they must investigate other word-wall words on their way to locating the particular word they seek.

individual books are less intimidating to a small child than those heavy basals.

Teachers always ask me, "What can I do? My district uses a basal and I have to use it and all the its ancillary materials or I will get in trouble."

My answer comes from personal experience. I suggest that the class moves through that common material quickly and together, using an SBE until the entire grade-level lot is "covered." Everyone reads together, and everyone does the workbook pages together with kids helping kids. It makes the ordeal far easier, and the half of the class who might struggle with this text that is above their reading level, happily works with a friend, learning a little about literacy along the way. We do it quickly so that we have time for what is *really* important—real books!

Grist for Discussion

Make a list of ways in which you could scaffold individual students during their reading. Number these in order of importance, that is, from the one that would predictably produce the best results to the one that may not produce many results. Discuss why you have numbered them in this fashion.

Chapter 4

The Cues Teachers Use

Mr. Henry tried to break it down into little bits, thinking six letters at a time would be good. But I said, "No, son, I want to see all the letters. I want to put them together." Mr. Henry said, "So that's what we did and by the second day, Mr. Dawson was set. He learned his letters in a day and a half. Then we moved on to phonics. You know, breaking words into small parts and sounding them out. Then Mr. Dawson said, 'I've waited too long, son, show me some words that makes sense.'"

GEORGE DAWSON AND RICHARD GLAUBMAN,
LIFE IS SO GOOD

A Sensitive Dance

It is surely a sensitive dance that we teachers do as we scaffold novices during oral reading, a time when we must sense and address each child's particular needs. The teachers in the following chapters show how sometimes that support is very subtle, while at other times it is a complete interruption. Sometimes scaffolders take total ownership, while at other times they place that ownership in the hands of the reader. The best of these scaffolders incorporate myriad gestural messages. They sometimes use their hands and sometimes use their words, and many times use both in synchronicity. All teachers responded to not only the decoding process but also the content of what was being read. It is really quite amazing all that goes on when a teacher and a novice reader get together with a book!

It is indeed a fine line that we walk with every learner—the tightrope that runs between too much and not enough. Too much mediation can color the transaction with "I don't trust you" and "You don't do anything right," while too little mediation can shade it with the insensitivity of an uncaring adult. The interesting aspect is that no two tightropes lie along the same path. While assessing each reader's moves, the scaffolder must sensitively dance forward *leading from behind*.

Leading from Behind

Verbal guidance seems to be one of the teachers' primary tactics for teaching children strategies and scaffolding them through print. They simply lead the readers through orally, similar to the way in which we teach learners any of life's skills. They are right there with the reader, leading from behind. Much like Vygotsky (1978) suggested, they allow the child the autonomy to forge onward, but when the road gets a bit bumpy they join the reader, leading him over the humps. They are sometimes ahead of him, sometimes behind, and sometimes right with him. Again the metaphor of dance seems closest to what was observed.

I watched Hannah, a veteran first-grade teacher, dance with grace and finesse. She and each of her students shared the reading event so closely that at times it was difficult to discern where one began that the other left off. This printed page will not do justice to such a transaction, but let me offer it anyway.

Sitting close beside each other, Hannah and her novice reader share a one-sentence-per-page big book called *Things to Love*. After the child reads the following sentence, notice how Hannah uses both voice and gesture to scaffold:

STUDENT: *(reading)* "Tom and his friends love to make music."

TEACHER: Oh, I think so! *(continuing to move her finger on to the next few words . . .)*

STUDENT: *(reading)* "The chicks love to sing along with the music."

TEACHER: I think so! *(glances over at the reader)*

STUDENT: There they are! *(pointing, to reference the picture)*

TEACHER: They *are* having a good time, aren't they?

STUDENT: Uh-huh!

TEACHER: Wow! Good!

STUDENT: *(taking this positive appraisal as a sign to continue)* Big H- H- Hel-

TEACHER: *(Masking the "-da" part of* Hilda, *indicating the child should respond by phonetically stretching through the word. Once the reader attempts the first syllable, the teacher moves her finger onward to the end of the word and waits.)*

STUDENT: *(blending through the whole word, the reader decodes)* Hel- da

TEACHER: *(correcting slightly and almost synchronistically, while validating)* Good—Hilda—good job!

What a sensitive dance this is! Hannah's pointing finger stays out in front of the reader, pulling the novice onward, while her voice celebrates every small effort, every approximation. This teacher stays in front of the reader, behind the reader, and with the reader—all at the same time!

Imposition or Invitation?

Scaffolding involves a learner and a teacher. However, when the one in power, an author (-ity), imposes her will upon the intentions of the other, the reader, the result may not be synchronous because the child may cling tenaciously to his own I-centered worldview. He may *not* want to dance and may feel like he's being dragged out onto the dance floor. There is a basic issue here of receptivity—a receptivity that may or may not meet the teacher's intention. An author (-ity) can impose her own script again and again, but unless the reader is receptive, the imposition evokes little success.

For example, young preword reader Cameron enjoyed saying the title of a book and its author, so he would repeat it over and over, rather than turning the page and moving on into the text. After several attempts at leading from behind and issuing invitations, Cameron's mom gave up and turned the page for him, saying, "Let's read *this* page now." She took control and pulled the child forward.

In another situation, first-grader Sami was pretend-reading *Over in the Meadow* (Keats 1999) when his teacher asked him to point to the words. Because Sami was still unable to match speech to print, the teacher laid her hand over the child's, invited him to read with her, and showed Sami how the spoken words matched the print on the page. The teacher had taken control of both the pointing and the reading. Yet, she did it sensitively through an invitation.

I use these two cases because they are exemplary of what occurs during the scaffolding of readers. Indeed, sometimes there needs to be an authority who can take over and model the process. Novices do need teachers and parents to step in and take over. Nevertheless, preceding that imposition with an invitation is a far gentler way to begin any scaffolding.

Opening with Invitations and Corrections

No doubt that is why most teachers began their scaffolding session with an invitation. Lani's student had selected his own mediation text, obviously by invitation, but notice all of his teacher's other invitations that encourage the reader to share some of his life and likes—to connect with his mediator and the text. Here and there throughout this section Lani's voice exhibited a lilt that bordered on teasing; and then, each time she leaned forward, the child would look up shyly and smile. It seemed as if he and his teacher knew something that I, an observer, did not. In other words, they had a relationship that was special for the two of them, but might not include an onlooker.

We join Lani and her novice reader as the child sits down and rests his selected expository text about amphibians on the table:

STUDENT: *(Opens book to title page, looking it over. He's in control.)*

TEACHER: Frogs and toads. Hm-m, is this part of that same series you've been reading? Why did you choose this one? *(Reaches over and turns the book back to its cover, imposing her control. She is always logging information—the title and author—for record-keeping purposes. This whole scenario does not seem to be anything out of the ordinary in this classroom. Both teacher and child seem very comfortable with this, even though a video camera is staring them in the face!)*

STUDENT: Because I like touching frogs. And I like animals.

TEACHER: You like what? *(no inflection)*

STUDENT: Because I like touching frogs and I like animals.

TEACHER: You like animals? *(The teacher, who has been taking notes up to this point, stops long enough to look the child in the eye for her question. He suddenly looks up at her and the beginnings of a smile that appears on his face tell me that these two know something that I do not. Afterward, the teacher goes back to her logging; the reader goes back to his book, but then she adds)* How do you think I knew that before you told me? *(reader grins again)*

STUDENT: Because I've been taking a lot of these books out.

TEACHER: Yeah, you've also taught your mom a lot about animals that she didn't know by reading to her, didn't you? *(leaning forward to look at the child as she speaks)*

STUDENT: *(glances up with an occasional shy smile in response to the kind words and personal connections)*

We can see that already, at the very beginning of the process there is a give and take, an ownership that's tossed back and forth. For although the teacher seems to be setting the agenda by authoring the comments, the comments are child-centered invitations and connections. The entire event rests upon the *child's agenda, his interests, his life.*

Opening with Imposition

However, now let us look at another opening scene. In this beginning episode Julie has selected a book for novice reader Jose—yet without his input. Ironically, Jose has selected a different book for the occasion—a well-rehearsed one that *he* wants to read. We join them as Julie is reminding this novice reader about the strategies he can use. Compared to the previous dyad, notice the difference in this reader's response to his teacher's scaffolding efforts.

TEACHER: Okay, before you read this, what can we do if we come to a word that we don't know? What if we come to a word that we don't know? What are some things that we can do? *(Both teacher and child have a different book!)*

STUDENT: Do it at the end.

TEACHER: What do you mean, "Do it at the end?"

STUDENT: When you're done here at the period, go back to the beginning. *(hits the end of the first sentence on the page of the teacher's book that is on the floor with the point of the book that he is holding)*

TEACHER: So—uh—we'll read along and if we come to a word that we don't know we'll read to the end? *(slight nuance of upward pitch here denoting a question, but goes on)* And then we'll go back to it, okay? And see what we think would go there. Okay? *(As the teacher reviews this process with the child she points to the beginning and the end of the sentence on the first page of the text that he will read. When she finishes with the final question, however, she reaches over and rubs the student's back and leans forward to look him in the face—and probably to catch his eye for he is not looking at her, but still at* his *book. He has not responded to her question and this lack of response could be a sign to use a different cue to elicit a more positive reader response. Teacher used a voice cue, to no avail, so she is now resorting to gesture or touch, which she explained during the follow-up interview. Still receiving no response, goes on)* But I want you just to do—*(continuing to rub his back and look him in the face but he still has not responded)* to do your best for this, okay? *(still no response, so she moves to sit closer and to also create a new avenue for the relationship by referencing the book he is holding)* Were you practicing this one? *(now touches his book)*

STUDENT: Uh-huh. *(Glances up for an instant—finally responding. The relationship has changed.)*

TEACHER: *(smiling in response to his gesture while offering a compromise)* You know what, let's read a little bit of this first *(her book)* and then we'll read a little of this, too, because I know you've already practiced this one. Okay? *(Throughout this episode the teacher continues to rub the child's back and smile, while pointing to the matching text each time she changes reference.)*

STUDENT: *(Leaning toward teacher, the reader agrees:)* Uh-huh. *(begins to read teacher's book)*

No doubt Jose felt that Julie was imposing her will on him; and as a consequence, the relationship was suffering. At first, her student would not even make eye contact. It was obvious that this bothered Julie because of the way in which she continually tried a variety of emotive gestures to move the relationship into harmony; that is, she looked at Jose, moved closer, rubbed his back, touched his arm, smiled repeatedly, and even offered some invitations that were similar to Lani's. However, because imposition had set the agenda, Julie's student did not wish to dance until the relationship was adjusted. It is indeed a sensitive balance that drives a harmonic reading relationship.

Creating a "Flow" Experience

For optimal results, every scaffolder should seriously consider a novice's intentions. This is actually the crux of the mediation act. It is the transaction that takes place when an *intentioned learner* joins the mediator-teacher in a textual dance.

A Gentle Relinquishing

Nevertheless, mediation often begins with and has a sporadic undercurrent of teacher control, whereby the teacher authors various episodes within the ongoing process. However, some episodes are also led by the child with the teacher right in step, and most often assisting through gestural facilitation, an analogic response that does not have the interruption potential of spoken scaffolding. Sometimes these textual partners transact in such a synchronous manner that it is impossible to tell whose leading whom. This harmony is caught within hand dances and also through the music of combined voices. One can often see such transactions develop at a time when the reader is experiencing the more difficult sections of text, during a time of struggle. Yet, as teacher and student move through this challenging period in togethership, their dance through difficulty creates a united flow toward the greatest growth.

The Fruits of a Flow Experience

And perhaps it is for this reason that most of the videotaped novice readers appeared captivated by their mediating experience, sometimes carrying the book with them long afterward. They had been presented with a challenge and, moving with their teachers, had scaled the mountain before them. As Csikszentmihaly (1990) would say of every *flow* experience, "It provided a sense of discovery, a creative feeling of transporting the person into a new reality. It pushed the person to higher levels of performance . . . In this growth of self lies the key to flow activities" (p. 74). That is why slightly challenging texts have a positive influence on the scaffolding experience.

"When goals are clear, feedback relevant, and challenges and skills are in balance, attention becomes ordered and fully invested" (Czikszentmihaly 1997, 31). When the teacher and student unite in this sensitive and caring dance, one can almost feel the learning taking place. The process becomes smooth and flowing. They both appear intensely involved and focused. And they begin to move as one, rather than two, and the process becomes a magical textual ballet.

How a Text Can Affect Flow

A teacher who has stood in the shoes of her learner will be one who can more readily move in harmony with that individual (Noddings 1984). To know a child's strengths and weaknesses, to know her likes and dislikes, her background knowledge, or anything else regarding that individual, is undoubtedly to pave a more harmonic mediation path. Not only decoding, but also comprehension will be enhanced by the questions a teacher asks and the connections she helps a reader to make (Harvey and Goudvis 2000). Questions and connections help solidify reading relationships.

But then there's also the text. Because a reading relationship will always include a text of some sort, it too will influence the unity of the whole. The text itself provides authored harmonies—those of genre, orthography, spacing, illustrations, language, beliefs, and many other influences. Such textual qualities always affect the harmony of the mediation process—positively or negatively. It's important that teachers of reading possess knowledge related to such text qualities, which will enable them to predict and to move more fluently between and among textual cues.

A poor text-reader match can shade the reading relationship like a dark cloud. Although first-grader John is of Irish descent, he is stifled by a book published in Ireland—one that his teacher selected for him to read aloud. The syntax of this text is occasionally dissimilar from the way in which American syntax unfolds. In the sentence: "That is very like his farm horse," John hesitates before and after *very*. He reads, "He works on a farm. That is . . . very . . ."

To some, it might appear strange that John, whose sight vocabulary was quite large, would hesitate before the words *very* and *like*. Yet, this insecure novice was probably questioning his decoding ability of these easy words, because the sentence did not make sense syntactically. We do not usually say "very like." No doubt that's why John's teacher stepped in to explain the meaning of the sentence. Accordingly, the more foreign the text, the more often meaning and syntax will need to be cued, but also the more difficulty the reader may have.

Every text has particular potential for particular readers. Perhaps a student who has just come from Ireland would need fewer cues in this text. From this perspective it becomes evident that what evolves into orchestrated harmony for one teacher-student dyad might create a chaotic dissonance for a different pair—depending upon the book, as well as the sensitivity and knowledge of the mediator. Indeed, each experience is rife with influences.

Accommodation and Assimilation of Experiences

The Teacher-Mediation Spiral in Figure 4–1 presents this grand myriad of influences. Mediators themselves receive signs or messages from their ongoing experiences—cues that influence their scaffolding decisions. All are important considerations that precede our scaffolding actions, for as Piaget suggests, each learner evolves by *accommodating* and then *assimilating* (Ginsburg and Opper 1988) his selected signs or messages from his environment. This is just as true for the teacher who is learning to facilitate the needs of the reader, as it is for the reader himself.

Within the realm of literacy, Harste (Harste, Woodward, and Burkett 1984) explains a similar idea through the use of a *linguistic pool*, a literacy reservoir belonging to all human beings into which they receive and then assimilate reading, writing, listening, and speaking experiences. Within every literacy experience, an individual dips into her ever-increasing pool, working from existing knowledge to construct new knowledge which, in turn, through another round of accommodation and assimilation, deepens the pool. Thus, our literacy pools are ever increasing in a variety of ways.

Balance Between the Emotive and the Rational

Growing in both *emotive* and *rational* experiences is an important issue here. It seems that teachers who lack emotive/aesthetic abilities in mediation may have trouble creating flow experiences or they may have difficulty conveying a love for reading. However, they might also have difficulty receiving and accommodating the messages from the child whose gestures may be signaling: "This isn't working" or "I'm very tired" or "I'm extremely frustrated." So emotive experience is an important facet of both teaching and learning.

Just as important, however, are rational experiences. It is knowledge that provides the mediator with a linear perspective of the process. It allows her to categorize concepts and to talk about them. It allows her to select from the repertoire of her own language pool and to lay the pieces alongside her demonstrations for the child. Rational experience shapes learning in a different, yet equally important, way.

Emotive and Efferent Relationships

As Figure 4–1 spirals out of the cues the teacher is using and on to be accommodated and assimilated, it also depicts the path toward which the cues will unfold and flow into a scaffolding act. That is why the mediation arrows flow outward (to be received by the reader) at the bottom of the spiral. We could also overlay a Reader spiral atop the Teacher Mediation spiral, for indeed, the student would be receiving both emotive and rational cues.

Rational/efferent and emotive/aesthetic experiences find form within the mediation act. It is a time when cognitive, scientific knowledge can harmonically transact with subjective, sensual, feeling experiences. When we balance mediation behaviors using both realms it is often difficult to discern who's in control. And, as a matter of fact, it no longer matters!

Demonstrating the Cues Readers Use

Teachers provided many spoken and gestural demonstrations for their novices. They gave examples of how readers sound when they read, how they use multiple methods in decoding an unknown word, how they connect the text to their own life, as well as many other facets of the reading process.

Juel (1996) paired college-age poor readers with first-grade at-risk children, and she found that, even in that situation, those who modeled and scaffolded were successful in helping first graders to read. That's why, when my students seem confused about a strategy, my first response is always, "Uh-oh, I haven't modeled it enough."

Think-Alouds as Demonstrations

One of the most common kinds of demonstrations is a think-aloud, a method that science tells us is effective (Pressley 2002). Teachers make covert processes overt when they share aloud how readers think, how they move through the process, where they look, how they connect the text to their own life or another text, and how the text makes them feel. They use think-alouds to support every cueing system.

Julie does this when her struggling reader miscues *wheel* for *well* as he is reading *The Wishing Well*. Julie had already explained the concept of wells to this novice during prereading, yet he still stumbled. But his teacher intuited that a semantic problem remained. She therefore resorted to a think-aloud. She said, "You know what I thought of? A wishing well, because sometimes I throw things in there *(pointing at the well)*—like throw a penny in there *(swishes her hand outward as though throwing)* and then make a wish and it might come true. Just like when we wish on the falling stars." Julie is demonstrating how good readers make connections to what they already know, and in so doing this teacher undergirds the reader with a sound comprehension strategy, along with some background on wells.

Julie knew that a story called *The Wishing Well* would hold far less meaning if its reader did not understand this crucial term. She also realized that she needed to scaffold the story's underlying concept of wishing to receive good luck. The few seconds it took for this think-aloud made a world of difference for this confused reader. His eyes brightened, and he dove back into the text.

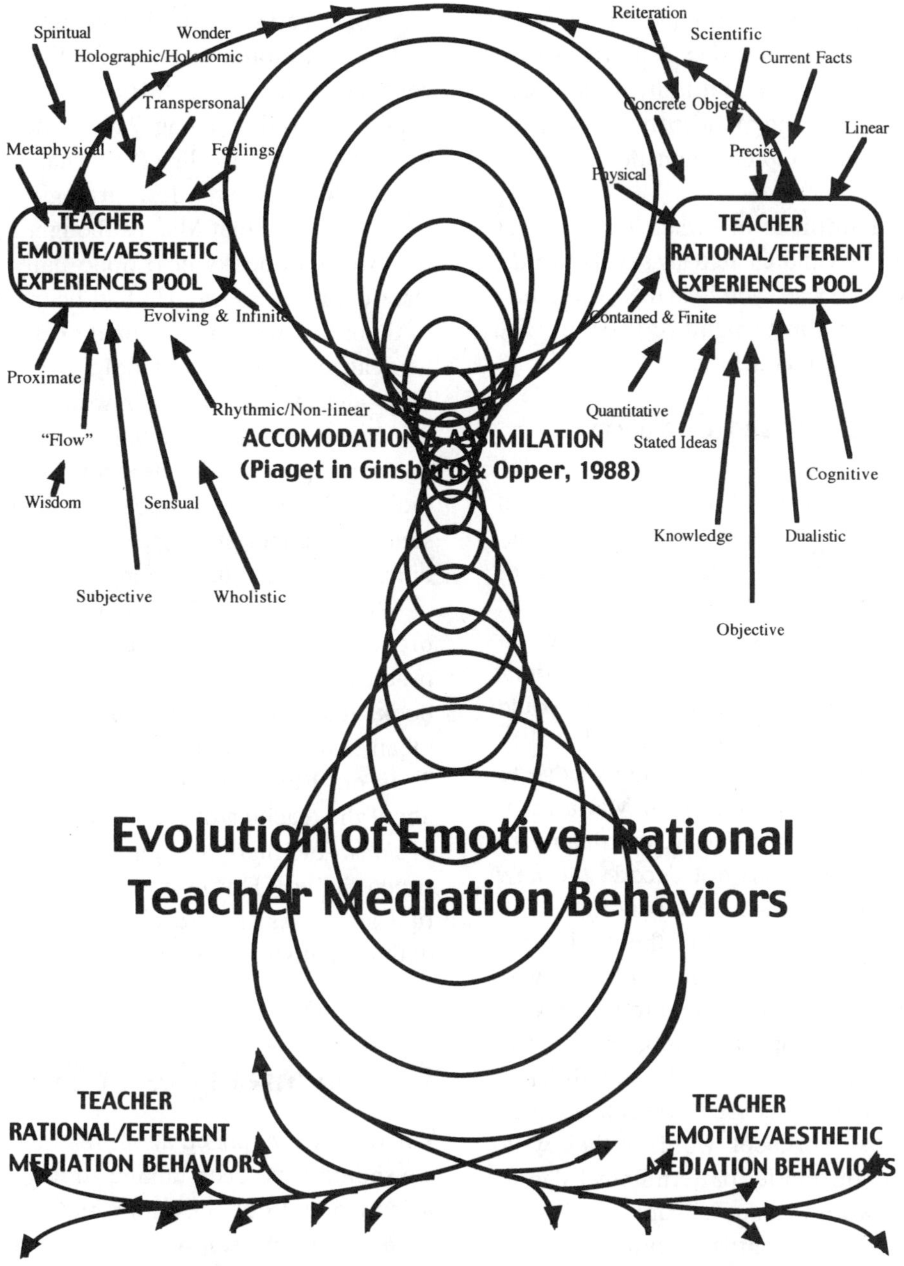

Figure 4–1. *Emotive-Rational Teacher Mediation Spiral*

Demonstrations Point the Way

I realized the impact of my own modeling one day near the end of our Read-A-Book period. Kids love it when I act like an investigative reporter, so that day I took out the camcorder and interviewed a variety of readers about the unknown words they had come across during their reading. I asked many of them the following: "Did you come across any words you did not know?" And then after most responded yes, I went on to request, "Show me that word, please?"

After Kelly flipped through her book to show me the word, I asked, "Kelly, what did you do when you did not know that word?"

Kelly responded, "I did what you did when you help me with words."

"What's that?" I prodded.

"I read more *(pointing to where she read)* and then I went back *(pointing again)* and got it." Kelly somewhat proudly remarked.

The amazing thing is that Kelly's answer was not just coincidental, because there were several kids on that tape who mentioned, "I did what you do." When we model and explain why we are modeling, readers quite naturally follow our demonstrations and independently apply those behaviors. We are helping them deepen their literacy pools.

But it still surprises me when I watch that tape and hear the children actually say the words: "I did what you do when you help me." Those first graders even had a metacognitive grasp of *why* they were choosing that behavior!

Workbooks Narrow and Condition Responses

One conclusion I have drawn after years of teaching and studying reading is that just because a student can bark back an answer does not mean he can use that skill independently. Let me explain this through a story. Our district ordered phonics workbooks for all first graders. Yet, again and again, I'd have students who could fill in the phonics blanks appropriately, but they would have trouble applying that knowledge to the actual act of reading. That is, Maria completed her entire short *A* page, then came to reading group, and could not decode the new word *snap*. Her responses were conditioned to and reliant upon the context of the workbook, and she did not understand the skills in a way that allowed her to transfer them to a new situational context. Kids appeared to memorize the spellings *before* they grew into the sounds. They were conditioned responses. Therefore, they could spell those workbook words in their writing, but could not transfer pattern knowledge to decode a new word in a new situation.

We should not confuse conditioned responses with the ability to apply and transfer skills and strategies *in action*, that is, in the context of a real, unrehearsed book. It's fairly easy for a teacher to condition a child in such a way that he responds automatically to particular cues. Even parrots and monkeys can do that! Children will understand the process far better if we scaffold them *within the context of authentic texts*.

The trouble with workbooks is that they narrow a reader's experiential options; whereas, real reading offers a multitude of experiences. Real reading provides a context in which a choice must be made, and readers soon learn that the more cues to direct that choice, the more likely they will decode correctly. They learn reading is a process, not a conditioned response.

I once had a new student come into my room, and after a month or so in our literature-based curriculum, he asked, "Mrs. Cole, when are we ever going to do reading?" Now, this was a child who was by then reading fairly challenging books all day long. After a few strategic questions, I came to realize that Marcus thought reading was the two workbooks he'd done daily in his last classroom experience. He had been conditioned to think that way, and it would be a while before he realized that he was doing reading all day long—even without filling in workbook blanks. In my experience as a reading specialist, I had a number of parents who also thought that kids who did not do daily workbook pages were missing something important. I guess they, too, were conditioned to think that reading is workbooks.

Nevertheless, it is authentic literature that provides the much-needed opportunities for practicing the process, and it is in those good books that scaffolding works best. This does not mean that kids do not need explicit instruction. They do. But useful instruction is really more about the teaching of *strategies* than the teaching of *skills*. And there is an enormous difference between the two. However, before I lay out the actual strategies that teachers do use, let's first define what strategies are.

Cueing Strategies or Skills?

For years we've talked about reading skills when we should have been talking strategies. You see, an individual only develops high levels of skill because that person possesses the strategies to get him to those skill levels. Thus, strategies become the driving force behind skills. In the following, you'll see how skills relate to more of those conditioned responses.

The Difference Between Strategies and Skills

The essential and important difference between skills and strategies is the *level of student autonomy*. Don Holdaway's (1979) *Foundations of Literacy* succinctly but thoroughly explains this difference. He tells us:

> The major difference between a "skill" and a "strategy" is the coordinating control of a human mind operating in pur-

> poseful, predictive, and self-corrective ways. The major difference, then, between "skills teaching" and "strategies teaching" concerns the presence or absence of self-direction on the part of the learner. In skills teaching the teacher tells the learner what to do and then "corrects" or "marks" the response. In strategy teaching the teacher induces the learner to behave in an appropriate way and encourages the learner to confirm or correct his own responses—the teacher does not usurp the control which is crucial to mastering a strategy. (p. 136)

Taught skills often appear as conditioned responses; whereas, strategies are needed for authentic reading experiences, because unlike workbooks and worksheets, real reading exhibits an unconditionality and must, therefore, be processed in a mindfully active manner. A conditioned workbook student will never understand all the options that a reader of authentic text possesses, because a workbook student is never privy to that grand myriad of possibilities that only real text contains.

Holdaway also suggests that skills teaching focuses on the pieces and parts of language, rather than on whole text. Skills teaching is more imposed, limited, and abstract—learned or reinforced by test-driven curricula. Consequently, when teachers scaffold through a skills approach, they tend to emulate a workbook by asking, "And what vowel sound does an *I* make? A short *I*? A long *I*?"

Strategy instruction differs, for it is more inclusive, embedded within larger situational contexts. Holdaway suggests that "our definition of teaching needs to move over towards inducing individual learners into mindful action rather than providing them with a pre-packed kit of rules" (p. 99). Phonics rules are primarily applicable on a prepared workbook page, but not in real reading (see the research of Venezky 1970; Clymer 1963).

Scaffolding Strategies?

What does strategy mediation look like? Let's examine two brief instances of reader application of strategies. In the following examples it will be obvious that there's been previous teacher modeling and instruction. Notice how the scaffolder encourages student autonomy in strategy use that will live on long after this particular reading moment.

TEACHER: What can we do if we come to a word you don't know?
STUDENT: Reread to get a running start.

And in another example:

TEACHER: What do you think would make sense there?
STUDENT: Lion, 'cause they're in the jungle and it starts with *L*.

Both of these teachers induce the learner toward mindful action. No rules are mentioned. Because their teachers had demonstrated for these two readers *how* to use a variety of decoding and comprehension strategies, and because the readers internalized these, they could now be asked to take charge, to actually use strategies in an unrehearsed text.

Why Strategies?

We can see the part that metacognition plays here. Indeed, skills can be learned through stimulus-response activities; however, strategies are most often learned within the contexts in which they can be put to use. It is only through strategies that skills can come to life; that is, without strategies skills are dead. And, although we outgrow some skills, we never outgrow strategies.

For instance, most proficient readers do not, when approaching a double-voweled unknown word, say to themselves, "When two-vowels go walking . . ." It is distractions such as this that move readers down dead-end avenues and away from print's context. Readers with strategies would respond to an unknown word by skipping it, and then returning, or they might search their memory store for another graphophonemically analogous word or look for known chunks. Or perhaps they would reread the previous section. After all, when was the last time *you* used the two-vowels-go-walking rule to decode an unknown word?

Teachers Encourage Strategy Use

When readers had trouble with a word, most teachers in this study demonstrated or encouraged the use of dozens of micro strategies, instead of teaching skills; that is, they invited the

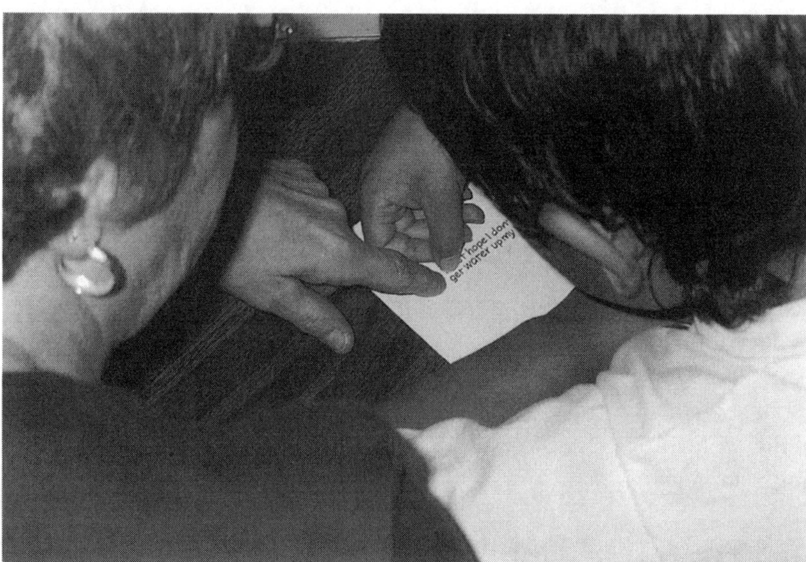

Linda and a reader work in the micro context.

child to check the picture (S-S) before reading, to reread (S-S), to sound it out (G), to cover up part of the word with her finger (G), or to relate the word to the context in which it was embedded (S-S). They said, "Let's read and find out" (S-S), or "Check and see if it makes sense" (S-S) or "Does that sound right?" (G or S-S).

But they also offered just as many macro strategies, inviting readers to question the text, make a connection, or retell a part. Teachers also invited the students to crawl into the shoes of the characters, to feel the feelings, to think the thoughts (P or S-S).

Most teachers have a menu of scaffolding behaviors, which can be found at the end of this chapter. It was these that they scaffolded. If a student had been relying upon primarily one cue, most mediators asked the reader to try another strategy. They used and reused their pointer finger, inviting students to return and reread or skip and read forward or check the picture. They indeed covered the strategy gamut, from micro to macro.

Scaffolding Micro-Process Strategies: Decoding

Throughout this book, I have demonstrated the grand number of cues that influence the decoding of words. At the top of this list of influences are graphophonic and semantic-syntactic cues. It is these cues, then, that teachers offer in-process to novices, but they keep meaning in the forefront; that is, they focus on *word-level semantic strategies*. (This does not mean that they eliminate cross-checking that incorporates graphophonics, however.)

Teachers use semantic micro processes to scaffold unknown words, strategies specifically related to the micro level. Through both words and gestural behaviors teachers scaffold readers to check the picture, reread for a running start, or skip, read on, and then reread the sentence.

How Teachers Scaffold Novices in Decoding Strategies

Although all teachers were involved in some way that helped readers focus on decoding strategies, I noticed how greater quantities of modeling and specificity occurred during novice reader scaffolding than during that of the fluent readers. That is, fluent readers were allowed more decision-making autonomy, while novices had those decisions made for them or with them.

For novices, who perhaps aren't capable of internalizing micro-macro strategies and metacognitive acts, teachers scaffold more specifically. At various points, Lani did this when she mediated, "Let's read that sentence again so we get the meaning," "Let's look at the picture," "Hm-m-m. Did that make sense?" and "Maybe we should go on."

The remainder of this book provides ample examples of ways in which teachers scaffolded their novices toward such semantic matches and cross-checking behaviors. Most used scaffolds that located novices within a micro context, yet nudged them toward chunking and the macro world.

How Teachers Scaffold Fluent Readers in Decoding Strategies

When teachers met with their fluent readers, they offered more autonomy. That is, they seemed to *expect* metacognitive behaviors, and their fluent readers generally obliged. For example, in the following Lani trusts that her fluent reader's decoding strategies will independently support him. This dyad is just beginning *The Great Kapok Tree* (Cherry 1993), when Lani offers only a very general metacognitive nudge by asking:

TEACHER: What are you going to do if you come to a difficult word? *(puts the reader in charge)*

STUDENT: Try to sound it out. And if that doesn't work I'm going to look at the picture, and see if that gives me any clues. And if that doesn't work, I'm going to skip it and then come back to it. *(It's obvious that this reader knows the answers to the teacher's question, but can he actually apply these behaviors? In this case, the answer is yes.)*

TEACHER: Well let's start out. *(trusts this reader enough to let his answers suffice)*

Leslie and Allen (1999) also indicated a difference in the scaffolding behaviors of teachers, depending on whether they were helping novices or "more advanced" readers. In their research:

> Beginning readers were encouraged to cross-check using initial sounds and picture clues. More advanced beginning readers were told to try a word beginning with the same sound(s) and and then finish reading the sentence in order to cross-check with meaning clues (i.e., to ask themselves, "did that make sense?"). More advanced readers were taught to use beginning sounds, rime patterns, and meaning to figure our an unknown word. (p. 408)

These strategies used to decode unknown words and taught to first graders today will be used by them for the rest of their lives. Every time a mature reader confronts a reading obstacle, he will reach into his bag of strategies and pull out the best one for the job—automatically cross-checking. You see, reading strategies are not all that different—whether someone is reading *Little Red Riding Hood* or *MacBeth*. Readers use similar decoding strategies on all kinds of texts throughout their lives (see eye movement research, such as that of Paulson and Freeman 2003). That is, unknown words are solved in a similar fashion, whether one is six or sixty. Nevertheless, the influence of the macro context for fluent readers makes micro-level tasks far easier.

How Teachers Lead Novices Toward Chunking: Transitions into the Macro Context

Becoming mired in the micro process uses up much-needed memory space for the macro level, so scaffolders stretch novices toward chunking behaviors. That is, they slide their finger under an entire phrase drawing the reader forward, because until that reader learns to chunk, macro processing and comprehension will be difficult.

When teachers focus *only* on the decoding of individual words at the expense of larger chunks, readers come to believe that reading is only about getting the words right (Goodman and Burke 1980). Yes, we do want readers to decode accurately, but we also want to move them beyond that word level—ASAP!

You will see the ways in which teachers consistently draw readers forward beyond individual words. They seem to have an internal compass

How Teachers Scaffold Toward Phrase-Chunking

Teachers most frequently encourage chunking through gestural and intonational scaffolds. Quite often such scaffolds hold a kind of synchronicity with the reader's behaviors, so that most of the following can be accomplished in tandem with the oral reading act.

- Teachers slide their pointer forward, slightly ahead of reader's voice.
- Teachers tap the end of sentence, calling readers forward.
- Teachers use read-along tactics to demonstrate chunking.
- Teachers use read-after tactics to demonstrate chunking.
- Teachers celebrate success by inviting a quick sentence reread.
- Teachers reread entire sentence with reader's miscue in it.
- Teachers offer keep-going strategies.
- Teachers consistently praise to build confidence.

Writing Reciprocity: Reproducing Predictable Language Patterns

It was the second month of school, and the kids were getting more involved in journal writing. As I read over their shoulders, I noticed that Jennifer's entry sounded like a poem, so I responded, "Jen! I do believe you have written a poem. Listen, everybody!" and I went on to read for the group what Jen had composed: "girls / are you a girl / yes I'm a girl / do you like girls / yes I do like girls."

Afterward, I asked, "How about if I put your poem on a poetry chart with the rest of the poets?" So by the end of the day, Jen's poem hung alongside Jack Prelutsky's.

The next day after journals, Bryan announced, "I wrote a poem, too!" And he read: "boys boys boys / I am a boy / Billy Joseph / and Jesse is a boy / a lot of people / are boys." Everyone clapped and we honored his poem on a similar chart.

It isn't surprising that the very next day Kelli shared a similar poem that she decided to call "Kids." She read, "Kids! Kids! / A lot of people are kids / Kids like to play / All day / They swing / And slide / See! / I told you / Kids play!" This time, however, I asked the kids which words should go on each line. With their help I composed the chart right there as a model.

The next day, Michael constructed his own poem in lines, "School": "school! school! / school is fun! / there are a lot of schools / schools! / you work / and play / and you do fun things / school!" I could scarcely believe how many kids were using Jen's language structure as a model. But it's also important to note that these first graders already had experience reading the poetry of published authors, which hung about room. Before long, our room was flowing with our very own poetry.

that points toward chunking strategies, so that by the end of first grade, we find kids reading in lengthier, meaningful syntactic units instead of individual words. Peter Duckett's (2002) eye movement research of first graders' reading demonstrates this shift away from word-by-word fixations. It is not surprising then, that the teachers of novices continually scaffold chunking behaviors.

Linda scaffolds text meanings with a reader.

Scaffolding Macro-Process Strategies: Comprehending

Although macro strategies work best when readers have moved beyond word-by-word reading with its focus on the micro context, teachers still weave their scaffolding with strategies that best serve macro processing. At times they scaffold novices into the macro context with a quick review, or they reread or read on a bit, enough to provide a greater perspective all at once.

It is especially at those times that they take comprehension strategies out of their scaffolding bag and weave them into the fabric of the transaction.

After readers *integrate* micro meanings, macro processing helps them to *summarize, elaborate*, and *extend meanings* (Irwin 1991). Readers do this through the use of comprehension strategies. When I survey the scaffolding transcriptions for these strategies, they just

Comprehension Strategy Cues

Teachers continually scaffold readers toward comprehension strategies they can use at the macro level of text. Such strategies are more apt to involve a paragraph, a page, a section, a chapter, or even an entire story. Teachers scaffold novices toward:

- asking questions of the text and its author;
- making connections to events, characters, etc.;
- visualizing, imaging, or reenacting parts of text;
- siphoning out the important ideas;
- making inferences backed by evidence;
- summarizing and synthesizing sections of text.

(Pressley 2000; Owocki 2003; Pinnell 2002; Harvey and Goudvis 2000; Keene and Zimmerman 1997; Pearson et al. 1992; Irwin 1991)

pop out all over the place. I honestly believe that most teachers teach at least one of these strategies every time they meet a child with a book—and they seem to do it without even thinking about it.

For instance, let's look at some comprehension strategies that Lani uses while scaffolding her novice and her fluent readers through their self-selected books.

The first three examples—synthesis, inference, and visualization—develop during Lani's transactions with her fluent reader, who was reading *The Great Kapok Tree*. The last, questioning the text, develops while Lani is scaffolding her novice reader.

While the fluent reader has very little trouble with decoding, notice how Lani scaffolds the use of comprehension strategies, focusing the reader on the macro context.

Synthesizing

TEACHER: Can we stop a minute, Bill? *(reaches forward to grab left side of page and lift it slightly. Then leafs back a page or two by lifting a few the pages.)* Can you tell me what the story is about so far?

STUDENT: So far it is about a tree and two men *(teacher turns back to previous page to invite use of picture cue to support comprehension)* coming into the forest and one left and the other man stayed *(teacher, sitting with elbow on table, rests her hand upon the side of face in a relaxed stance)* and tried to chop down the tree and then fell asleep.

Unlike this scaffolding situation, I find that one of the best times to ask kids to synthesize is when we, ourselves, have *not* read the text. In such situations, questioning is more authentic, because we really *don't* know the answer. How many times have you and your friends or family synthesized stories, movies, or TV shows for each other? Unfortunately, teachers most often request synthesis to test—and kids know it. When our inquiry is honest, the reader responses are even more mindful.

Inferring

Now watch how Lani continues her scaffolding when she encourages inference:

TEACHER: Okay. Let's go on now. Has he met anyone?

STUDENT: Uh-h-h . . . the boa. *(pointing)*

TEACHER: The boa constrictor. What's his feeling?

STUDENT: That the kapok tree is his home, and it was also the home of his ancestors. *(Teacher's elbow rests on the table as she holds her chin in her palm again. But when he finishes this sentence she jots a note down, and then crosses hands atop each other on the table, peering over at the page of reference.)*

TEACHER: Uh-huh.

STUDENT: Whatever his ancestors are. *(initiates a wonder)*

TEACHER: What do you think they are? *(leading into an inference)*

STUDENT: Um-m-m. *(Teacher is smiling, enjoying this moment.)*

TEACHER: Probably elephants . . . elephants, giraffes? *(leading into inference)* Who might the boa constrictor have for his ancestors? *(leading again)*

STUDENT: A snake?

TEACHER: *(gestures with palms up to mean, "Why not?")*

Lani uses a very common inference nudge here: "What do you think?" This encourages readers to gather evidence, synthesize it, and then infer or predict, which Irwin calls elaboration, because they are "inferences not necessarily intended by the author" (1991, p. 4). That is why readers need to back them with evidence.

Lani also uses another common inference nudge when she asks, "Who might . . . ?" Verb forms that incorporate *might* or other postulations pull readers into prediction, inference, and triangulated evidence because asking "might questions" almost requires a reader to provide an explanation for his answer. (See *Knee to Knee, Eye to Eye* [Cole 2003] for more on this.)

Visualization and Imagery

In this next example, notice how Lani moves from the micro to the macro context, incorporating drama and imagery along the way:

TEACHER: When you read it you said "whipped."

STUDENT: whipped *(miscueing, but pointing at the word* wiped*)*

TEACHER: whipped *(Repeats and then sits and waits with her hand on her cheek in a kind of observational stance offering autonomy. Sits like this for over ten seconds)*

STUDENT: *(subvocalizing, sounding through)* w-whipped . . .

TEACHER: You still like that word, huh? Whipped. *(points to the next word)* Read on and see. *(bounces her pen along over the next few words, presumably indicating: These are the words you should read)*

STUDENT: "off the sweat that—"

TEACHER: Okay. Show me how he would do that? *(encouraging imagery and drama)*

STUDENT: *(actually whips—not wipes—his hand, in a flash, across his forehead in what looks like a fling of the wrist at the end)*

TEACHER: He whipped off the sweat? *(has a touch of humor in her voice and a large smile on her face, while the child looks thoughtful, trying to figure it out)* That's right *(with an upward pitch on the end of right)*—except . . . that the word is *wiped. (points again at the word)*

STUDENT: wiped—

TEACHER: I suppose—I suppose, Billy, *(reenacts Billy's whipping movement and laughs as she does it, realizing now that it actually could be* whip*)* that you could actually whip sweat off, *(laughing aloud)* but that's *wiped* not *whipped. (pointing at the word again as Billy throws a proud smile her way)*

Young children love the reenactment and imagery that reading can offer. It is also surely a way in which we can scaffold them toward thinking differently about what they are reading. Billy will, no doubt, remember the man in the jungle and how he wiped (or whipped?) the perspiration from his forehead. Along with it will come many other ideas about what a jungle is like.

Questioning the Text

Perhaps there is no comprehension strategy offered more frequently than questioning the text and its author because questions are what drive our reading. They keep us going to see what will happen next, did we predict accurately, and how do all those pieces fit together? Wondering about events and people becomes the thread that weaves together the tapestry of text meaning.

Lani's scaffolding here is a perfect example of a natural movement toward questioning the text—an easy and natural place to start with novices. So it is that we join her with her novice as their investigation into the world of *Frogs and Toads* begins.

TEACHER: Okay, Want to start reading this? *(stops in her page-turning to ask)* Do you think you are going to find out anything?

STUDENT: Um-hum . . . *(mutters and nods in positive response while teacher backs off, no longer touching the book, yet does not explain)*

TEACHER: (*scaffolding*) Is there anything you wonder about frogs or toads? See I'm wondering now about something you said. *(leans forward intentionally to look the child right in the eye when asking this question)* You said frogs are bigger than toads, right? *(Nodding her head, she now crosses arms and rests them on the table, looking toward the text in an invitational manner, which must be a common nudge for readers to read on in order to validate their hypotheses. It is with this nudge that her reader enters the text.)*

One of the reasons I like this example is because grist for the investigation emanates from a previous statement made by the child. Yes, the teacher asks the question, as she scaffolds this novice toward such behaviors. Nevertheless, Lani knowledgeably gathered the grist for that question from the reader himself. Oh, that we could always follow Lani's instructional lead!

The following chapters provide many more instances of the ways in which teachers scaffold comprehension strategies. Yet, we can thank Lani for the wonderful backdrop she has provided.

The Micro-Macro Tango

In the following chapters, teachers repeatedly incorporate strategies into scaffolding acts. Notice how they move through each scaffold using a kind of micro-macro experience. That is, they help readers move in and out between the word-level or micro context and the more global macro context—and then back in again.

So it is that when a reader has trouble decoding a word—one whose meaning may be in question—the scaffolder will sometimes slide that reader out into the macro context, helping the novice make a personal connection before she guides him back into the micro for another try. At other times, we might observe the teacher asking a few questions, leading the reader into independent inquiry and problem solving. Or she may summarize or review what's occurred, so she can nudge the reader toward a meaning-based inference. Sometimes, teachers combine a couple of strategies. Through such strategy instruction and scaffolding, kids soon learn that there is a lot more going on during reading than just sounding out the words on the page.

Scaffolding Metacognitive Behaviors

Teachers continually encouraged learners to be captains of their own ships in both the micro and macro world. In order to do this, readers needed not only to monitor their reading but also to know how to facilitate any problems. This, in turn, required lots of strategies.

Sustaining Behaviors

All of these strategies serve to sustain the young reader when he is on his own. That's why *putting both the macro and micro processes into the hands of the reader is our ultimate goal.* In so doing, we will have worked ourselves right out of our scaffolding job.

There are numerous ways in which we can encourage readers toward these behaviors that sustain reading (Pinnell 2002). Some of these are listed below.

This list provides many scaffolding options. Yet, we can overdo the scaffolding, too. Once word readers gain a little confidence and show us they are ready to go it alone, we need to back off and just watch them do their thing. There's a considerable amount that can be learned from such experiences—for both the novice and the teacher.

No Mediation is Still Mediation

Occasionally, the absence of a mediation behavior would actually act as a strategy itself, in that

Scaffolding That Helps Readers Sustain Reading

Teachers guide students toward independently sustaining their own reading when they demonstrate the following behaviors and ask questions that lead novices to:

- more rapidly decode unfamiliar words,
- monitor semantics, syntax, and graphophonics through cross-checking behaviors,
- correct miscues,
- gather chunked meanings into wholes,
- predict upcoming events,
- maintain fluent behaviors,
- and adjust reading to the situational context.

if the reader miscued and was allowed to continue, the teacher could observe and assess the youngster's self-correction strategies. Lani served such an intention when she asked her reader during prereading, "What are you going to do if you come to a difficult word?" Afterward, she allowed this reader almost free reign in decoding.

This may mean that a novice could miscue and keep going. He may destroy meaning without blinking an eye. Let's hope not, but if a novice does not use strategies when he should, such an omission still offers the observer an important piece of information—one that may evoke further scaffolding related to red flags.

Indeed, reading authorities such as Goodman (Goodman, Watson, and Burke 1987) espouse this omission-is-still-information strategy as an important clue to a reader's proficiency. Such observations and assessment information direct teachers toward their next instructional strategy.

The "Tell" Category

I have decided to travel a divergent theoretical road regarding the "Tell" (give-the-student-the-word) category of former research. It now seems very obvious that the reason the Tell category seemed too difficult to squash into one of the three given rubrics is because it, like gesture, falls into all of them.

To What Cue System Does Tell Belong?

Let me explain. When a young reader comes upon a word such as *judicious*, most teachers will probably resort to the Tell cue, a scaffold that merely settles the reader's point-of-miscue struggling. What is imperative is that we look at the reason *behind* this Tell cue. What prompted it? When we discover that, we discover the cueing category to which it belongs, that is, what brought it into being. In this case, it is probably the plural—categories—for it seems that one would tell a beginning reader this word, *judicious*, because (1) the reader would not know the meaning of it, and correspondingly, (2) he cannot sound it out (G). But furthermore, if we notice that he is starting to fret or bore of the activity, and therefore needs an emotional (P) cue, it would then fall within that system.

Consequently, if a student is struggling to sound out the word and he just cannot do it, so the teacher tells him what it is, that is considered to be a (G) cue. However, if it is graphophonemically comfortable, but would not be a part of the child's vocabulary, then it will be designated as (S-S). Occasionally, it does not seem reasonably related to either (G) or (S-S), but seems more congruent with (P). So Tell can find its way into all three categories, or its purpose may actually align with more than one at the same time.

Many researchers have designated the Tell cue to be the most frequently demonstrated teacher mediation behavior (Singh 1989; Allington 1980; Speigel and Rogers 1980). Unfortunately, none of these studies actually thoroughly described or provided examples for what Tell actually is. We must assume then that Tell is merely providing the student with the unknown word; therefore, if the teacher precedes Tell with another cue, then, in comparison to past feedback research, I must say that there was only a very minimal quantity of (what has been termed) terminal feedback in this current study. Indeed, *most of these first-grade teachers used sustaining feedback*.

Why Don't First-Grade Teachers Use the Terminal Tell Cue?

Perhaps this research offers a different perspective because of the way in which the study was initiated. The informants knew that I was coming into their regular classrooms to observe and videotape the way in which they actually mediated a child through the text. In other words, they knew I was trying to learn what teachers do to help novices. If all they did was tell children words, it would not provide much information. On the other hand, when I collected that first set of videos from K–2 teachers, the second-grade teachers did indeed use the Tell cue without sustaining feedback.

I can't help but think that first-grade teachers use few Tell cues for another reason. Maybe they are pulled into sustaining feedback through their yearlong challenge to develop a roomful of readers. Using only Tell with novices is not going to demonstrate the process very well. These little ones need to be shown—up close and personal—how the process works. Tell just won't do that.

Gestural Cues

Demonstration seems to be the key that unlocks reading's door. And the most frequent demonstration used with novices proved to be fingerpointing. Yet, although I was well aware of the fact that I continually cued novices to words and their parts using fingerpointing, I had no idea of just how important gestural signs actually are.

We think nothing of gestures, because they seem almost instinctual. We tend to take them more or less for granted, only noticing them when they are overused or exhibited in an atypical manner. Yet, many linguists suggest that we receive as much as 90 percent of our meaning through gestures (Searchinger 1995; Griffin 2001). *A Dictionary of Gestures* (Bauml and Bauml 1975) has 250 pages of the various types—and these are just the most common ones!

Furthermore, until I read Marie Clay's (1979) and Don Holdaway's (1979) work no one had ever mentioned gesture's important role in the teaching of reading—neither my professors nor textbooks nor reading manuals. Yet the entire scaffolding act is driven by two very important gestural effects. One regards gesture's role in *emotive bonding*, while the other focuses on gesture's use as a *marker*. Both are extremely influential aspects of all novice reader scaffolding.

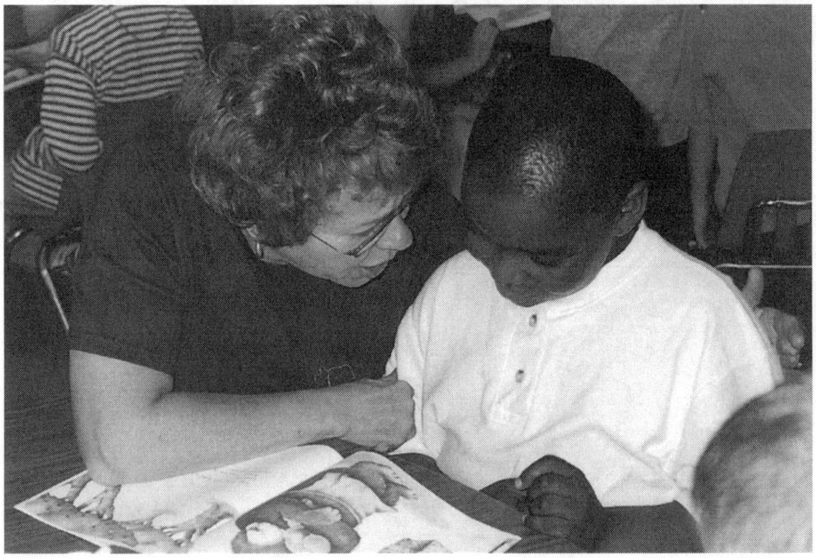

The Importance of Gesture for Emotive Bonding

Our inner, human emotions transform our faces and our body stances. Such subtle messages are important to the scaffolding act. In *Steps to an Ecology of Mind*, linguist Gregory Bateson (1972) suggests that "language is first and foremost a system of gestures," and by eliminating verbal language "it would make life a sort of ballet—with dancers making their own music" (p. 13). Bateson has described a teacher scaffolding event!

This ballet plays on the emotions of both the giver and the receiver. Gentle pats, shy smiles, body stances, and other gestures undergird the entire reading relationship and keep it flowing. Transcriptions are woven with the threads of compassionate gestures—smiles, touches, pats, nods, voice inflections, closeness, and gentleness. I cannot even imagine a scaffolding act devoid of the emotive bonding gesture offers.

Thus, throughout each transcription I offer interpretations of emotive gestural behaviors to lend a descriptive perspective to a very subtle, but influential process. As a matter of fact, I bet after reading this book you will be able to identify various teachers by their emotive bonding techniques alone! Chapter 7 delves into this topic in considerable depth.

The Importance of Gesture as a Marker

From a baby's first recognition of faces, hand and finger gestures (for example, pointing) are indispensable markers. These marking gestures serve meaning throughout our lives. Just as we teach babies where to look by pointing, we also teach readers where to look. There's a humorous cliche: "Cut off her hands and she won't be able to talk." And I must add, nor could she as effectively teach a child to read.

Linda's close relationship shines through as she teases her reader.

Thank goodness Marie Clay's *Reading Recovery* (1993), along with its related methods, helped give the act of pointing its place in the sun—and rightly so. Yet, as I did workshops related to this research, many teachers still responded, "I thought I was supposed to *discourage* pointing!" But just as many acts in life, there is a time and a place for pointing, and when a novice is just beginning, she *needs to point and so do her scaffolders* (Holdaway 1979; Clay 1979; Ehri and Sweet 1991).

Evidence of Pointing as a Marker in Other Language Systems

As a matter of fact, this is true for novices learning the language system of other cultures, too. I had an experience while visiting a school in another country, which revealed this behavior to be a common one.

My daughter and I were backpacking India about seven years ago when I decided to call on some schools and request permission to visit. When I telephoned Tagore School in Delhi, a woman kindly invited me to visit the very next day. The principal took me from classroom to classroom, where beautiful children sat in disciplined rows with open books before them. When we entered a classroom of six- and seven-year-olds, I asked if the children could read something to me. The teacher smiled obligingly and invited a young, proficient reader to come forward and read aloud from a colorless Hindi reader. The others followed along at their desks.

The text was written, and thus read, in Hindi, which was completely foreign to me. I only wanted to watch how children and teachers interacted with texts. Sure enough! The kids at their desks kept their pointer fingers moving in time with the reader—that is, *most* of the kids did. Here's what I wrote in my travel journal that day:

> I noticed some children—especially the girls—pointed left-to-right, word-by-word, while others were pointing, but were on a different page! To me, the English-speaker, the reader's phrasing sounded somewhat strange, as she read in short, clipped language chunks. The teacher did facilitate a few children. She marked the place for them with her finger.

Thus, similar to novices in this country, some of those Indian children apparently had not developed wordness either. Those who could not match the words of the reader with those on the page were scaffolded by their teacher. I might have been in India, but it sure felt like same old, same old!

So children and their scaffolders worldwide use gesture as a marker—one that comes in handy when they are first learning to read. But gesture also has other significance within the scaffolding act.

Gesture: An Analogic, Noninterruptive Cue

A unique and significant quality that makes gesture so facilitative in teaching reading is that it is silent, less intrusive, and noninterruptive. It is an *analogic behavior*. That is, through pointing we scaffolders can stay right with the reader, continually supporting him without any *voiced interruption*. Or, like Hannah, we can stay slightly ahead, encouraging forward movement. Considering that our intentions are focused toward fluency, these noninterruptive behaviors are indeed an important cue. They help us to quietly slide in and gesture the student to reread, or to jump over the unknown and then read forward again—all by the orchestration of analogic finger dances.

Linda pointing to a spot on the page.

Gesture Supports All Cueing Systems

Furthermore, gesture can be used to support all four cueing systems. For example, when a teacher covers part of a word with her finger, it is a (G) cue; when she points to the picture, it is a meaning cue; and when she looks a child in the eye or pats his hand, it is a (P) cue. These pragmatic-emotive cues set the scaffolding into action, and then they remain the connective glue that holds the entire process together.

Multicultural and Gender Differences in the Use of Gesture

Furthermore, there are great gestural differences between cultures. *Interactional boundaries* can differ significantly. And this is not only true of diverse ethnic groups, but such differences also exist between genders. For instance, women tend to be more comfortable in face-to-face encounters, while men usually speak elbow-to-elbow, throwing quick glances sideways (Searchinger 1995).

It therefore seems quite clear that in any relationship the meanings and emotions scaffolded through gesture can be both positively or negatively influential. Thus, gestural signs can make or break a reading relationship, and that is why I treat them as a significant cueing behavior. Chapters 5 and 6 are hued with gestural marking, while Chapter 7 thoroughly addresses emotive behaviors.

Linda points to gesture a reader over a hump.

A Summary of the Cues Teachers Use

Indeed, there are a vast number of cued reader behaviors, and there are just as many teacher scaffolding behaviors that support them—both gestural and voiced. The table on pages 62–63 provides a kind of overview, or menu, of some of the most common teacher cueing behaviors. The lists have been categorized to provide an organized background for what is in upcoming chapters.

Monitoring a Student's Oral Reading

Indeed, there are a grand variety of scaffolding behaviors related to every cueing system. Yet, it's imperative that we know about reading behavior, itself, before we try to scaffold it. That is why Chapter 2 of this book precedes the rest of the chapters. It discusses what readers do when they read. Only after we know what's going on inside the reading act can we facilitate it in some way.

One of the ways to actually internalize those reader behaviors is by administering a ton of individual oral reading assessments. As a matter of fact, my friend, Mary Shea, shared a somewhat humorous anecdote related to this overlearning. She said that after a couple of weeks of giving running records to large numbers of students in her school, she found herself monitoring the priest's reading during a Sunday service! So using assessments can actually condition us to observe reading behaviors every time we witness someone reading—even our clergy.

There are many individual, yet informal ways to assess a child's oral reading. From such individual monitoring there is much to learn. Miscue analysis (Goodman, Watson, and Burke 1987) and running records (Shea

The Cues Teachers Use

Graphophonic Cues:

Word Structure:

Teacher reminds child: "Remember what 'ing' says."
Teacher suggests: "This part of the word is a little word."
Teacher asks: "What word did we just have that ended the same way?"
Teacher covers part of word with finger.
Teacher encourages, "Close," when a child has almost decoded.

Initial, Medial, and Final Sounds:

Teacher covers up all but beginning of word and asks, "What's this much say?"
Teacher asks, "What is this sound?"
Teacher cues: "The *W* sound? What is it?"
Teacher suggests, "Sound it out."
Teacher suggests, "This word begins like *go*."
Teacher points to specific letter for a response.

Rhyming and Riming:

Teacher suggests: "This word rhymes with *mother*."
Teacher asks: "What word did we have that rhymes with this?"
Teacher suggests: "Cover the beginning. What's left?"
Teacher reminds: "Look at the end part."

Spelling:

Teacher expects child to make the sounds for the letters as she spells through the word.
Teacher tells child a letter; for example, in a *b/d* confusion.

Syntactic Cues:

Fluency:

Teacher rereads whole sentence over after child stumbles.
Teacher suggests that child rereads a portion.
Teacher slides finger under part cueing child to reread it.

Cohesion:

Teacher questions referential pronouns (e.g., she, he) to ascertain whether child understood the anaphoric relationship.
Teacher refers back to previous portion of text to make connections to latter portion.

Grammar:

Teacher asks, "Would *you* say that?"
Teacher suggests, "Read that again to see if it sounds right."
Teacher uses finger to bring child back to reread sentence.
Teacher rereads miscued sentence with a questioning inflection (hoping child will hear its grammatical offensiveness).

Punctuation:

Teacher rereads sentence emphasizing punctuation in voice.
Teacher draws attention to a particular punctuation mark.
Teacher points back to the period, question mark, etc.

Inflection:

Teacher rereads to demonstrate inflection.
Teacher asks: "Is that the way s/he would say that?"

Meaning Cues:

Semantic Match Cues (Micro Context)

Teacher points to picture for decoding a major text component (nouns, verbs).
Teacher suggests that child skip the word in question and go on to gather meaning.
Teacher models a semantic technique or way to process text.
Teacher provides a semantic cue in the way of a question: "Where did he look?"
Teacher encourages, "Close—" when child is close to meaning.
Teacher rereads distorted sentence with questioning inflection.
Teacher stops child to explain meaning of word.
Teacher slides finger past unknown word and on to next word, for keep-going cue.
Teacher encourages child to reread sentence when it doesn't make sense.
Teacher asks, "Does that make sense?"
Teacher encourages child to guess, sometimes suggesting, "What would make sense there?"
Teacher supports child when she hears inflection in his voice that means sentence is not making sense.

Comprehension Strategy Cues (Macro Context):

Teacher prompts reader to question the text or author: "Why did they do that?"
Teacher demonstrates and prompts wondering: "Hm-m-m. I wonder why that is."
Teacher demonstrates a personal connection to text: "I like to do that, too."
Teacher asks prediction question as page is turned.
Teacher prompts a synthesis: "Okay, let's discuss what's happened so far."
Teacher suggests reader stand in the shoes of a character: "How would you feel?"
Teacher provides a meaning clue from previous section, such as "Remember, the author said he was always afraid of the dark."
Teacher stops child to create a mini-discussion connecting the reader to meaning.
Teacher suggests: "Let's do a picture walk to see what the story's about."
If child reads miscued sentence which still makes sense in the macro context, the teacher does *not* correct him.

Pragmatic Cues:

Environmental Influences:

Teacher reminds reader that they just had that word/concept in another subject.
Scaffolding is interrupted by someone or something in the room.
Teacher asks reader to change the way he is sitting.
Teacher refers to wall visual in room.

Teacher-Student Relationships Influences:

Teacher reinforces with praise.
Teacher encourages (e.g., "Go ahead.")
Teacher displays joy in the process, such as laughter.
Teacher attempts to control child's attention, direction, focus, etc., by fingerpointing.
Teacher touches, pats, or in some way demonstrates affection or reassurance.
Teacher sits close to child, or even cuddles her with her arm.
Teacher's responses are kind/inviting.
Teacher mirrors behaviors of child.

Textual Influences:

Teacher invites choice of text within parameters.
Teacher refers to supportive structure of text, such as the table of contents, headings, etc.
Teacher compares text to another similar text.
Teacher refers child back to previous page, paragraph, or sentence.

2000; Johnston 2000; Clay 1985) are two oral reading assessments with which we can monitor and produce a written record of a student's oral reading, his miscues, self-corrections, and such. One of the hidden rewards in using these assessments is that they help raise our everyday level of awareness related to reading behaviors. They teach us how, where, and why to observe while they increase our understanding of reading relationships. They internalize the process for us.

I like the way Yetta Goodman (Goodman, Bridges, and Goodman 1991) explains that internalization:

> The more you know about miscue analysis itself, the more you know about the reading process, the more you can help a child who has problems. Once you are aware of what is involved in miscue analysis, you are always listening with what I call a "miscue head" you have the scheme of miscue analysis in your head. (p. 100)

And the earlier this takes place, the better! Decades ago, in my undergraduate experience, I was involved in a study that offered me the interesting opportunity of assessing a whole city of second graders using the Gilmore Oral Reading Assessment. Alongside all those readers, I—like Mary Shea—internalized the qualitative side of that quantitative experience, and I lived off it throughout my career. Mindful scaffolding can, indeed, be a natural outgrowth of such assessment experiences.

Coming Up Next

Throughout the remainder of this book, I invite you to investigate how teachers employ proactive scaffolding, model strategies, work toward student autonomy, and use gestures to complement and supplement their voiced interventions. Learn about what works and what doesn't.

In the next few chapters we'll take a closer look at specific cues within each of the cueing systems. What specific cues do teacher use? How do they support novice readers along their journeys through text? What do they say? What do they do?

Grist for Discussion

In the following, a student is reading the sentence "I like socks on my chair," from *My Messy Room*. Find all the cues proffered in this transcription. To what cueing system does each belong? Discuss the effectiveness of each teacher cue.

(We join this dyad when the reader gets stuck on the word *socks*.)

STUDENT: I like . . . *(reads but stops just before the word* socks*)*

TEACHER: Hm-m? What is the beginning sound first and then we'll go picture hunting. S-s-s-. Hm-m? What in this picture starts with *S* sound? Do you see anything? Starts with s-s-s-. If sounds aren't working, let's try something else. Let's jump right over it. "I like blank" *(leaves off with an upward, invitational inflection)*

STUDENT: *(finishes)* "on my . . . chair."

TEACHER: Okay. So she likes something on her chair that starts with s-s-s-. Do you see anything on her chair that starts with *s*? What are those?

STUDENT: *(points to the socks and says)* Socks.

TEACHER: Okay. Let's check our work though. *(gestures a rereading by fingerpointing back to the sentence beginning)*

STUDENT: "I like socks on my chair. I like books on my bed." *(points and rereads correctly)*

TEACHER: Outstanding!! *(celebrates as she pats the student's hand)*

Chapter 5

How Teachers Scaffold Meaning and Syntax: Micro and Macro Processes

If reading is about mind journeys, teaching reading is about outfitting the travelers, modeling how to use the map, demonstrating the key and the legend, supporting the travelers as they lose their way and take circuitous routes, until, ultimately, it's the child and the map together and they are off on their own.

ELLIN KEENE AND SUSAN ZIMMERMAN,

MOSAIC OF THOUGHT: TEACHING COMPREHENSION IN READER'S WORKSHOP

After working with children for over three decades, I have many delightful stories about how easily kids can be confused by words, sounds, and meanings. One time Anthony ran up to me, gave my jacket several hard tugs and exclaimed, "Mrs. Cole! Mrs. Cole! Dierdra is writin' in the butter!?"

"Butter?" I pondered aloud.

"Yes! Look! Look!" he said as he tugged me across the room. "She's doin' what you said *not* to do. She's writin' in the butter!"

After teachers work with kids for many years, we can usually untangle these confounding moments. But this one had me baffled. So I continued to be led by Anthony until we finally came to Dierdra, who just seemed to be innocently writing in her journal—and there were no dairy products around.

Yet, Anthony continued to complain. Finally, frustrated because I remained complacent about the unknown misdemeanor of Dierdra, he jabbed his finger to a spot on her journal page.

The margin! Dierdra had written in the margin, not the margarine! And certainly not the butter!

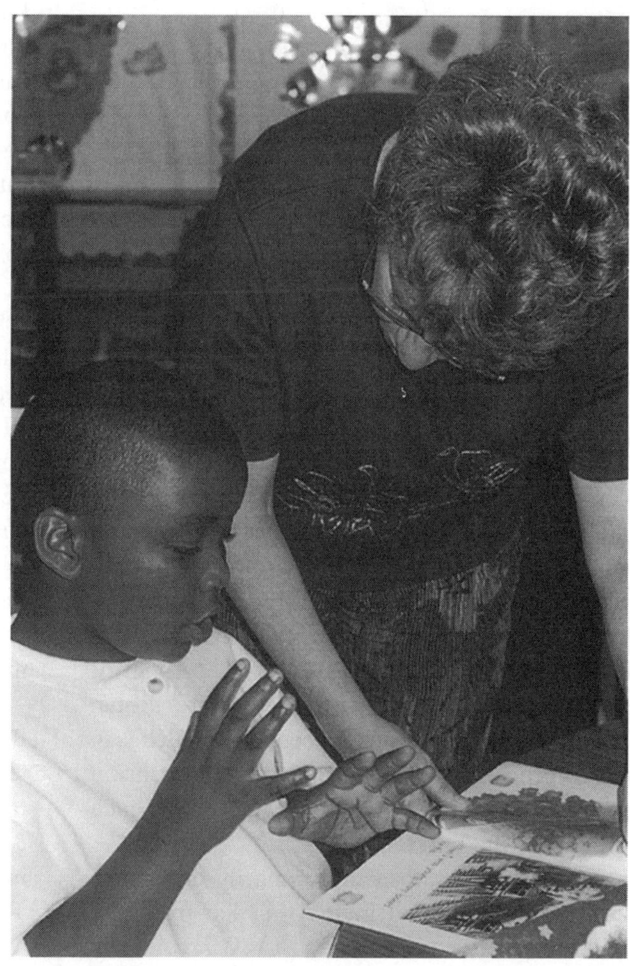

That week I had been focusing these novice first graders on spacing and neatness and had mentioned the margins for about three seconds. Nevertheless, Anthony picked up on it, and had become our room's "margarine" policeman.

Another common kindergarten and first-grade faux pas can be seen in this word: *wunsaponatim*. About eight out of ten novices who encode *once upon a time* using phonetics, do it in a similar fashion (which I actually applaud for its close letter-sound correlations). How are they to know it is actually four words! It is only after I show them the four words, pointing to each, that they exclaim, "Oh-h-h-h!" The meaning of that abstract phrase eluded them, thus, the spelling did, too.

Children who have only been on the face of this earth for six years have many confusing moments in literacy. That is actually part of the joy of teaching first grade; that naivete, that innocence, is a quality I so enjoy and cherish. But I always try to embed the curriculum and the day with meaning, because without it, we all get lost in the butter.

Considering the importance of meaning in general, semantic-syntactic (S-S) cues remain utmost in importance, because it is they that are central to the entire literacy process. After all, they help everything else to make sense, and when meaning breaks down, everything else does, too.

Macro and Micro Processes: Interdependent Meaning Makers

This chapter will focus on both the micro processes, which include word decoding, and the macro processes, which include comprehension strategies. Meaning and syntax are vested in both of these interdependent processes. While the micro processes involve, primarily, word units and local cues, the macro processes involve, primarily, larger syntactic units with their more global meanings. Readers reach for semantic matches in micro processing; they reach for comprehension in macro processing. Obviously, however, each influences the other.

Nevertheless, focusing primarily on sounds and words will steal memory space from the macro meanings, and focusing primarily on larger chunks of texts containing numerous miscues will confuse the entire process. Novices need to get good at both!

Meaning's Relationship to Fluency

Don Holdaway (1979) suggests that "The major reason why predictive and meaning-oriented drives must operate at the center of any efficient strategy is that they provide the necessary conditions for fast automatic performance" (p. 99). When the flow of words slows or takes on a different tempo or timbre, the reader is sending a metamessage to the listener, "This isn't making sense." It's like a song being sung slightly off-key—we notice it immediately and want to do something about it. And when the off-key reader was a novice, teachers did tend to rescue fluency.

In this regard, I was fascinated by the astute responses of the teachers I watched. Even when kids were fairly fluent, teachers seemed to notice almost imperceptible changes in their students' fluency patterns. The child may have appeared confused for only a second, or maybe the reader just altered his pace a tiny bit, or he changed his intonation pattern. Regardless, all teachers noticed these nuances, and their gestural behaviors told me they were ready to scaffold, if needed.

As Kara watched her video footage, she asked that it be stopped momentarily at a point where she was explaining a bit of the story to her reader. She focused my attention, pointing out, "There's another cue . . . I just didn't want her comprehension to break down." What Kara helps us to see here is how she attempted to rescue a young reader's (S-S) flow *before* that child experienced failure. Julie, Lani, and Hannah also did this on occasion. They followed their instinctual sense to support, to rescue dysfluency or a miscue before it occurred.

When I discussed this with the teachers themselves they said that they know when a child "isn't getting the meaning." Most obvious to them was that the reader's fluency starts to break down. Thus, fluency affects meaning and meaning affects fluency, and both affect scaffolding. The relationships are close ones.

When a Slower Pace Actually Enhances Comprehension

The strategies the reader uses affect meaning perhaps more than the pace at which he reads. We all know that when we are reading and come upon a strange term or concept, we slow down, think about it, maybe reread, or we read on and then return. During such meaning-gathering periods, we do not sound very fluent; however, we are interrupting our fluency for a very good reason, that is, to *sustain meaning*.

Whereas, if we did not understand and kept going at that same steady pace, we'd sound good, but meaning would no doubt suffer. In that case, implementing strategies that make us sound less fluent can actually aid our comprehension, because almost all readers slow down to implement time-consuming strategies when they come upon a nonmeaningful section of text. This means that several readers could read the same material at different rates, yet still comprehend in a similar fashion.

Yet, although slowing down to implement a strategy can support comprehension, it can also indicate to a scaffolder that the reader is experiencing some kind of trouble. And when that reader is a novice, it might be a good time for the teacher to jump in and rescue meaning or fluency or both—a decision that is not always an easy one to make.

Why Teachers Enter to Save Fluency for Novices

I watched Jane make the decision to jump in when she noticed a change in her novice's inflection. It was only a nuance of difference, but Jane noticed and accommodated. Afterward, Jane and I watched a segment of the video together. We heard her novice stumble, after which an immediate inflection and intonation change occurred. Almost synchronistically, we heard Jane begin to read along with her novice reader.

As we were watching the event via video, Jane pressed Pause and commented to me, "I don't know if he's enjoying this right now. Do you think he's enjoying it?"

Instead of answering her question, I asked her another, "Is that why you're reading *with* him now?"

"Yeah," agreed Jane. "I think he's getting frustrated and isn't getting it." Jane sensed her reader's meaning might be slipping—along with his patience—so she saved him. She understood that fluency and meaning are directly related, and that if the fluency was slipping, then meaning probably was also. Nevertheless, maybe Jane would have waited were it not for her sensing a change in reader attitude.

Wait Time: A Sensitive Scaffolding Decision

Wait time varies, because some transitioning preword readers need lots of support, that is, a guide by their side catching them before they fall. But if we do not give novices some wait time, how will they learn to use strategies, to correct their miscues, to go it alone?

Teachers respond in different ways to wait time. Instead of interrupting, many wait until the page is about to be turned to ask about a miscue. They correctly assume that once the page is turned, it is unlikely the reader will go back.

That's what happened when the following reader miscued on the word *sometimes* in the sentence: "Sometimes he changes at lunchtime just to show off."

STUDENT: "Some he ch- changes at lunchtime just to show off." *(Glances at the picture as she finishes, appearing to verify the print with the illustrations. Then, just as quickly, reaches for the edge of the page to turn)*

TEACHER: *(stops the page-turning to comment)* Okay, when I heard that part it didn't quite make sense to me. "Some changes at lunchtime." *(reiterates the reader's words)*

STUDENT: Oh, *sometimes*! *(says with a slight grin as she observes the text)*

TEACHER: There, just like what I do. When I read something and it doesn't make sense, you need to—

STUDENT: go back.

TEACHER: *(makes a circular motion with her finger over the text)* Yes, go back.

It was obvious to Kara that this reader was going to move on without self-correcting her miscue, so the teacher stepped forward to scaffold. However, she waited for the page-turning.

Not all teachers step in to correct. Natasha's fluent reader was reading *The Amazing Bone*, by William Steig, when the reader miscued on the word *instead*. He read, "It was a brilliant day. Instee- . . . It was a brilliant day inst- eed of going straight home from school . . ." but then the reader continued to read. He did not self-correct, and the scaffolder did not stop him.

When Natasha and I watched the video of this reading, I stopped it at this spot and asked, "Now, 'It was a brilliant day and insteed of going to school' does not make sense, and you didn't correct him. Why not?"

We know that Natasha understood fluency's effect on the macro context and meaning when she responded, "I thought he would catch it himself. I expected him to catch it and so I thought I'd wait and see what happened." Natasha gave her more fluent reader greater autonomy to *self*-correct his miscues. She knew that when readers have a chance to gather a larger unit of text—the entire sentence or paragraph—meanings solidify, readers realize their own errors, and they self-correct. This child's lack of response to that miscue makes us wonder about his meaning making.

Readers sometimes *do* recognize their miscues, but feel no compulsion to reread and self-correct. Nevertheless, they have *internalized* that self-correction. Adults also choose this route sometimes. We just don't take the time to go back every time we blunder—even though our brains have indeed self-corrected. We would not want novices to make a habit of this, though.

The Relationship Between Interruptions and Meaning

There are myriad ways to enter the act and help novices—some resemble a sledgehammer effect, while others are barely noticeable. In *Knee to Knee, Eye to Eye* (Cole 2003) I discuss the difference between *interrupting* and *piggybacking*, and I believe it is applicable here, as well. That is, when we gently slide in to help, we are piggybacking and it is not intrusive. However, when we obtrusively jump in and jolt the reader out of the context and his stream of thought, it is interrupting.

Notice the way that Julie enters to decode and simultaneously meld meaning. She and her fluent reader are reading *The Reluctant Dragon* when the child struggles with the word *volume*.

STUDENT: *(reading)* "But his little son, when he wasn't helping his father, and often when he was as well, spent much of his time buried in big vol- vol-"

TEACHER: Volumes. That means like—um—many books, many books compiled into one, volumes? *(Here the pitch of her voice rises slightly to connote a question, to which the student responsively nods, yes, meaning, "Yes, I understand it now." And thus reads on.)*

If this had not been caught via video, an observer would hardly have noticed it occurring, it was slipped so subtly into the the reading act. The more harmonically we can slide into the process to save fluency and to ground comprehension, the more secure the reader will be. Sometimes blatant interruptions are indeed necessary, but it is best to avoid them as much as possible. One way to accomplish this is to handle potential stumbling blocks *before* they occur. Another, whenever possible, is to use gestural instead of voiced interruptions.

The Noninterruptive Quality of Gestures

As I mentioned earlier, gestures are a unique and wonderful scaffold because they are not voiced; therefore, they are fairly noninterruptive. These silent pointing and body behaviors painted the background of every single teacher-reader scaffolding event. And quite often the gestural intention was to secure the text's meanings.

To help make meaning more concrete, teachers pointed to pictures, to places in the room, to features on themselves or the child. Some teachers even incorporated hand movements to gesture a word's meaning. That is, Lani pointed to her own chin and the child's chin to denote *chin*, while Natasha signified another part of the body, *leg*. Coupled with graphophonics, most—but not all—of these gestures supported meaning.

Sometimes gestures actually got in the way of meaning when the word was still unknown after the gestured behavior. That's because the reader focused more on decoding the gesture than decoding the word! (Chapter 8 discusses this to a greater extent.)

Gestures are usually more facilitative if we keep them implanted in the text itself and draw readers toward macro meanings. Therefore, it seemed that the most effective gestures contributing to the meaning were those that scaffolded a flow forward, a nudge toward chunking, or the pointing guidance that directed a reader to check the picture or to return and reread.

Catching Readers Before They Fall

Some teachers, like Hannah, seem to intuit potential stumbling blocks, so they respond *prior* to that seeming problem. For example, before beginning a new page with her novice, Hannah prepared the reader for an upcoming word: *hopscotch*. The teacher had predicted that this particular child might be intimidated by the word's length. So knowing it was coming, Hannah used a pictorial cue prior to the time that the reader met the word.

At another time, Hannah let go of the page as her fluent reader approached the word *persuading*. Knowing full well that this was no first-grade word, her gesture, this time, indicated a concern even before her words were uttered and also before the reader's miscue took form. Hannah's gestural response indicated a potential miscue, and her prediction was correct. But she quietly slid in just before the word, reading along with the child until he moved past it. Such graceful scaffolding is not surprising for a teacher whose intuitions are grounded in thirty-two years of teaching over eight hundred children to read!

Interrupting for the Sake of the Whole

Sometimes fluency does not break down; nevertheless, we still see teachers interrupt the process. Such scaffolders say they are trying to rescue meaning *before* it is lost. They feel that a particular concept or term will ground the reader, and without it, the child may become more and more confused. That is, without that conceptual background, the macro meanings may be lost.

This is a common occurrence when reading aloud to preschoolers. Stories often need a bit of semantic glue to hold them together in a meaningful manner. Yet, we slide in and out with our scaffold as quickly as possible, so as to keep the meaning in flow. For example, while reading aloud the book *Madeline* by Ludwig Bemelmans, I scaffolded the concept of an appendix for four-year-old Delanie. Without it, the remainder of the story may have been confusing, for the term is central to the meanings vested in the latter part of the book—the operation, the scar, and the moral of the story itself.

Lani does this in the following when she interrupts her novice reader at the unknown word to briefly interface with an explanation. Her novice was reading *Frogs and Toads* (Butterworth 1990), a book about animals all over the world, when he miscued on the noun *Australia*. Therefore, the teacher not only told him the word, but also added some background knowledge. Lani first exclaimed, "Wow! You are really close!" Then she quickly added, "That's the name of a country. It's also a continent. It's where this animal would live. You were very close to it—it's *Australia*."

With an entire section of text gathering its substance from that continent, the teacher felt compelled to develop the concept for the reader. She interrupted for the sake of the whole—but she kept it brief.

Interrupting to Define Strange Terms

Lani also rescued her fluent reader when the child was trying to apply a two-vowels-go-walking phonics rule to the noun *ruins*. In this case, of course, that rule wasn't working. The scaffolder began her explanation in this way, "*Ruins*. Sometimes words are hard to figure out because you don't know the meaning of them. . ." and she went on to define *ruins* for her first grader.

Lani assumed that this reader had scant knowledge of what ruins are. He may have continued to decode this five-letter word as one syllable throughout the text had his teacher not stepped in to scaffold him with its correct pronunciation, as well as its meaning.

Another strange-term scaffolding took place when Kara's student was reading *The Principal's New Clothes*. After the child read "Mr. Bundy is the principal of P.S. 88," Kara jumped in quickly for the following eight-second scaffold:

TEACHER: Ya know what, Let me tell you about P.S. P.S. here *(pointing to* P.S.*)* doesn't mean the P.S. when we do letters. This is the short way to say public school. Some schools don't have names like Glendale or Willowridge. Some schools are just called Public School and then a number. See there it is up there, Public School 88. *(pointing to the picture)*

These brief strange-term explanations occurred throughout all scaffolding. Who's to say, however, whether readers may have eventually come to understand the term without the teacher's support? Yet, when we are there beside a novice for such a brief time, why not offer a hand and our heart when it feels appropriate?

Keep Interruptions Brief and Subtle!

We know that scaffolders do interrupt readers, and often with good reason. Marie Clay (1993), who focused much of her work on novices, would suggest that interruptions be as brief as possible. Certainly the slide-in scaffolding that keeps a beginner afloat would *not* be considered an interruption.

However, disrupting fluency always has the potential of disrupting meaning, so having a five-minute conversation midtext may inflict as much harm as the good that was intentioned. As a matter of fact, Clay suggests that we have kids take words apart *only when necessary*. That is, save most of the lengthier sound-it-out lessons for reading-group instruction. Or at least wait until the child has finished reading. Allington (1980) found that teachers interrupt struggling readers far too often, and this led him to suggest that we should avoid interrupting fluency.

Ultimately, interruption will depend upon the reader, the book, and the scaffolder. Careful consideration of this matter can only enhance the reading relationship.

Between-the-Pages Scaffolding

To circumvent during-reading interruptions, teachers frequently waited for the natural page-turning interruption. For instance, I stopped Brandon at page-turning and said, "Hang on a minute. We need to check something that you didn't fix. You said, 'Mother Bear has yarn to do.' She does have yarn, but this word starts with *w-* instead of *y-*. Yarn would start with *y-*. Right? Mother Bear has *w-* work to do. What's that word *(pointing)*?"

When I first begin guided reading groups, I always ask readers to read only two pages at a time. We then stop for a quick review and introduction to the next two pages. Baby steps.

Between the pages or at the end, teachers summarize or review what's been read, constructing the macro context. For example, during a small guided reading group, as the readers neared the end of the story, I asked, "Now, what was Beth's problem that needed to be solved?" And after the group answered, I asked, "Did it get solved yet?" During page-turning, I grasp the chance to ground the novices in story structure.

It's also a time when we can flavor upcoming text to make it more predictable. For instance, when Billy was near the end of *The Giving Tree*, I interjected, "Oh, here comes the sad part." We continually add these tiny pieces of meaning to keep the flow as well as the reading relationship intact.

Thus, page-turning can be a convenient scaffolding moment, and as long as it is brief, it is less intrusive than interrupting in the middle of flow. Most of these scaffolds were tidbits of only a sentence or two, just enough to keep meaning afloat.

Scaffolding Meaning Through Proactive Mediation

Rescuing a reader even before he ever enters the reading act is most optimal. That's why all teachers grounded novices in text background *proactively*, that is, before the reader came in contact with the text. They did this before the child opened the book and at page-turning, providing meanings that aided prediction and, thus, fluency.

When teachers introduced a story before reading, they scaffolded meaning through a variety of methodology: providing background information, focusing on picture clues, modeling readerly behaviors through demonstrations, presenting (S-S) strategy briefings, and offering sensitive emotional support.

Novices Received More Prereading Prep

Teachers prepare their novice readers far more than their fluent readers. They said they do this to put the reader at ease, to build confidence, and to keep the emotional response positive.

Julie dedicatedly prepared her novice reader, and later, as she was watching the video, she volunteered the following: "I prepared him more . . . because I know he's not an advanced reader and I sensed he was a bit nervous . . . [The fluent reader] is very confident . . . I knew that she really wouldn't need it." Notice how Julie sensed or intuited a nervousness in this child that an observer might not sense. She therefore tried to accommodate the reading relationship through gesture and by undergirding with more background. She allowed a lengthier warm-up period in which she developed story schema in order to accommodate certain "sensed" changes in the child.

In both time spent and depth of scaffolding, novices received more prereading scaffolding than fluent readers—scaffolding that would support the *process* of reading, the *content* of what was to be read, and the *interest* and *confidence* of these readers.

Prereading Background Development: A Proactive Strategy

Teachers used a variety of instructional avenues to support their readers prior to the reading act. They introduced story structure, made connections, discussed vocabulary, reviewed illustrations and photos, and offered related information to develop schema. They did this to make the text more predictable, because the more predictable it is, the easier it will be for the novice to read.

Story Structure Aids Text Predictability

Story structure is an important prereading consideration. If the text is a narrative, scaffolders introduce the characters (who may have strange names) and setting, and they entice readers with the story's unknowns that will need to be solved. If the text is expository, however, they explain that readers will be reading for information, and they make certain that the young novices have the prior knowledge upon which they can build. Lani did this before her novice read about frog and toads.

Sometimes teachers grounded readers in story structure prior to the story itself; while at other times this occurred in a flash, during page-turning. Either way, it occurred prior to the reading act, thus undergirding it with meaning and predictability.

Writing Reciprocity: Using Story Structure and Choice to Scaffold Writer's Block

It was writer's workshop, but Rowanda sat staring out the window, while his pencil remained in its groove on his desk. I stooped down and whispered, "Rowanda, what would you like to write about?"

"I don't know," Rowanda distantly responded.

Rowanda had just finished writing a wonderful piece, but he was intimidated by all upcoming possibilities; that is, he just could not imagine that his next piece would be as good as the last. Thus, when asked about his new topic, he could only mutter, "I don't know."

When writers experience these I-don't-know periods, I can help by offering choices related to story elements. That's why I began with, "Do you want to write a true story or a make-believe story?"

"Make believe," he said after a few seconds.

"Okay, fiction. So who do you want to have in your make-believe story? A giant? A king? The hulk? A witch? A dinosaur?" and I continued, offering just a few more. But, once I saw the writer soften, I stopped and let him choose the first character.

"A dinosaur," Rowanda responded, devoid of enthusiasm.

"Okay, what other characters should be in this story with a dinosaur? A giant? An alien?" I scaffolded.

I continued to support Rowanda in this fashion through all the rest of the story elements, that is, setting, problem, events, resolution. Each time I offered a choice of several; each time I wrote his choice down on a sticky note in the corner of his desk. When we were finished he had the main elements of a good story. That is, Rowanda had the macro context.

I talked with him a bit more, asking questions related to what might happen next in this story, and for each of his answers I responded back with a related question, as though the idea was actually his. Before long, I invited, "Look at all your ideas for another great story! Let's think of a good first sentence. Maybe, 'Once upon a time,' or ' There was once,' or 'A long time ago.' What do you think?"

As Rowanda responded, he also reached forward to pick up his pencil, and I knew this writer was again intentioned. So I left him to create the details for his story from the macro context we had constructed together. Sooner or later, just like others, Rowanda would realize that all stories have common elements that help guide our pen.

Content Connections Aid Text Predictability

Patty spent a period of time with her novice reader preparing him for a book from Ireland that she had selected. She connected her reader using everything from world geography to his own family lineage. She made a textual connection to similar books he'd read by recalling the characters "with unusual names." Thus, when the reader began, he was well grounded in prior knowledge.

Before reading, Jane and Julie both connected readers to the author of the story through previous texts of that same writer. Teachers reviewed the author's works, discussed favorites, and invited students to make their own author connections, all of which helped develop related schema, and it demonstrated how readers make connections between texts.

Hannah connected her novice reader to the story characters' nicknames through uncovering the relationships among meaning, pictures, and print. She pointed to the picture of a little mouse and asked, "What do you think they call him? What kind of animal is he?"

"A mouse," answered the reader.

"And what sound does he make?" the teacher went on.

"He squeaks," the novice responded.

"Squeak! Squeak!" the teacher mimicked. "So what's a good name for him?"

"Squeaky," the reader concluded correctly.

Later, when this reader encounters that word, it will hopefully be in his literacy pool.

Teaching Vocabulary Aids Predictability

Teachers focused heavily upon prereading vocabulary introduction. They had an uncanny ability to predict which words would serve as stumbling blocks to meaning, decoding, or both. I especially like Hannah's intuitive responses in this regard. For example, before her novice began to read, Hannah suspected the child would have problems decoding *hopscotch* (Hannah told me this during video viewing). Therefore, she used a proactive strategy.

Hannah pointed to the picture of a child playing hopscotch and asked, "What's that called?"

"I don't know," the reader answered, but then her eyes told us that she was pondering the question.

So Hannah went on, "We'll see if you can figure that out by the time you read the rest of this page."

"Hopscotch!" exclaimed the child. As the teacher suspected, she remembered after all.

When I was scaffolding a small group during guided reading, I continually mentioned the names of characters about to be introduced, because I know names are often difficult. I saw a name that I knew would give the readers a problem, so I said, "Look at this girl *(pointing)*. Her name is Laura. Please find her name on the page before you read on. Then let's see what Laura's making."

Picture Walks Aid Text Predictability

Pictures or illustrations are an important part of beginner texts, and novices need to understand how those pictures elevate the level of predictability. That is, pictures can help them predict meanings and decode unknown words through semantic matching. It is no surprise, then, that most teachers previewed pictures *before* the reader entered the reading act. Several teachers mentioned the relevance of the cover illustration to the story. Then, they skimmed through the text's illustrations for a page-by-page *picture walk*. All of this grounded the beginner in story schema.

For example, Lani invited a picture walk prior to listening to her novice read about frogs and toads. As they discussed the photos, the teacher used questions, such as "What do you think this is about?" and "What is happening here?" to connect the reader to that which he would read. Therefore, the student had an *overview* of the story's content *before* it was read. The novice would have a semantic head start, which would support both confidence and comprehension.

Julie invited her novice to investigate the picture prior to the story. She had a suspicion that he did not know about wishing wells, which is a key understanding to comprehend the story called *The Wishing Well*. Let's investigate how she uses the picture proactively to solidify the concept.

TEACHER: Now, we are going to look at the picture. *(circles the picture with her finger)* What are you thinking? *(but the novice does not respond)* The Wishing— *(pointing back up to the title for each word)* What's that? *(points down at picture of well and quickly retracts her hand)* What do you call that with water inside? You know what you call those things? *(quickly circles the well three times with her finger and then lifts her hand to use it for gesturing through the rest)* Like Jack and Jill up the hill—they got the water from this. *(waits a few seconds)* It's called a well. *(circles the well again three times with her finger)* You don't see too many of these *(points at well)* nowadays—one that's got the water in it. And the string rolls *(rolling gesture with hand)* down and water collects in the bucket and you roll it back up. They used to use a lot of these *(tap, tap, tap on the picture)* in the olden times. Not so much now.

The picture was an important resource for this prereading prep. Imagine explaining a well to a first grader without the picture! We can be grateful that all early reading texts have illustrations. Nevertheless, even with this prep, the novice stumbled on the word *well* during his reading.

Demonstrating Readerly Behaviors Through Modeling: A Proactive Strategy

Teachers could readily be seen modeling *readerly* behaviors for a student. Some of these were just a common part of their daily read-alouds, but other behaviors were implemented for a particular purpose. Teachers modeled looking at the picture; they modeled feelings related to characters, reading with inflection, rereading to capture a flow, as well as many other (S-S) behaviors. Thus, when their readers entered a text, they could follow their teacher's lead.

Throughout Hannah's scaffolding she repeatedly preread and reread words and sentences with noticeable inflection, modeling an almost dramatic performance that she hoped her readers would mirror. She never said, "Do it this way," yet her expressive way became contagious after a while. Sometimes Hannah would slide right in with her reader, softly and in unison, yet emphasizing inflections, intonations, and rhythms. This seemed to draw the reader in, moving him toward fluency—a fast-moving and exciting scaffolding event—one that was even fun for an observer!

Semantic-Syntactic Briefings: Proactive Micro-Macro Strategies

Prior to the reading act, teachers nudged readers toward strategy use. Sometimes they explained and demonstrated the strategies for their students, while at other times, they expected readers, themselves, to explain the strategies they would use. Some of these strategies, such as cross-checking, were related to micro processing; whereas, others were related to the macro context and often involved chunking or comprehension strategies. Let's investigate these.

Proactive Micro Strategies

Teachers readied their students for a more independent reading act by reviewing strategies that could be implemented when readers encountered an unknown word. Some had a list of these posted in the room. Most began by inviting the learner to review previously taught strategy options, and students responded with both (S-S) and (G) strategies. For example, teachers prompted:

- "When we come to a word we don't know, what are some things we can do?" (Kara)
- "Before we read, what will you do when you come to a word you don't know?" (Julie)
- "If you get stuck on some words, use some of the strategies you know." (Jane)
- "What do you think (it) is going to be about/happen next?" (Patty)
- "Where else can you go for help (the picture)?" (Ardith)

Now one cannot help but notice that most of these questions require a metacognitive response; that is, the teacher did not tell a child what to do, but instead, using an open-ended question, just reminded readers that there were strategies that should be used. They left the ownership of choice in the hands of the student. This is important because it is indeed the student who will be using the strategies, yet in order to do that, he must have already been taught *when* and *how* to use them.

Nevertheless, students who answered, "Sound it out," as the one-and-only strategy were nudged by their teachers to consider, "What else?" They did not want readers anchored to only one cueing system, for they knew that as long as novices stayed glued to the micro pieces of text, meaning would be at stake.

Proactive Strategies That Transition Novices Toward Macro Processing

Teachers consistently scaffolded readers toward a broader palate of cueing—scaffolds that would lead novices toward chunking and its more global enticements. Some teachers had charts with strategy guidelines that were read prior to the reading act. Most often, they reminded students that "if you get stuck on a word, there is more you can do than just sound it out." They mentioned the following:

- "Reread to help me understand it."
- "Reread that sentence a little faster if it was choppy the first time."
- "Skip the word you don't know, go on, and then come back to the capital letter."
- "Think about what you've read so far."

So these scaffolders were helping novices decode unknown words, and at the same time they were nudging these young readers forward, out of that micro world and into the macro. For it is there that novices would come to understand and apply more global, comprehension strategies.

Emotional Support That Undergirds Meaning: A Proactive Strategy

As might be expected, teachers provided emotional support for their students before reading even began. One could not help but notice that as the actual reading act approached, all of the teachers tended to move their bodies closer to the child. This gestural support was probably most noticeable in Julie, who even later fretted aloud about how a child might feel regarding her corrections, reading before a camcorder, and such. It's not surprising that Julie would demonstrate gestural nurturing to complement her words of support. And she demonstrated it right from the start.

As we viewed her scaffolding video after the session, I asked Julie to "notice your gestural behaviors. Your arm is around him and you're leaning down. What do you think about that?"

She immediately responded, "I think I'm saying to him with my gestures, like 'Don't worry about this, because we'll do it together; and if you have trouble, I will help you.'" This teacher knows that kids (and adults) can't think when they're nervous. A gentle touch might help make everything right.

Perhaps children just need to feel someone is there for them. As Hannah said, "I do that so the student knows [I'm] with her and so she knows she's not alone." I call it adding a touch of magic to the act.

Pictures Help Prepare and Predict: Micro-Macro Perspectives

Teachers showed novices how reading the pictures prior to the text will serve to support their decoding. They laid the groundwork for this in a number of ways.

Verb Prep Through Pictures: The Micro Context

Scaffolders drew attention to pictures to lay the groundwork for vocabulary. "Look. What's she doing in the picture?" was a common scaffold that drew novices toward vocabulary related to events occurring. This helped ground a novice for the action vocabulary found in upcoming verbs.

Noun Prep Through Pictures: The Micro Context

Teachers sometimes added a meaning cue for an upcoming noun that might be an unknown, "Do you know what that's called *(pointing)*?" Textual illustrations seemed to be very fertile ground for both conversations and meaning related to people, places, and things.

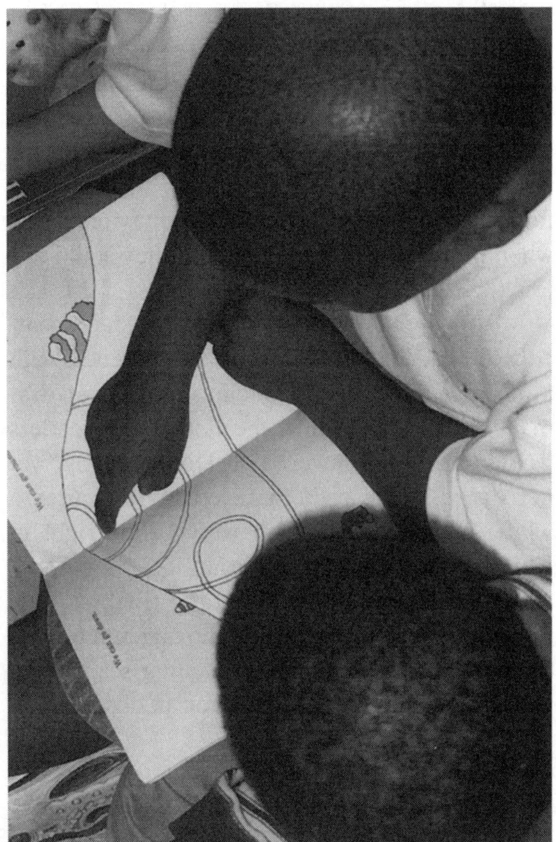

Partners use the picture to support the text.

Schema Prep Through Pictures: The Macro Context

Pictures are wonderful supports for both character and setting background. That's why Jane focuses her reader on the picture prior to reading. She begins:

TEACHER: Let's take a look at what he's doing. *(indicates where to look by pointing in circular motions around the page with her forefinger)* He's in bed. Do you think he's getting up or going to sleep?
STUDENT: Getting up.
TEACHER: Okay, I think he's getting up, too. How does he look? Does he look surprised? Does he look angry? Does he look happy?
STUDENT: He looks surprised.

So before the reader even begins to read, he already understands a good bit about the setting for the story, and he has a sense of the character. Drawing readers' attention to pictures is an important habit to instill.

The schema prep that pictures provide is not only for novices. It is just as important for students reading content-area books, such as history, science, and technology. Publishers go to a great deal of trouble and expense to extend and supplement the text in this manner, and they expect readers to use those resources. Therefore, it's a habit worth instilling early!

Prediction Prep Through Pictures: The Macro Context

Teachers also laid the groundwork for upcoming elements in story schema. Mostly, they used illustrations to help them reach forward, to predict what was about to occur. "Uh-oh! What's gonna happen to him next?" was a very common question. They were teaching novices that reading is a process in which we continually predict, then read on into the macro context to confirm or nullify those predictions.

Pictures Help Bring Meaning to Confusion

In the following, notice how Jane also references her novice reader to the pictures. Especially consider her invitations to think and the locus of control. This episode begins when the reader is finishing a sentence in a Little Critter text (Mayer 1986). The reader is unsure of the word *tired*, because she has confused pictured characters. However, the illustrations are about to help her:

STUDENT: *(reading)* "until she was . . . um . . . um . . . tired?" *(with tentative inflection)*
TEACHER: That's right. Until she was tired. *(validating, but sensing confusion through the reader's hesitation and voice inflection, points at a smiling, excited Critter and asks)* Does that make sense?
STUDENT: No. *(shaking her head)*
TEACHER: You know why? 'Cause, does she look tired? *(pointing to a jubilant Little Critter)*
STUDENT: *(shakes her head no)*
TEACHER: No, but you know what? That's what it says. *(referencing picture and then reviewing)* If I let her go on the swing until she was tired— *(rephrasing author's words)* Who's tired? *(Now she cues to the other character in the story who is tired, so the child accepts this invitation and points to that creature, and thus answers the question and, ideally, her own character confusion.)*
TEACHER: Why is *she* so tired?
STUDENT: 'Cuz, she's tired of pushing her. *(Bingo! Through the teacher's strategic questions and references to pictures, the text now makes sense to this reader.)*
TEACHER: That's right! She's tired of doing all those things on the playground with her. Right? *She's* the one that's tired! *(validating)*

Jane used the picture to clear up a confusion in the mind of the novice. But she did it cleverly, through a problem-solving technique—no doubt one that she hoped the novice would use independently someday.

Pictures Help Cue Unknown Words

Hannah orchestrates between picture and print in a wonderful flowing manner to help the reader construct the local meanings and inferences needed to remember a noun. Her novice, who is reading *Things to Like* by Richard Scarry (1987), stumbles on a story character's name, *Fingers*.

Hannah immediately references the picture, where we find an octopus and duck, but it is the duck who has lots of fingers protruding. Hannah points to this strange duck-like creature and asks, "Why do they call him Fingers?"

"He has lots of fingers," responds the novice.

"Yes, look at all the fingers he has," reinforces the teacher.

"Just like an octopus!" connects the reader.

"That's right! So they thought a good nickname for him would be—?

"Fingers!" The novice responds and continues reading the sentence.

Hannah and her novice helped lay several meanings in place through picture connections in this little vignette. Many illustrators are quite purposeful about the way they lead youngsters into meaning with their artistic creations. That's why pictures are an important cue.

In this previous episode the teacher kept responses anchored to the picture for her inexperienced novice. She offered explicit cues that would lead the novice reader forward with plenty of help. But now notice the difference in scaffolding in the following episode where the novice is a bit more experienced. Here, invitations are more open, the cues are more diverse, and the picture is saved as the final key to unlocking the unknown word.

We join this dyad at a point where the reader has miscued on *began*. (The text reads: "Billy went back in his room and began to dress.")

TEACHER: Do you want to go back? *(offers an [S-S] invitation, but then rereads for the student)* "Billy went back to his room and—" *(models orally while pointing to the words and then leaves off with an upswing to her voice, but then covers the* -gan *part of* began*)*

STUDENT: *(does not apply [G] cue offered by the teacher, but instead uses his own favorite keep-going strategy, Say Blank)* "—blank to dress."

TEACHER: *(interrupts)* Why don't you check out the pictures and *see* what he is doing? *(no pointing, just an open cue to use the pictures)*

It's apparent that this teacher offers her reader more autonomy and cue variety. She is less specific in her leading, and less wordy in her explanations. This is true of most all of the fluent-reader mediators. As a matter of fact, when we compare the amount of spoken mediation for the novices with that of the fluents we can easily see that, in general, teachers take more seconds-per-word when mediating the novice reader (see Figure 5–1). Does this align with the way in which we teach other skills in our daily lives? Do we allow more skilled baseball players, swimmers, and writers more autonomy with less specific guidance?

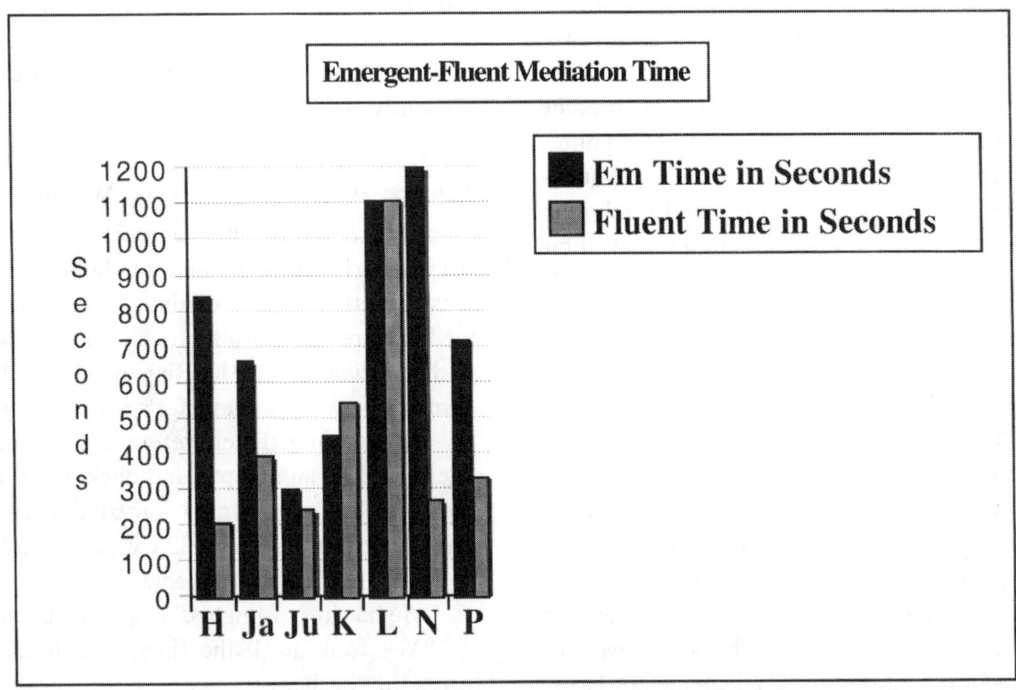

Figure 5–1. *Emergent and Fluent Spoken Teacher-Mediation Times*

Fluency and Meaning: A Symbiotic Relationship

We know that chunking leads to fluency, which then develops the macro perspective that leads to comprehension. That is why chunking and fluency cues are woven in and out and throughout the scaffolding of novices. And dysfluent reader behaviors made it fairly obvious when assistance was needed. Thus, dysfluency became the teacher's cue to step in and scaffold. That focus on fluency ran like an undercurrent through the entire reading relationship.

Teachers laid the pathways to fluency in a number of ways. The last chapter of this book investigates all of these pathways, but at this point we are mainly concerned with the way in which their scaffolding of fluency helped students make semantic matches and aided them in understanding larger units of text.

How Teachers Modeled Fluency for Macro Meanings

Novices need fluent models. When they listen all day to primarily beginning, word-by-word readers, they have few demonstrations to emulate. It's therefore important to provide lots of fluent modeling.

Sometimes we hear teachers say, "Read it faster." But fast does not necessarily connote fluent, even though many think the two are synonymous. They reach for the term *faster* because they understand that very slow, word-by-word reading seems to distort meaning. We have already discussed why this is usually so. Yet, merely telling a child to read it faster does not help. However, there are some ways to scaffold these slow readers.

One of the important scaffolds teachers offered was modeling. Teachers themselves supported the macro context for the novices, giving them something they could not, at that point, capture for themselves. Teachers merely modeled a sentence or two in a fluent and meaningful manner. They did this by reading *before*, *after*, and *with* kids.

How Teachers Reread in Meaningful Chunks

Closely related to modeling is rereading. Hannah is a wonderful example of a teacher who demonstrates rereading for fluency. She uses some tactics that have become a natural part of her transactions.

On every single page Hannah focused on fluency with zealous and yet harmonic voice and gestures. She approached chunking in two ways, (1) by reading *with* her reader, but leading toward more fluent behaviors and (2) reading *after* her reader to again demonstrate and celebrate what chunking sounds like. The novice haltingly read, "Kitty. . . loves . . . Pickles," and Hannah immediately chunked the three words into one syntactic unit, celebrating, "Kitty loves Pickles! Good job!"

At other times Hannah approached fluency in a little different manner. That is, when her novice reader read haltingly, Hannah did not reread to model, but invited the child himself to reread for fluency. Notice the combination of fluency scaffolds that Hannah uses in the following, when her novice carefully decoded the word *Babykins*.

Hannah first responded, "Good! Babykins!"

The student went on to read "—has fun building a tall tower."

But before they turned the page, the teacher praised and reread, "Pretty good! Has fun building a tower." Then, Hannah invited the student to reread, "Can you read that again? Baby—"

The student slid right in and reread, "Babykins has fun building a tall tower."

Once again, Hannah celebrated her reader; this time with, "Wow!"

Hannah knows that word-by-word reading bogs down the short-term memory and keeps the reader in the micro context. So sometimes Hannah models, rereading, while at other times she invites the novice to do it. Either will nudge this child toward larger syntactic chunks and their macro meanings.

How Teachers Use Macro Processing for Micro Meanings

Teachers also used *keep-going strategies* in their thrust toward macro meanings—ones that might cue a previous semantic mismatch. Jane's novice reader got stuck mid-sentence reading a Little Critter book. Watch how Jane implements the skip-it strategy.

STUDENT: *(reading)* "My little sister w-went. . . wanted. . . w-w-" *(struggling with* wanted*)*

TEACHER: Okay, why don't you skip it and go on, and then we can come back to it. "My little—" *(begins pointing to words)*

STUDENT: "sister wanted to go to the park" *(Teacher takes finger away.)* "Mom was too blank so I said 'I'll take her.'" *(Teacher is pointing to each word again as the child reads.)*

TEACHER: What do you think? *(rereads for the child)* "Mom was too what?" *(points to the word she's referencing)*

STUDENT: Busy.

TEACHER: Excellent!

Notice how the macro meanings affected the micro context for this child. This time the teacher had to lead the novice through the strategy, but with this kind of success, perhaps the next time this reader will use it on her own.

One important part of this skip-it strategy, however, is the return to reread. In this example, the teacher did the return *for* the child. Without that last step of returning to reread, some students develop a habit of just skipping unknown words and then forgetting about them, which takes an enormous toll on meaning. The return after skipping shows students that rereading provides the fluency flow and semantic grist needed to identify unknowns on that second time through. That is, an (S-S) strategy guides the reader toward meaning and fluency, which then interacts with the available graphophonic cues. The more cues, the more clues!

How Teachers Use Semantic-Syntactic Drama Cues for Meaning

Some teachers felt that using a particular voice inflection would help students remember a word or phrase, and Marie Clay (1993) also suggests using exaggerated voice to focus a reader's attention. One teacher commented, "I think the more dramatic you make it, the more they remember it."

Hannah mentioned after viewing that she blended through words with her reader because "then the [unknown] word wouldn't sound so silly," meaning that, to young readers, a haltingly read word or phrase may still be incomprehensible or, as she said, "sound silly." This may give a novice reason to pause, but Hannah slides in and accompanies her readers forward, letting them know that all is well. In other words, the teacher's added fluency helps give the sentence and the whole relationship more meaning.

Mini-Lessons Inside the Act

Occasionally, teachers take readers back for a context-related mini-lesson. In the following the student had miscued on the word *does*, substituting the somewhat synonymous verb *did*, and the teacher used the miscue as the substance for an instantaneous mini-lesson grounded in both graphophonics and meaning. Watch how she keeps meaning in the forefront.

The teacher returns to that section of text, pointing and repeating what the child had read earlier.

TEACHER: *(repeating after child)* "But mommy *did* not." The word *did* would make sense to you? But can I ask you a question, though? It makes perfect sense here, and if I said that, I would keep going, too. And making sense is always the number one job, but if I were to ask you again to look at that word closely, could that be di- d? *(stressing that final sound)* No, it couldn't be did *(pointing under the* S *in* does*)*. I'll tell you what the word is because it is one of those tricky words that is not even spelled the way it sounds. It's so tricky. *(reads while pointing to each word)* "But mommy *does* not."

Teaching inside the process like this can be very effective. Nevertheless, a reader will lose sight of macro and micro meanings when during-reading interruptions are frequent or lengthy. On the other hand, saving them for long afterward will remove the lesson from its meaningful context. Bottom line: keep inside mini-lessons brief and infrequent.

How Teachers Scaffold Comprehension Strategies: Macro Processes

Much of the preceding part of this chapter was closely related to semantic-syntactic strategies used within a micro context and triggered by local unknowns. Even so, we saw how teachers helped readers reach forward to grasp the bigger picture. It is within these macro meanings that readers learn to use comprehension strategies that will help them construct global meanings.

Interestingly, in her seven thousand minutes of classroom observations, Dolores Durkin (1978–79) found that comprehension was actually taught *less than 1 percent* of the time. It seems teachers confuse the *product* with the *process*. That is, many teachers think that a worksheet of comprehension questions to be answered by students is teaching comprehension, when it is actually assessing the product.

Nevertheless, it is difficult to teach comprehension strategies within the process without imposing blatant interruptions, because these more complex processes are almost impossible to gesture. Trying to do so would no doubt only draw the reader away from the context, rather than bringing him closer to it. Therefore, teachers primarily scaffold comprehension strategies before the reading act, during page-turning, or after the reading has been completed.

Teaching Comprehension Strategies Between the Pages

Jane slips meaningful comprehension strategies in between page-turns with her novice reader, who is reading *Just Me and My Little Sister* by Mercer Mayer. Watch what happens as Jane demonstrates story synthesis and then how her reader makes connections to the text. Both great comprehension strategies!

Story Synthesis and Story Connections with a Novice

Story Synthesis:

TEACHER: *(at page-turning, slips in to synthesize)* He's having a hard time keeping up. It looks like he's falling. *(points to the picture of child falling and then looks back to child in an invitational manner)* He's being dragged, right? He can't even keep up with it. *(turns the page and the student interjects to make connections)*

Making Connections:

STUDENT: I did that before!

TEACHER: *(now turns page back since child is making a connection. A very sensitive dance here—a caring dance)* Did you? That happened to me, too! *(another honest connection)*

STUDENT: My cousin ran so fast he—I had to hold on so I couldn't fall off. I hanged on and I was swinging around. *(laughing)*

At this point the teacher laughs, too, as she turns the page again and quickly leads the novice back into the act; she does not want to sever the contextual ties to the novice's text memory store. It is interesting how effectively the book itself becomes a mediator for such flowing continuations.

Three Kinds of Connections That Support Comprehension

It's always wise to have a sense of where you are going before you get there. No doubt that is why teachers made connections that would tie readers to the context of text, while at the same time, they developed an interest in the story or the book being read by connecting many of the text's ideas through mini-discussions. Teachers themselves seemed to be *living* the text experience. That is, they were not separate from the student-book event, but actually an integral part of a *triadic transaction*.

Lani demonstrates these connections throughout her transactions that often take place between the pages of her novice's expository text. Most teachers did use this five-second page-turning intermission to ground comprehension. Observing these brief and connected transactions, I find it difficult to dub them an interruption. They instead appear to be part of the textual fabric.

We just saw how Jane and her reader connected to the events in a story. But there are actually several ways in which we can encourage readers to connect stories to their own prior experiences and knowledge, all important comprehension strategies. Let's look at each of these.

How Teachers Scaffold Connections to Life's Experiences

One of the fundamental ways in which we comprehend is by connecting the new to the old, the unknown to the known. Teachers often connect their own lives and the lives of their students to what is being read—a key comprehension strategy (Keene and Zimmerman 1997).

Sometimes, teachers offered questions that helped the child make connections to his own life, such as "What would you do if . . . ?" Jane asked her fluent reader, "What do *you* do in the morning?" and "What would *you* do if you found one?" She was connecting the reader's life to the life of the story characters and events.

Kara asked her novice reader, who was reading (Packard 1993) *My Messy Room*, "Is this what *your* room looks like? I'm going to call your mom and ask," she teased.

Julie asked her fluent reader, "Would you like to be a shepherd? Would you like this job?" So regardless of the level of the reader, teachers tended to tie the book to the child's personal life, as well as their own.

When my reading group was reading about a child who made a shape book, I asked, "What shape would your book be about?"

Hannah led her novice toward such connections when a character was playing music. After discussing the character's actions, Hannah asked the reader, "Do you like music?"

The reader made an immediate connection, "Uh-huh! My dad turns up the radio really loud and then I like to dance!"

All teachers encouraged kids to connect what they were reading to their own lives. At times this meant connecting facts to facts; yet at other times, it meant connecting real-life facts to textual fiction. Regardless, making personal connections grounded new text in old meanings and helped strengthen the reading relationship.

How Teachers Scaffold Connections to Other Texts

All texts are like others in some ways. Some are very much alike; whereas, others differ greatly. Nevertheless, we can support young readers by connecting known similarities. Books about the same topic, from the same genre, a part of the same series, can actually offer textual scaffolding. We want to help readers make these text connections a common link in their reading act, because they add meaning, broaden schema, and evoke greater interest.

That's why Lani draws her novice reader's attention to the fact that his book is part of a series that he has already tasted. She says, "*Frogs and Toads*, hmmmm. Is this part of that same series you've been reading? Why did you choose this one?" Lani invites the reader to reflect on any connections that he may have already made when selecting this text from a known series. Then, she can build on his responses, and he himself can build on those connections as well.

Once I had steeped readers in my room in the patterns of predictable texts, they found other patterned books everywhere. Then, they compared the new text patterns with those of other texts. They could readily do this by the second month of school, but only because they'd been steeped in noticing patterned texts. It's the steeping that's fundamental.

How Teachers Scaffold Connections to Authors

Authors are a part of the reading relationship, too. And most novices have a favorite! They get hooked on Steven Kellogg or Robert Munsch or Dr. Seuss or hundreds of others. Some like humor, others prefer nonfiction, while many enjoy fairy tales. Certainly, the menu is bountiful. Yet, once we know a student's preferences, offering more books by that known author is a good way to create immediate interest and ground connections. After reading a text by a particular author, we have a feel for that author's style, vocabulary, sentence structure, content, and such. It therefore makes another book by that same author somewhat easier to read, to understand, and to connect to. This means texts by the same author will help scaffold novice readers. Consider Dr. Seuss. What three-year-old couldn't find more of his books once he experiences a few!

I readily use author connections during scaffolding—and Robert Munsch is usually a good bet! For example, one time an observer caught the following transaction on video during Read-a-Book, when I stooped down beside the desk of a young novice and offered him another book by a known author.

I reminded, "Remember, Robert Munsch? Want to read another one?" Feeling a bit intimidated, the reader hesitated to answer, but just shrugged, instead.

So I suggested, "Let me start you out by reading the first few pages, okay? See if it's like other Munsch books. See if you like it." I was leading toward potential connections that would build confidence.

And indeed it did just that. For after I quickly read the first few pages, the novice caught my eye with his smile. "What do you think," I asked. "Is it like his other books?"

"Yeah," responded the first grader.

I knew the relationship was growing, so I prodded, "How?"

“’Cause it’s funny. And it keeps repeating,” he offered, gaining confidence.

“Absolutely!” I agreed. “You even noticed the pattern that makes Munsch books easy to read. Why don’t you reread the part I just read and then keep going? If you have trouble, just raise your hand.” I left the young reader as he reopened his new Munsch book, preparing to add more connections to his Robert Munsch reading relationship.

Text connections are more thoroughly discussed in *Knee to Knee, Eye to Eye* (Cole 2003), in *Strategies That Work* (Harvey and Goudvis 2000), and in *Mosaic of Thought* (Keene and Zimmerman 1997).

How Teachers Scaffold Questioning as a Comprehension Strategy

Teachers readily draw students’ attention to the sense of what’s being read. Julie frequently asks her readers: “Does that make sense?” or “Do you know what that means?” Sometimes she does this to prompt the reader’s thinking, while at other times she uses this cue for her own assessment, to see if meaning is actually intact. But these questions focus more toward leading a student into chunking and out of the micro level.

Other questions emanated from and gathered their responses in the macro context. General in-process questions that could act as common strategies across texts are:

- What are you wondering now?
- Why did that happen?
- How do you think s/he’ll do that?
- Where do you think they’ll go next?
- Who do you think will win?
- Why can’t s/he do that?
- How do you think they’ll get there?

Notice how many of these begin with “Why do you think . . . ?” and “How do you think . . . ?” These draw readers to elaborate, yet they should not elaborate on pie in the sky. In other words, elaborations should grow out of evidence and then be substantiated or nullified by new evidence.

Lani, who earlier shared her comprehension strategies with us, seems to salt and pepper her mediation with questions, most of which were laden with rich science concepts that might seduce a wondering (or a wandering) mind. Lani led her novice through his *Frogs and Toads* (Butterworth 1990) expository text with a variety of fascinating wonders! Surely all these authentic questions paved the path toward the development of that novice’s own wondering strategies.

As I myself read to and with kids, I often interject throughout the text, “What are you wondering about?” In so doing, I demonstrate for kids that wonders nudge us to discover their answers as we read on. They keep connecting us to the text and laying the groundwork for comprehension.

Lani uses another tactic. She utters a subtle, “Hm-m-m,” as she and the reader traverse text. She is demonstrating the way in which readers ponder as they read. They ask themselves questions, which become the keys to comprehension (Pressley 2000; Keene and Zimmerman 1997).

We join Lani and the reader as the novice is finishing a page of expository text. Earlier, the youngster had predicted (inferred) that the frogs’ air sac would be filled with eggs, but now the text has not validated that prediction. Let’s see what happens.

TEACHER: Air, hm-m-m. *(pondering)* But what did you say before that you thought they filled it with? *(pointing)*

STUDENT: Eggs.

TEACHER: Hm-m-m. Could they do both? *(with pen pressed against corner of mouth in pensive consideration)*

STUDENT: I don’t know.

TEACHER: I don’t know either. *(shaking her head and shrugging her shoulders—an honest answer)* Let’s read on and find out. *(scaffolds toward reading for evidence)*

Here you can see how Lani has intertextual wonder-chats with her novice reader, weaving these ten-second conversations in and out in a natural way. These little book chats of Lani’s have a think-aloud structure; they demonstrate *overtly* the way in which people wonder their way *covertly* through books. In so doing, Lani uses several meaning cues to help lay the groundwork for what is to come. However, she does not do it through standard comprehension questions—that is, she does not use a teacher’s manual. She speaks with each child as a unique equal, one who is on a similar journey that has occasional brief way stations for shared wondering.

The fact that Lani's students chose to read expository texts is important here, because an information text can more easily be interrupted without harming meanings. As a matter of fact, some say that is how we should use expository text—for specific bits or pieces of information we might need, as opposed to reading them cover to cover. At any rate, Lani would never have interrupted a narrative with so many questions.

How Teachers Scaffold Inference Strategies for Comprehension

We teach readers to construct inferences from the title on. That is, even when readers are discussing a title, they are being drawn into the world of inferential thinking. After reading the title and checking the cover illustration, we ask them, "What do you think this story is going to be about?" Their answer will be an inference, constructed from the context of the cover and title.

Teachers continually ask, "What do you think is going to happen next?" Readers must then construct from what has already been read to infer what might occur next. Yet, they must build on solid evidence. We expect their maybes to be educated guesses.

Inferences carry an air of tentativeness, and often possess tentative verbs, such as *might*. Thus, we hear teachers ask, "What *might* happen next?" or "How *could* they get there?" These are often followed by responses that begin with *maybe* or *probably*, two words that researchers tell us are not often uttered in our classrooms.

Patty demonstrates how readers draw tentative conclusions and infer from pictures. After turning the page to a new picture, she says, "Okay, there they are having their little cake *(explaining the picture)*. And they went to the cake shop and next the pet shop. Maybe they had to go in there to get some pet food *(inference)*." Once they read on, they will prove or disprove Patty's inference.

Patty demonstrated for her reader how mature readers think as they process text. She did it through a think-aloud containing a tentative hypothesis. It is through such modeling that readers learn comprehension strategies such as inference. Novices need many such demonstrations.

How Teachers Scaffold Text Synthesis for Comprehension

One of the common practices that many teachers have is to ask a reader to "Tell me about what you've read so far." This is one of the simplest ways in which to lay the groundwork for synthesis or summary, both of which are key comprehension strategies.

Synthesis, however, more carefully considers the pieces and their relationship to the whole. Often, asking a Why? question moves readers toward synthesis. That is what happened when novice reader Anthony proudly finished reading *The Giving Tree* by Shel Silverstein.

The story ends with both the tree, now a stump, and the boy having grown old and tired. The tree, having loved the boy throughout the years, invites the boy to sit on her. And the book concludes with "And the boy did. And the tree was happy."

I asked Anthony, a tiny boy who had blossomed late in the year, "Do you think the boy is happy, too?" I used a "Do you think . . . ?", question which requires him to synthesize what he knows about the character and then decide what he thinks.

Anthony responded "Uh-huh," even though the old man does not look happy.

I agreed, but inquired further, "But why do you think the boy is happy?"

" 'Cause he has the tree to sit on and be with," Anthony said.

"Well, why do you think the tree was happy, too?" I asked.

Anthony smiled one of those sensitively knowing smiles and responded, "Because he finally has the boy to be with him."

"Yes, he sure waited a long time, didn't he?" I added.

Anthony had to synthesize the story to some extent to construct his answers. Indeed, I fear there are some adults who might not truly understand this beautiful story. Anthony did.

Synthesis also must occur when we ask readers to compare a story they are reading to another they've read. Readers must consider the pieces, their relationhip to the whole, and then their relationship to the pieces from the other whole. After Bobby read a somewhat basalized form of *Little Red Riding Hood*, I asked, "So Bobby, is this *Little Red Riding Hood* like others you've read?"

Bobby began thinking aloud to share the ways in which the two stories were alike, beginning with, "She takes food to her Grandma in both of them," and he continued to synthesize characters and events for their similarities and their differences.

Whereas we usually think of summary as a mere regurgitation of the storyline, synthesis is a step beyond. A higher level of thinking is required. Nevertheless, even first graders can do it.

Indeed, there are many comprehension strategies that help readers with macro processing, so it's beneficial for teachers to incorporate these into their scaffolding. However, readers need to eventually move into a metacognitive stance—one that finds them monitoring their *own* comprehension, implementing strategies, and clearing up confusions independently. Monitoring is perhaps one of the most difficult acts for young readers to develop—especially when they are bored.

Monitoring Comprehension, for, with, and by the Reader

The path to optimal comprehension is continual monitoring, first *for* the student, then *with* the student, and finally *by* the student. Teachers can demonstrate these behaviors for readers, but eventually students, themselves, must grow into metacognitive behaviors involved in monitoring.

Teachers often scaffold monitoring by sensitively questioning at strategic points in the text. They begin by owning the act in order to help readers understand how and why they must follow their teacher's lead.

Watch how Julie harmoniously moves her fluent reader toward a connection, an inference, and monitoring, as the child reads a section of *The Reluctant Dragon*. After the taping, Julie and I watched the video. It was then that she related the reason for her interruption. She said that the reader was reading so fast that she felt the child may not have been comprehending, and that is why she interrupts.

STUDENT: *(reading and rocking in time with the rapid music of her own words)* ". . . as much as he liked; and instead of frequently getting a cuff on the side of the head, as might very well have happened to him, he was treated more or less as an equal by his parents."

TEACHER: Do you know what they mean by that? *(pointing to the phrase "treated as an equal" and sliding her finger under it twice within the blink of an eye)* "Treated as an equal?" Treated as an equal by his parents? *(interfacing with a question to clarify)*

STUDENT: *(leans back, pulls her head into her shirt and slowly lifts her shoulders, which would probably indicate to the teacher that this reader doesn't know, yet doesn't really want to say so, or is not sure that she doesn't know)*

TEACHER: He was so proud that his parents were proud of him because of what he could do. *(As teacher explains, the student becomes noticeably nervous, unsure—probably due to the interruption. But notice now that the teacher makes a personal connection to the life of the reader and thus mends the relationship)* Probably like your parents are proud of you because of what you can do. You like to read a lot, right? *(leans forward to look into the face of the child, to salve all wounds, and as she asks this question, the child looks up with a responsive, pleased facial expression and nods her head)*

STUDENT: Uh-huh.

TEACHER: And your mom's proud of you about that. Yeah?

STUDENT: *(nods to affirm again, smiling)*

As we discussed this section of the video, Julie noticed how she stopped the reader by touching the text. She said she did it "just to go back and check to see if she understands."

"What do you have up your sleeve by rereading that little section there? So—uh—why did you do that?" I asked.

"I still want to keep checking to see if she's able to relate it to her own life experience," she explained."Does she know what it means to be equal with someone? Does she know what it means to be equal with her parents?"

This prompted my mini-synthesis of the situation, "Okay, so this is like a form of assessment almost. It's instruction and assessment melded together, because you're actually seeing if she's understanding it. *(Julie is nodding in affirmation)* Am I correct that this is your way to monitor that?"

"Uh-huh, just to see if she's reading for meaning," she reiterates."Does it have any significance to her? Does she relate to that?

I always ask: Do you know what that means? And when I need to, I come up at the end with an example."

I noticed that during the videos of my own scaffolding, I, like Julie, continually asked readers comprehension monitoring questions, such as "Do you know what that means?" and "Does that make sense?" and "Do you understand?"

This is such a great illustration of how everything is woven together into a vibrant, living relationship. This is not just monitoring. It is not just connecting. It is more than comprehending. It is a relationship of all of the above and more. And this is why basals and scripts just will not make the grade! How could they monitor in this fashion? How could they make such intimate connections? How could they salve wounds? How could they scaffold individually? Let's face it, they can't! Only *teachers* can do that.

A Fine Balance

From the very beginning, we interface each child's life with meanings. The pieces that lose their meaning seem to fall by the wayside, gone and forgotten. It's through meaning that children learn to navigate this world, to communicate, to read. As the teachers in this chapter have demonstrated, the ways to help kids construct meaning are limitless.

Yet, for a preword reader who does not even notice words yet, we cannot focus *only* on meaning, because to do so would be to ignore the page's graphics, which is actually what's being read in the first place. It is a fine scaffolding balance between the meaning, the syntax, and the graphophonics that is necessary for optimal novice progress. We can help readers make meaning as they read, but we also need to help them notice and then decode words. Novices need scaffolding in all of this. That is why the next chapter focuses on graphophonics.

Grist for Discussion

Text Used for Upcoming Transcription

> My little sister wanted to go to the park.
> Mom was too busy so I said I'd take her.
> So we went to the park, just me and my sister.
>
> My little sister wanted to play basketball but the hoop was too high.

Read the transcription below. Mark all (S-S) cues, then examine each one to decide if the cue helped the reader. Was macro processing used? Afterward, discuss how you might have scaffolded this reader in a different manner.

Jane and her novice reader are are beginning *Just Me and My Little Sister*, a Mercer Mayer book. Jane has just incorporated some proactive mediating to scaffold meanings prior to reading. Pleased with her reader's connections, she responds:

TEACHER: Great! Okay. *(opens to first page of book and continues to hold text)* Let's see what Little Critter is going to do with his little sister. There's Critter *(pointing to pictures)* and I guess her name is Too. I didn't even know that! That's a funny name! Okay—

STUDENT: "My little sister w- went- wanted w- w" *(struggling with* wanted*)*

TEACHER: Okay. Why don't you skip it and go on and then we can come back to it? *(slides her finger past the word in question)*

STUDENT: *(reads)* "blank to go to blank. Mom was too—"

TEACHER: *(interrupts)* Okay. Let's go back *(pointing to words, gives the reader a head start by rereading)* "My little—" *(continues to point but signals reader to take over)*

STUDENT: "—sister wanted to go to the park. Mom was too blank so I said I'll take her." *(Teacher is pointing to each word as the child reads.)*

TEACHER: What do you think? Mom was too what? *(points to the unknown word)*

STUDENT: Busy.

TEACHER: Excellent! As you can see, Mom is working there, right? *(points quickly to the mom and then starts to turn the page)* You did a nice job figuring out that word. So Critter is going to take sister because mom is so busy.

STUDENT: *(continues reading)* "So we went to the park just me and my little sister."

TEACHER: What does the sign say? *(points to signs in picture one at a time)*

STUDENT: "To the park. This way. Keep going." *(afterward, returns to the text)* "My little sister want- wanted to play basketball, but the . . . blank was too . . . blank."

TEACHER: Okay. But the what? *(pointing in circular motions around the picture)* Let's see what that would be. "But the—" Hm-m-m. What do you need when you play basketball? It has a ball *(pointing)* and what is this? *(pointing at the hoop)* Do you know what this is called?

STUDENT: The hoop?

TEACHER: The hoop, right! *(rereads for child and fills in unknown word)* "But the hoop was too—" what?

STUDENT: Hard?

TEACHER: Alright, she's getting on top of her brother, there. *(pointing)* So the hoop is too— He's going to make her taller so she can get to it. So, the hoop is too— what?

STUDENT: High!

Chapter 6

How Teachers Scaffold Graphophonics: A Micro Process

I was made to read without explanation, under the usual fear of punishment. And on a day that I remember it came to me that "reading" was not "the Cat lay on the Mat," but a means to everything that would make me happy. So I read all that came within my reach.

RUDYARD KIPLING,
SOMETHING OF MYSELF: FOR FRIENDS KNOWN AND UNKNOWN

A System of Letters and Sounds

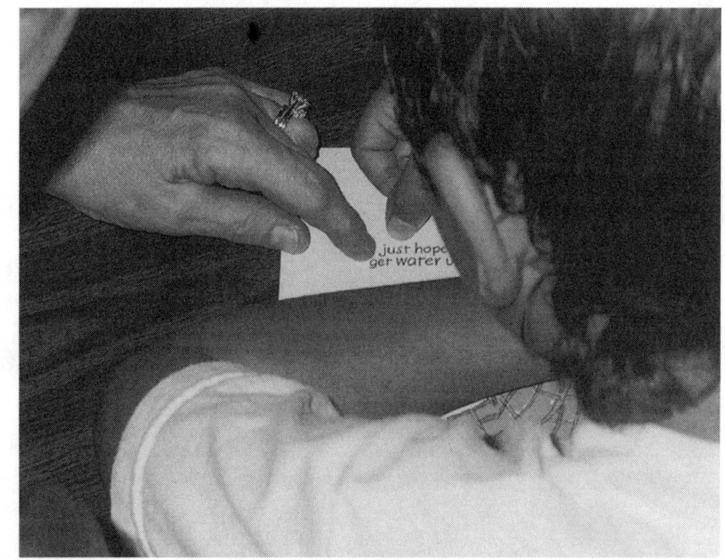

Our system of reading uses English orthography. Other cultures use a different print system, while individuals without sight might use Braille to receive the page's message. Essentially, all of these systems relate to message in some way.

In many systems, as in ours, spoken sounds are assigned to specific symbol arrangements. For instance, there is a common spoken sound for the following symbol or letter arrangements: -eight, -ing, and -ote. Thus, symbol arrangements can be read aloud—spoken—because of their sound potential. This makes ours a *graphophonic—symbol-sound*—system. Some orthographies, such as the Kanji ideographics of Japan, are not graphophonic. We are fortunate that ours is, because it gives readers one more major cue to use in decoding.

Before Graphophonics: Preword Reading

Long before a child comprehends those sound-symbol connections, he may "*reenact*" (Holdaway 1979) a book experience and begin "talking like a book" (Clay 1979). That is, young children understand that reading is spoken and that it has something to do with meaningful language and books, so they use "reading-like behaviors" (Doak 1985; Holdaway 1979) and mimic what they have seen others do. At this stage in development, reading a story and telling a story may appear to be identical processes.

Researchers say this is *tacit knowledge* of language, that is, these *preword readers* have "only a functional awareness . . . [a kind of] unconscious, intuitive knowledge that a language user has of the rules and conventions that underlie the structure of the language" (Roberts 1992). But eventually, this young novice comes to understand that those words coming out of his mouth have more to do with the print part on the page than the picture, and thus he transitions from preword to word reading, a cognitive leap that, due to its importance, Henderson (1980) calls a "watershed event" (p. 9).

During this transition from preword to word reading, the novice comes to realize that those words being read to him from his favorite book do not differ with each reading, so he begins to *mumble read* along with the scaffolder. As he memorizes texts, he will move on to *cooperative reading*, when he and the adult will chorally read the memorized story. Only a brief step away is *completion reading*, when he can finish the reader's sentences, and shortly afterward he will *echo read*, a period when he repeats sentences or phrases immediately after his scaffolder (Doake 1985). Throughout this early developmental period, preword readers move from picture matching to page matching to eventual print matching.

The Transition out of Preword and into Word Reading

Sooner or later, especially if the novice has a scaffolder who points as she reads, this young preword reader will begin to analyze and copy more of his scaffolder's print-related behaviors. He will begin to notice the print part of the page and move toward an eye-ear-voice match. But it still may be some time before that child is able to perceive word junctures marked by the spaces between words. Some kids even try out other methods; for instance, they might try to follow the lines or dots they see in the print (Harste, Woodward, and Burke 1984). As a matter of fact, full recognition of that one-to-one correspondence of speech to print doesn't take place until most kids are well into school's formal reading instruction (Roberts 1992; Ferreiro and Teberosky 1982; Holden and MacGinitie 1972). The transition can be a lengthy one!

During their transition into the concept of wordness, children begin to recognize words that have concrete references, that is, nouns and verbs (Roberts 1992). Yet most novices continue to have trouble matching the *word boundaries* of spoken words to those of their print partners. And abstract functors, such as *the*, *by*, or *if*, usually instigate this confusion. As I said earlier, that is why preword readers might identify *once upon a time* as only one word. Its abstractness eludes them.

Yet, many first graders who are indifferent to these word boundaries are still able to orally

Writing Reciprocity: Scaffolding the Phoneme-Grapheme Match

Once kids begin to learn the written alphabet and are reproducing some sight (memorized) words to support their illustrations, they soon find the need to expand their writing. It is then that they make a language leap that takes them onto more independent ground—a leap that moves them into *invented spelling* (Graves 1983; Calkins 1986). This invented-spelling independence finds novices trying out words for themselves by listening for the sounds in a word and encoding those sounds into their approximations. Most often, however, the product is less than accurate, yet still readable—especially by a first-grade teacher.

To scaffold word-writers toward independence in phoneme-grapheme matches, we lead them through a series of questions, starting with: "What do you hear first?" a question that initially needs our scaffolding support to answer—depending on each child's level of confidence.

Next, I invite, "Write that letter."

Then, "What do you hear next?" And most often at this point, we scaffolders must stretch the sounds so that the novice can perceive the phoneme-grapheme match. Upon the encoding's completion, as a validation, I always slide my finger under it, blending what was written. Never mind the correct spelling at this point, a time when our focus is on developing independence.

Gradually this developing writer is pulled toward fluently encoding spoken sounds into their decodable printmates. Once they have internalized this process of "What do you hear?" and "Write that down," we know they are a giant step closer to understanding how language works.

reproduce easy, patterned books. Marie Clay's research demonstrates that a "child can begin to read words with only a limited knowledge of letters; [and] he can read text with only a limited knowledge of words" (Clay 1993, p. 24). It may therefore sometimes seem that novices are further along than they actually are. So we need to remember that this is a *transition period*, a time in which kids lop back and forth between preword and word reading; so just when we begin to assume a novice has speech-to-print match, we discover that he can still become confused. His pointing may get ahead of or behind his spoken words, confusion sets in, and we observe that he still manifests some behaviors of a preword reader.

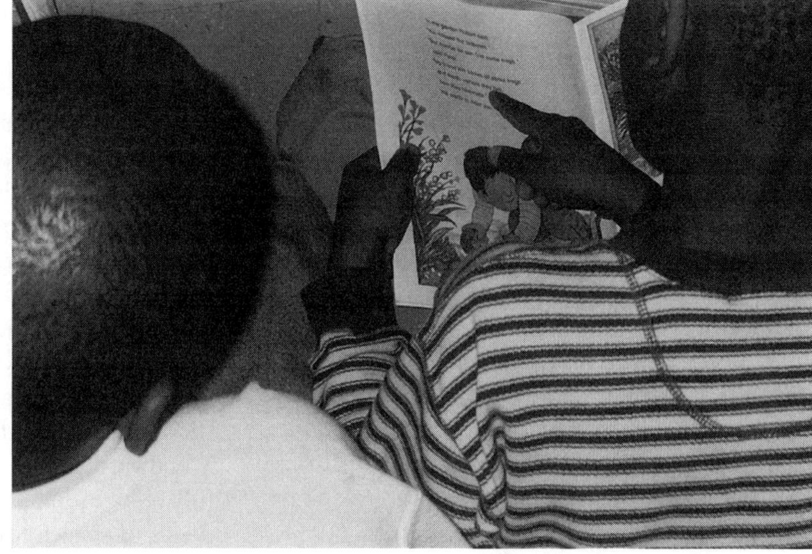

Pointing is important for novices to keep their place.

When a child begins to match what he is saying to the words on the page his reproductions take on an arhythmical quality (Doake 1985). This becomes a cue that he may be ready to begin pointing to words, which would allow his teacher to observe exactly how close his matches really are. Fingerpoint reading requires preword readers to "pay closer attention to the print" and the word boundaries (Ehri and Sweet 1991, p. 445). Therefore, "Point to the words!" becomes a kindergarten and first-grade mantra. Yet without adult assistance, novices easily fall into confused pointing behaviors. These transitioning readers need help with *word-to-word tracking*, and that is when scaffolding is essential.

In and Out of Printmatch: The Transition Continues

It was always a chaotic period at beginning of each year, a time when practically every first grader was learning word-to-word tracking. I felt like I needed twenty hands and a good pair of roller skates, as I dashed from child to child moving their little fingers to the appropriate spot on the page of the text that we were chorally reading. For most kids, learning the basics of matching only took a week or two, but even now I laugh just thinking about how crazy I must have appeared to an observer.

This beginning freneticism no doubt also occurred in the classrooms of the first-grade teachers I videotaped. As a matter of fact, while viewing the scaffolding tapes, I observed teachers mediating novices who did not demonstrate a completely consistent graphophonic match. These readers could track most of words most of the time, but they did not pay close enough attention to the features within the words. It was then that the scaffolding teacher focused on graphophonic cues. And they did this in a variety of ways, both spoken and gestural.

Preword reading precedes graphophonic cueing. Consequently, this chapter transitions from preword scaffolding behaviors to a more thorough investigation of graphophonic scaffolding. And certainly with good reason!

Graphophonic Cues Remain in the Limelight

The graphophonics cueing system has claimed headlines and controversy throughout the twentieth century and now into the twenty-first. Educators continue to debate its use, misuse, and abuse, while parents voice concerns, even in newspaper columns, screaming, "My child isn't getting enough phonics." With so many cueing possibilities, one wonders why we don't hear the public clamor about their children not getting enough meaning. It's always phonics! Nevertheless, although some would have it be the miracle drug to cure all of education's ills, graphophonics is only one cueing mode that transacts with and influences the other modes. Yet, it does hold a place of importance in the cues readers use. Therefore, its scaffolding is also important.

As a matter of fact, over the course of my study, I watched as teachers again and again used the graphophonic cueing system to scaffold novice readers. There is no doubt in my mind now that graphophonics is by far the most used first-grade cueing scaffold. So if this work is any indication of teacher mediation in general, one thing is fairly certain: the public can stop worrying about phonics, because (at least in first grade) teachers *do* use such cues, and they use them in abundance. This was also a finding in the research of Wong, Groth, and O'Flahavan (1994).

Recently, however, phonics has even become a federal government issue. The National Reading Panel (NRP), a government-financed group, researched the components of successful reading approaches. After dedicating about half the pages in their document to phonics, they still warn that teachers must not "allow phonics to become the dominant component not only in the time devoted to it, but also in the significance attached. It is important not to judge children's reading competence solely on the basis of their phonics skills" (NRP 1999, p. 11).

Do not be misled by corporate seduction and fancy phonics ads. Instead, remember that the report tells us that phonics should be only a part of a *balanced reading program*. For some easy-to-use guidelines related to phonics and what the NRP report actually indicates, see Elaine Garan's books, *Resisting Reading Mandates* (2002) and *In Defense of Our Children* (2004).

That is also the perspective that my work takes. Phonics is an integral and necessary part of the entire cueing system. But it is only a part and not the whole. Readers need it, but they need much more to process print, which was made clear in the previous chapters of this book.

The Phonemic Part of Graphophonemic Cueing

When we closely investigate the term *graphophonemic*, we see that it is made up of *phonemic* (sounds) and *grapho* (symbols or print). Therefore, a concept, such as *phonemic awareness*, omits the graphics, which means that phonemic awareness relates to sound awareness, that is, what a child hears or, better yet, how he perceives what he hears. If a child has a lesson in phonemic awareness, the lesson would focus on hearing the likenesses and differences in words, or perhaps repeating particular sounds. There are no graphics involved—only voiced sounds.

As I suggested earlier, I believe that if reading is a graphophonemic process, we do the process an injustice by dissecting this term, because the symbols and the sounds have a symbiotic relationship. That's why it is much easier to teach a child the *B* sound by presenting that sound's relationship to its written counterpart (Adams 1990). After all, it is not a reproduction of "Buh, buh, kuh, buh" that we are trying to achieve. We want readers to use a *B* sound when they encounter a word with a *B* in it. Why separate the two?

Kids need the tacit knowledge that preschool literacy experiences allow—stories read aloud, playing with pencil and paper, reciting songs and rhymes—rather than drills on sounds, so that they will acquire a tacit or preword knowledge upon which they can build as they transition into word knowledge. And tacit word knowledge occurs well before an explicit understanding of words (Roberts 1992; Karmiloff-Smith 1986; Ferreiro and Teberosky 1982). Preschoolers know what words are; they just cannot explain it. In fact, they will not be able to construct an explicit definition of word until they are in upper elementary school (Papandropoulou and Sinclair 1974).

Once we move into graphics, we can *show* novices every sound through its printmatch. Therefore, spending periods of time breaking spoken words—without their print counterparts—into separate sounds seems like we'd be spinning their wheels in abstractions. And indeed research bears this out (Adams 1990). As we see kindergarten curriculum requiring kids to isolate and segment phonemes, we would do well to remember what else Adams found: "Further, among normal readers, the ability to count the phonemes in a syllable is only beginning to stabilize by the end of first grade. The ability to delete, transpose, or add phonemes to a syllable continues to develop at least through high school. Thus, full attainment of phonemic awareness also takes considerable time" (1990 p. 54).

Therefore, the more cues, the better! We need to match those words to their concrete printmates. That's what reading is all about. Why would we separate the hearing from the seeing? Why not use both modes? Besides, conquering the graphics part is no small task!

The Graphics Part of Graphophonemic Cueing

There's not much more to graphics than that which meets the eye. Yet what meets the eye of the novice is perceived in a somewhat different manner than that which is perceived by a mature reader. Preword readers must first learn to notice words, and then novices must learn to look at those graphics in a certain fashion. As a matter of fact, in many areas of learning we must learn to look in a particular fashion if we want to develop a skill in that area.

Scaffolding Noticing Behaviors

You may find this example somewhat humorous, but it illustrates how even adults can look at something, yet at first not see it. It involves nits, those tiny iridescent, whitish eggs that lice lay near the root of a hair. I guarantee that the first time an individual is shown a nit, she will not see it. That's because most people have not learned to *look* at nits. I remember identifying a nit in a child's hair while his mom watched, yet at first she could not see it. Then, suddenly she screamed, "Oh, my gosh! They're all over the place!" What she could not see at first was "all over the place" one minute later—once she noticed one.

That's what happens with novice readers and words. They cannot identify the word *the*, but the next thing you know, they are finding *the's* all over the place! They are not sounding through the *T-H*. And they may not even know letters yet, but they can still identify *the* and they are on their way into reading, because once they have a large enough collection of words and instruction, novices begin to make connections to likenesses and differences within that personal collection. And it's but a short leap from noticing words to applying graphophonemic cues.

Identifying a Word Through Its Configuration

This means that even before a child begins to understand how spoken phonemes match print forms, she is able to discriminate one word from another through each word's *configuration*. That is, preword readers notice something about a word's shape, which helps them in identifying it again.

But they also are cued by the word's context. That's how preschoolers know all too well the familiar McDonald's and Pepsi signs. They use the context in which the word resides, as well as the configuration of the word itself. But they do this without noticing many of the details, so that when those well-known words are modified in some way (for instance, changing the *D* in McDonald's to a *P*), most preschoolers will not notice. That is, they will continue to read the modified word as McDonald's (Masonheimer, Drum, and Ehri 1984).

This lack of attention to details is common to all new learning. That's why a botanist notices far more in a daisy than I do and why a geologist can rapidly identify rocks. I may even mistake a daisy for a similar flower, because I have not attended to all of its *distinctive features*, which include far more than white petals and an orange, bumpy center. That's because I have not hung around with daisies enough to know them up close and personal. I only have tacit knowledge.

Even as mature readers, we sometimes use configuration and context to read. Once when we were traveling to Myrtle Beach for a vacation, we became stuck in traffic in a city not far from our destination. Unsure of exactly where we were, we strained to see the sign that was far up ahead of us. Together, we determined what the next towns on our route were through their print configuration on the distant sign. We were much too far away to discriminate the individual letters, but we could tell by the shape and length of each word, as well as our background knowledge of the area; that is, the context we were in. We read that road sign much like some novices perceive words—by configuration and context.

Novices do not at first attend to the distinctive features related to the graphics on the page for the same reason I might confuse flowers. These beginners haven't hung around with books and print long enough. And maybe they haven't had a scaffolder to point out distinctive features, to help them notice the details.

This means novices may know the word *me* because it has only two letters that are both the same size. Or maybe they know it because it has two humps at the beginning. That's how children can identify some words even before they can identify letters. They use configuration. It's part of their tacit knowledge about words. But they must move beyond that, and we can help them by drawing their attention to distinctive features, along with the sounds they represent. Sometimes, however, our novice readers are not ready to be so analytical.

Fingerpointing: The Key to the Kingdom of Wordness

For some kids it takes a lot of experience inside text to understand its nitpicky features. Having novices fingerpoint to what they are reading is about the only way that teachers can monitor a child's level of in-process word awareness. Morris and Henderson (1981; Morris 1983) designated three levels of fingerpointing after having kids memorize a short text. Level 1 students exhibited no ability to point to words. Level 2 were transition students who used spacing cues to point, but tended to fall into monitoring syllables rather than whole words, and thus were "over-segmenting" (Clay 1993). Level 3 students could point to words as they said them and self-correct mistakes made on multisyllable words. It was only those readers at Level 3, the researchers contended, who had actually achieved the concept of word.

Teachers scaffold readers into wordness through a variety of avenues. Yet, for some, it becomes one of the most difficult concepts to acquire without some kind of one-to-one scaffolding.

Window the Word

It will come as no surprise, then, that one of the most common (G) cues is merely "Look at the word." Visit any first grade at the beginning of the year, and I guarantee this ruling will ring out regularly. And it seems especially important when we hear kids celebrating, "I can read with my eyes closed!"

Many teachers use masking: they ask a reader to cover everything except one particular word. Some teachers cut small rectangles of varying sizes in tagboard, so that only one word at a time will show through the window. This works far better when demonstrating with big books than with small, student copies, because it takes a while to find the right-sized window *and* the word.

Sometimes I ask kids to "window the word." I tell them to just use both of their pointer fingers to show me the beginning and ending of a given word. Marie Clay (1993) calls it "finger framing" (p. 22). After all, fingers are attached and far easier for first graders to manipulate. Masks are fun for big books—a novelty. But they take too much time away from the reading act when I am scaffolding.

How Kara Scaffolds Wordness

Kara used a different procedure to teach wordness to her novice reader. As the reader matched words while reading a sentence, Kara put up one finger at a time for each utterance that was a complete word. Watch how she models this in the following:

TEACHER: I notice *(reaches forward to point to the beginning of the sentence)* that you said "I—like—my—room" *(while saying each of these words that the child read, she holds her hand out in front, actually covering the text while releasing one finger at a time on her hand to denote counting)* There is one more

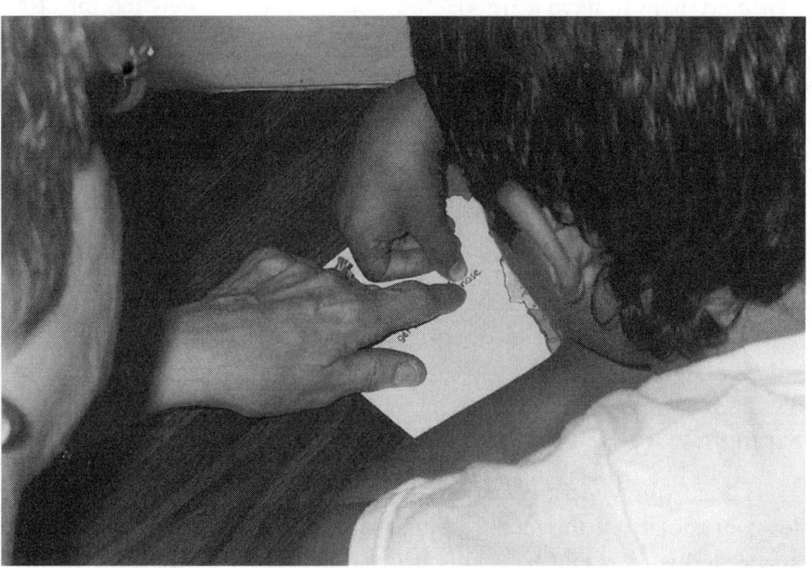

Reader and scaffolder "window a word" together.

word. *(points to* messy, *the last word in the sentence, the one the child omitted)*

It would seem that teachers spend a great deal of time and effort in kindergarten and first grade trying to get children to match spoken words to their printmates, helping novices grow out of preword and into word. But even at the end of the year, Kara felt the need to have this child focus by counting the number of words to make that *visual match*. For this novice, the concept of word was still a bit fuzzy. Again we are reminded that the transition can take a while.

Scaffolding Novices Who Don't Know All the Letters

I remember when reading programs barred a reader from moving forward in their program's series if that child did not perform optimally on the letter and sounds section of that book's post-assessment. When this occurred, teachers were expected to have the child repeat that entire book, all of its stories and everything that went with it (such as workbook pages). It was a grand way to turn kids off to reading—*if* the teacher followed that prescription. How silly it seemed to do this when the child *could* fluently read the text, but did not know the expected sounds or letters! Why not continue to teach letters and sounds, but move into a different text?

Indeed, as novice readers encounter new text, we often see gaps in what we might have expected them to have learned. Therefore, it will come as no surprise that, as I observed teachers scaffolding novice readers, many still had to help kids with letter identification—and you can probably guess which letters they were.

Notice how this teacher weaves letter scaffolding into the ongoing processing of text the student is reading:

STUDENT: *(reading)* "He made the bot . . . bot—" *(mired in the micro because it doesn't make sense)*
TEACHER: That's a *D*.
STUDENT: "Dot. He made the dot bigger."

I don't worry too much about these early letter confusions, but the media has parents overly concerned with would-be relationships between dyslexia and reversals. A recent *Time* magazine cover displayed a *b-d* on a chalkboard with a perplexed child observing it, along with a headline that focused on dyslexia. Yet, the article itself debunked this, calling dyslexia's relationship to reversals a myth. It's no wonder that never a year has passed that at least one parent did not ask me if I thought their child might have a serious problem because the novice continually confused *B*s and *D*s. Let me share the explanation that usually abates such worries.

I explain that from the time children are born a chair is a chair is a chair, regardless of the way in which it is turned. That is, knock it over and it's still a chair. There is nothing in their young lives that takes on a different name when we turn it around or upside down. Therefore, when novice readers encounter fifty-two (upper- and lowercase) letters, many of these youngsters just don't quite internalize how it all works. And no wonder! These symbols are different from anything they've ever encountered.

Furthermore, I tell the parents, research shows we don't have to be concerned about reversals until about third grade. This explanation draws a sigh of relief from most parents, but we all still continue to scaffold the kids toward correct forms.

Cueing Through Demonstration

It appears that there could be a relation between the scaffolding behaviors of teachers and the risk-taking behaviors of their students; that is, I watched the strategies of instruction become the strategies of language use. This modeling effect occurred in the Reading Recovery teacher-student interaction research of Wong, Groth, and O'Flahavan (1994) and also in Cambourne's (1988) investigations. Likewise, in this study it seemed that teachers who encouraged and modeled use of strategies had students who attempted to use these same strategies. Our demonstrations become those of our students.

More Pointing Demonstrations for Novices

The most common behavior of teachers in this study was one in which they used pointing as a marker, a demonstration tool to draw novices' attention to distinctive features. Teachers isolated both words and parts of words in a variety of manners. Patty pointed her marker over the text. Lani tapped with her pen. Julie circled with her finger. And they all used fingerpointing continually, but they also had their own ways of drawing attention to a word and its distinctive features.

All readers received such cues, but teachers finger-cued novice readers far more frequently. Three of the teachers were randomly selected in order to measure the amount of time their fingers actually touched the reader's book. There were moments when the teacher sat perched, ready to touch the page, but if she was not actually touching it, it was not counted, even though the child must have perceived her intention.

Patty used this touch-the-page pointing about six times as much with her novice reader as with her fluent, while Julie used it about eight times as often. Kara used it less than twice as much with her novice reader. Yet we can easily see that teachers do use this gesture far more with less-skilled readers, even when the more-skilled are also reading challenging texts. Figure 6–1 provides a comparative view among the three individuals.

Following the Leader

Teachers used more proactive, in-process, or sustaining graphophonemic mediation with novices than with fluent readers. Most of their leading behaviors were of this nature and involved gestural graphophonic cues as much as voiced. For example, when the reader slowed his pace, anticipating an unknown word, the teacher might point underneath the initial letter, or she might make that beginning sound for the reader to demonstrate what he should be doing. Or she may do both.

As in the children's game Follow the Leader, leading remains a kind of demonstration behavior, but one in which novices eventually play Follow the Scaffolder. Some of the children actually take on those demonstrated behaviors, so that as they are partner reading with another student who is having trouble decoding, these student-scaffolders reach over and cover part of the word, offer the beginning sound, or give some other cue to help the reader, just as their own scaffolder modeled. In so doing, novice followers become leaders. Chapter 3 offers an example of this when kids in my own room were partnering.

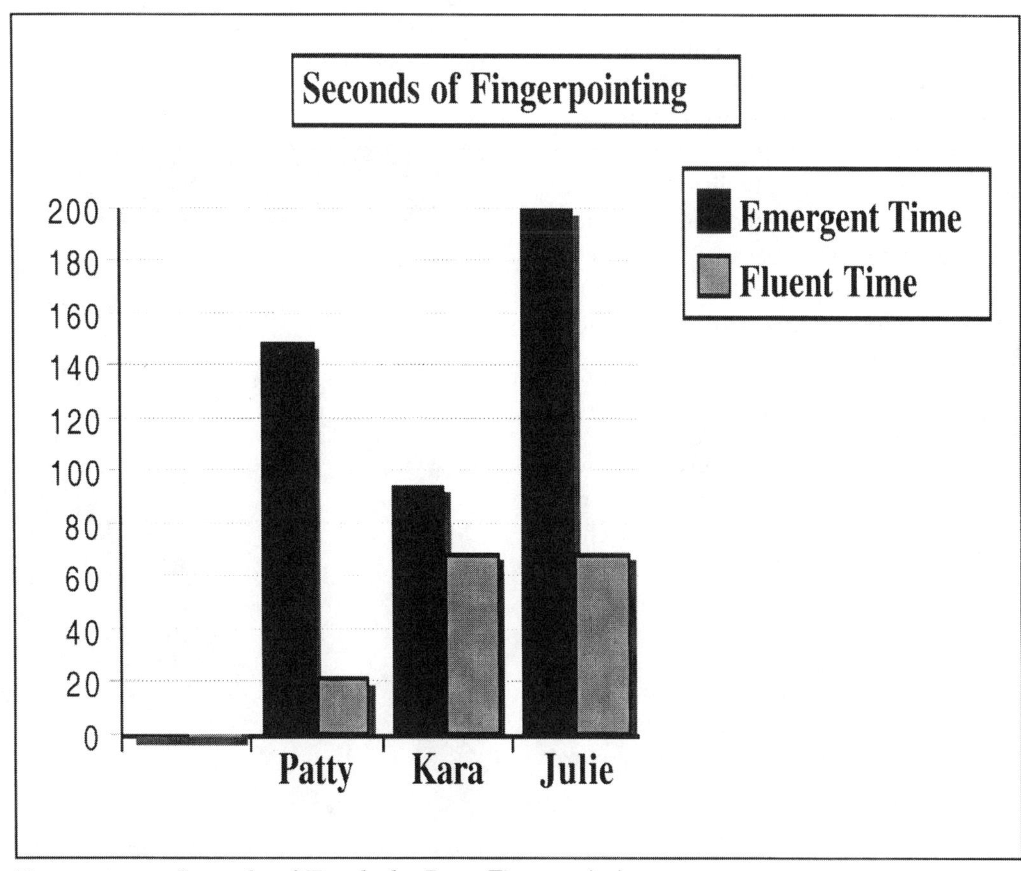

Figure 6–1. *Seconds of Touch-the-Page Fingerpointing*

When novices scaffold each other, we see that teacher fingerpointing behaviors have been internalized.

Graphophonic Strategies: Gestural and Voiced Scaffolding

It is difficult to separate gestural from voiced mediation. It's like trying to remove the rhythm from a song. Although there are some aspects of gestural mediation that I do want to mention separately, the rhythms of all voiced scaffolding were kept moving and meanings were enhanced through ongoing and abundant gestural behaviors.

The following is seemingly divided into two parts, gestured cues and voiced cues, but these can never truly be divided because they rely on each other for meaning. I did, however, omit many of the gestural behaviors from the voiced section to save a tree.

Gestural Graphophonic Strategy Cues

Teachers provided ongoing gestural (leading) behaviors to scaffold novices. Pointing, the primary marker, cued most strategies when teachers pointed to mark their place, to keep pace, or to draw attention to and mask parts of words.

How Teachers Gesture Graphophonic Cues

Although all teachers fingerpointed, the graphophonic cues they were referencing differed. For instance, to focus attention on a specific word part they covered:

- all but one letter (leaving only the *S* visible in *sung*)
- the root word (leaving *kins* visible in *Babykins*)
- the inflectional ending (leaving *bark* visible in *barking*)
- all but a little word in a big word (leaving *tail* visible in *tailor*)
- syllables in sequence moving from left to right (*im- por- tant* uncovering in sequence)

Sometimes their hand dances actually amazed me. They were indeed an intuitively orchestrated symphony of scaffolds. Yet, because the dance is so uniquely blended with other cues most researchers have completely overlooked the important contribution that gestures make in teaching novices to read. An omission in definite need of amending!

Obviously, it is easier to capture teachers' words in print than their gestures, which we can only attempt to describe. This especially inhibits quantitative researchers, but it also affected the writing of this next section. That is, more space in this book is afforded to the voiced cues. But

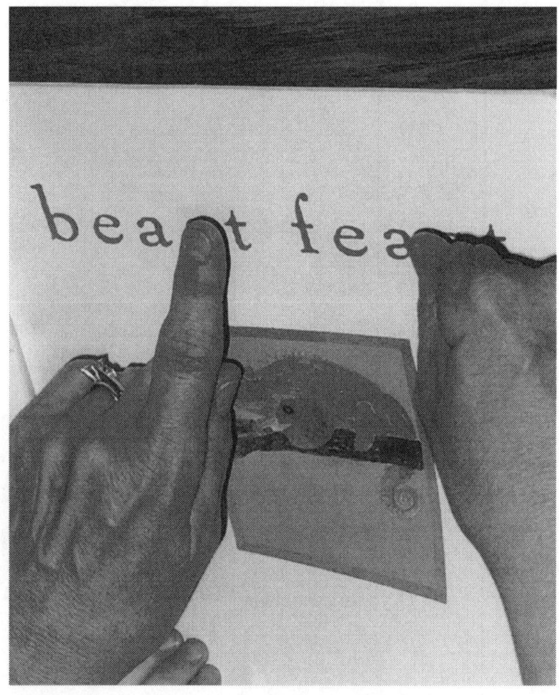

Linda covers end of words to focus reader on identical vowel sounds.

Writing Reciprocity: Encoding Syllables in Multisyllable Words

At first the phonemic awareness needed to encode a multisyllable word, such as *understand*, can be a real challenge for novices, so I focus writers on one syllable at a time by using mini–Post-its. It's effective, as well as fun.

First, we decide how many Post-its we need (by counting syllables), and then we encode each syllable onto its own little Post-it. Afterward, we move the syllable notes right under where they'll be copied into the novice's piece of writing.

We know when it's time to eliminate this sticky-note tactic and do the syllable encoding right into the text, itself—it occurs when we run out of Post-its!

please do not be deceived, for gestural cues are at least equal to voiced cues in their scaffolding importance. Furthermore, their silent message is less intrusive than a voiced interruption.

Gestural cues are far more inferential than spoken ones. In most cases students must have some prior knowledge of a gestured strategy before they can understand its message. For example, if a teacher is gesturing for a reader to return to the beginning of the sentence and reread, that reader would have had to have this strategy previously explained and implemented in order for him to understand the scaffolder's inferences. And this background knowledge is particularly true for graphophonic gestural cues.

Voiced Cues

Voiced cues are an integral part of the scaffolding process. Their pragmatic impact is inherent in the act, especially when teacher and reader trade the lead. And this is what occurred in every transaction I observed. I was not only watching a gestural dance, but also listening to a duet—one in which the lead moved back and forth, and at times was shared in a unique harmony.

Verbal Guidance/Leading

A large amount of the teacher mediation observed was indeed verbal guidance, often evident as teachers led novices through the words phonetically. They sometimes modeled, but at other times made suggestions that invited the young novice toward a certain behavior. Teachers used verbal guidance scaffolds in several ways. They:

- suggested which part of the word to look at,
- modeled how to sound a certain letter (especially the initial sound) or onset,
- found known little words within bigger unknown words,
- provided a rhyming word, and
- corrected miscues.

The chart below lists, more specifically, some of the verbal guidance that teachers offered during the mediation act. The chart also indicates times when verbal guidance was offered.

Common Verbal Guidance Cues

What Teachers Said	When Teachers Said It
"Check your ending."	When the reader had the word's beginning correct but not the end
"Sound it out."	When a student seemed afraid to move on
"Make it one word."	When leading the reader toward blending
"You are close."	When reader had almost decoded the word
"That's a silent letter."	When reader tried to attach a sound to a silent letter
"Let's try it again from the beginning."	When reader became confused inside the decoding act
"Look at the beginning of the word."	When reader wasn't focusing
"That's right! Good!"	While reader was blending through
"Let's skip. Let's go on and we'll come back."	When reader became frustrated using graphophonics

Linda helps a novice sound through an unknown word.

Voiced Cues Within Graphophonic Categories

Because our focus here is on children who are just learning to read—that is, novices—and because graphophonics incorporates sound, teachers used myriad voiced cues to scaffold readers toward graphophonic strategies. It therefore seems that these cues deserve a separate section, which might make cues easier to reference. The chart on pages 97–100 is structured for that purpose.

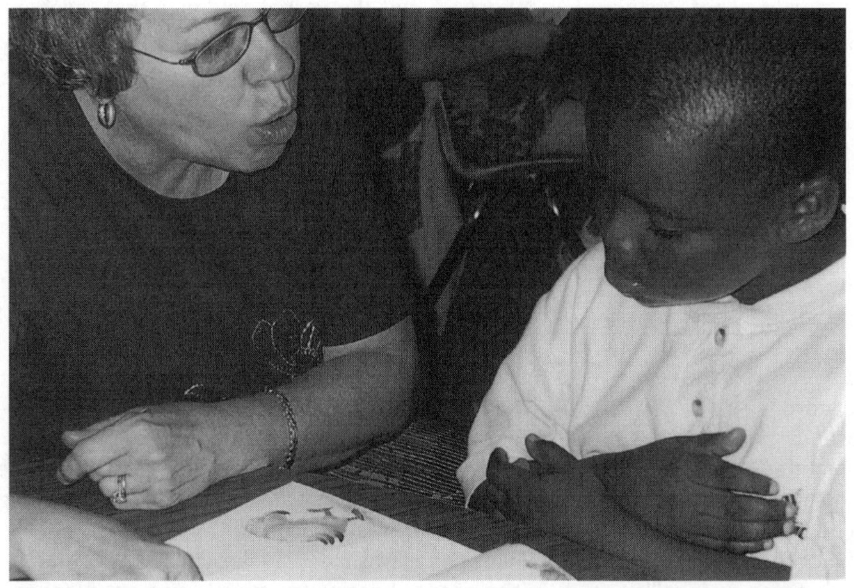
Here, the scaffolder draws attention to a vowel pattern by phonically stretching a long O.

Graphophonic Cues Teachers Used

The following demonstrates some of the specific cues offered within individual graphophonic categories. Please note that they are but examples—ones that may or may not have been effective. Which ones would you use?

Consonant Sounds

Initial (onset), final, and medial consonant sounds

The reader miscued *dark*, substituting *blankets*, so the teacher scaffolds:

TEACHER: All right. Let's look at that beginning sound. Do you know it? What is the beginning sound?
STUDENT: D- D- *(self-corrects* B *to* D*)*
TEACHER: Okay, D-D- k-, d-k- *(scaffolds using initial and final sound)*
STUDENT: Dark?

Silent Consonants

This is such a common example that most every teacher is committed to it. The reader is stuck on *know* in the following:

TEACHER: Let's look at this word. That word is a funny word because that *K* doesn't say anything at all. And the *W* doesn't say anything. Look at it, Josepi, the *K* and the *W* don't say a thing, and I don't know why they even put them there, because all you hear is the *N* and the *O*.

Consonant Digraphs

The reader is stuck on *petshop* in the following:

STUDENT: *(reading)* "He has food for the petsh—"
TEACHER: Pet what?
STUDENT: Pet-
TEACHER: What is that *S-H* sound?
STUDENT: St-
TEACHER: No, the quiet sound . . .
STUDENT: Sh-

Another reader is stuck on the word *those*, so the teacher uses analogy to scaffold the initial *T-H*, and she then moves on to encompass the vowel sound, as well:

TEACHER: T-H as in *the (hints)*
STUDENT: th-
TEACHER: It has an O. So-o-o-o, what? What's the sound of words that have an O? Th-? Th-? Th- ose. *(segmenting into two parts)*
STUDENT: "Those strange bumps . . ." *(blends the word and reads on)*

Vowel Sounds

Vowel Sounds in One-Syllable Words: Short Vowels

The reader is stuck on *shop* and has instead decoded *ship*, so the teacher scaffolds:

TEACHER: Almost. But there is not an *I* there. If there was an *I*, it would be *ship*. That's an *O*—a short O, and what says o- o- o- *(voicing short sound of* O*)*? Sh—?
STUDENT: Shop.

Vowel Sounds in One-Syllable Words: Long Vowels

The reader is stuck on the word *time* and has provided the initial sound t-. The teacher validates by saying, "It does begin with a *T*. What else do you see that you recognize?" to which the reader responds, "*I*."

STUDENT: Ti- *(blending using short* I *sound)*
TEACHER: Ti- *(demonstrating long* I *blend)* And then the *M*. T- i- m-. T- ime *(blending)*.
STUDENT: Time *(blends onset and rime and reads on)*

Another reader got stuck on the word *music*:
STUDENT: *(reading)* "and make loud m- mu-" *(using short* U *sound)*
TEACHER: M- u-, long *U*, mu- *(demonstrating two separate sounds, then blending)*
STUDENT: Music!

Silent Vowels

The reader substitutes *tack* for *take*, so the teacher scaffolds:

TEACHER: Let's look at that word again *(covers the final* E *with her pointer)*. This *E* says nothing. It is only there to make that vowel say its name *(pointing to* A*)*. Try it again.
STUDENT: T- Take *(successfully decoding)*

Vowel Digraphs

The reader is stuck on the word *down*, and substitutes *don't*, so the teacher scaffolds:

TEACHER: Almost. But that middle sound is -ow. Instead of do- *(using a long* O*)*, if you say -ow in the middle it becomes . . . ?
STUDENT: Down?
TEACHER: Right!

Vowel and Consonant Sound Blending

Consonant Blends

The reader miscues on the word *blow* in the phrase "blow out the candle." The preceding line was "Time to"; therefore, the reader evidently thought it was about time for bed, so she substituted *bed* for *blow*. But then she quickly returned to the initial consonant and gave the initial b- sound. Therefore, the teacher scaffolded:

TEACHER: B-L at the beginning *(hinting at the initial blend)*
STUDENT: B- B- *(still not blending)*
TEACHER: Bl- Bl- ow-ow.
STUDENT: "Blow out the candle and go to sleep, he said . . ."

Consecutive Unblended Sounds

Sometimes teachers talk kids through words using consecutive demonstrations prior to the decoding act of the student. In the following the reader is stuck on the word *while*, so the teacher scaffolds:

TEACHER: Okay, I'll help you. What is the beginning?
STUDENT: Wh-
TEACHER: Okay. Do you see anything else there *(pointing)*? It has a *W-H* at the beginning and an *I* with an *E* at the end *(pointing at each)*.
STUDENT: Will?
TEACHER: Almost, except now you want a long *I* so you want to say wh- i-i-ile instead—
STUDENT: "While I am . . ."

Other novices know the sounds, but they need a nudge to use them because they are not independent in their application yet. That's what happened when Linda was scaffolding Joey who got stuck on the word *made*. The teacher knew Joey was capable of making the sounds within the word, so she offered an open invitation without modeling:

TEACHER: Say the sounds you know.
STUDENT: m- a- d- *(sounding separate consecutive sounds and using a long* A *and then blends)*. "Made a face—a funny face" *(self-corrects)*.

Consecutive Blended Sounds

Brandon miscued *black* for *blue*. I scaffolded:

TEACHER: What do you think *(pointing)*, does it look like bl- ack? Huh-uh, it doesn't. Black would be bl- and then -a- would be an *A*. So it's what?
STUDENT: Bl- ue.

Later, Brandon came upon *black* and hesitated just long enough to blend bl- ack.

TEACHER: Good! I liked the way you went bl- ack. I heard you go: "There was a bl- ack one!"

It's helpful to let novices know when they have appropriately used a taught strategy. Time to celebrate!

Teachers often worked in tandem with a child, sharing the sounds through a word. This reader was stuck on the word *Aborigines.* Without a scaffolder nudge how would he know such a word! (This one always tickles my funny bone.)

STUDENT: Abor- abor - ig - nee.
TEACHER: Put it all together and see what you come up with. I think you're really close.
STUDENT: The Aborignee *(Not bad! But -rig- syllable rhymes with dig and he eliminated -in-.)*
TEACHER: It's *Aborigines*. Those are the kind of people who live in Australia. They're called Aborigine. Have you heard of that? *(reader shakes his head no)* Well, you've heard of them now! And it's a wonderful word to say. Try it. Aborigine. *(backs off and folds arms to gesturally to offer independence to the reader)*
STUDENT: The Abor- ern- er- g- rigine people, . .

(I could barely keep a straight face!)

Word Parts or Chunks

Chunks

The reader is stuck on *Daddy*, so the teacher scaffolds:

TEACHER: If we put the marker over this part (covering the -dy in *Daddy*), do you know that word now?
STUDENT: *(reading)* "Daddy likes to work."

In another case, the reader miscued on the word *patch* by substituting *pouch*. To focus the child on the medial vowel, the teacher did the following:

TEACHER: Okay, so when we come back here we see it's not *pouch*, but . . . is there anything alike here in this word and in the other word?
STUDENT: It's got a *P* and a *C-H*.
TEACHER: Okay, so you might have thought that it was *pouch*. But do you see this -at? Now, what could that possibly be?
STUDENT: Patch.
TEACHER: Yeah! But do you know what a patch of ground is?

Rimes (Phonograms; Families)

The reader is stuck on *small*, so the teacher scaffolds:

TEACHER: Can you sound it out? *S-M*. Sm- and there is a little word *all* and when we put it together what do we have?
STUDENT: Small.

Little Words in Big Words

For this common strategy most teachers use gesture as much as voice. They cover up all but the little word. Patty covered the silent *K* and the silent *W* in *know*, leaving only the little word *no*. She did it *for* the reader, but of course, just as often teachers simply ask, "Do you see any little words in that big word?

Indeed, reading authorities suggest that we adults work our way through unknown print primarily using this strategy. So although it seems valuable, perhaps we'd better first look to see if the little word inside will indeed help before we suggest this strategy to a reader—an issue that is discussed in Chapter 8.

In the following example the reader is stuck on the word *grinning*, so the teacher scaffolds:

TEACHER: Do you see any little words in that big word?
STUDENT: Yeah.
TEACHER: Which ones?
STUDENT: -ing.
TEACHER: Okay, -ing. That is an ending.
STUDENT: Oh, *in*.
TEACHER: Okay, so we have the beginning gr-, -in, -ing. Grinning. Have you ever heard of that?

Word Structures

Inflectional Endings (-ed, -ing, -es)

The student is stuck on the word *asked*, so the teacher covers the -ed ending with her pointing finger, and waits, saying nothing.

STUDENT: Ask.
TEACHER: And add an *E-D* to it. Ask-?
STUDENT: A-a-ask -ed *(two syllables, but then self-corrects)* Asked.

Compound Words

Compound words came up many times, and, in one case, a child drew attention to one before the teacher! Nevertheless, most compound word cues were gestural. That is, the teacher covered up one of the words.

Hannah's novice came upon the word *playpen* and stopped after sounding the *PL*. So Hannah immediately placed her finger under *play* and then just as quickly under *pen*, denoting two words or syllables. From there she pointed to the picture of the playpen, and asked, "What is this thing where we put babies and they can't get out?"

"I don't know," responded the child.

So Hannah covered *pen* to see if that would help, but when it didn't she scaffolded, "Pl- play-play-ay-ay" with an upward inflection as she slid her finger under *pen* and tapped.

"Playpen!" decoded the student in surprise.

"Good!!" the teacher called joyfully. "You figured it out! What a good reader!"

"I think its a compound word!" added the novice.

"Oh! I think it's a compound word, too! Play-pen! Good jo-o-o-b!" celebrated Hannah.

Prefixes and Suffixes

Re- is an easy prefix that I usually introduce early in the year. We have fun with it seeing how many action words (verbs) we can attach it to. Sometimes it gets kind of silly. Nevertheless, it proves helpful when a novice then encounters it in print, which is what happened in the following:

STUDENT: *(stuck on the word* redial) That's a funny word. Red—
TEACHER: Yes, but you already know the prefix. *(covers the root word)* What's this much?
STUDENT: Re-
TEACHER: Yes, now look at the picture. What's happening again?
STUDENT: She's dialing the number.
TEACHER: Exactly! So it would be re—?
STUDENT: Re- re- dial?
TEACHER: Yes, redial the phone.

Roots/Morphologic Structures

Novices primarily become aware of roots through common words to which affixes (prefixes and suffixes) or inflectional endings have been connected. Root words differ from chunks or parts because roots key the meaning of the term, while affixes and inflectional endings refine or guide that meaning.

The reader encounters the word *unhappy* and stops, so the teacher scaffolds:

TEACHER: *(covering the prefix with her thumb)* What's this root word?
STUDENT: Happy?
TEACHER: Yes. Now you know most of the word, so just put the beginning on *(slides her pointer under* un- *and waits)*
STUDENT: Un- happy.
TEACHER: Right. But slide the two together.
STUDENT: Unhappy.
TEACHER: Wonderful! A three-syllable word! A long one!

Syllabification with Open and Closed Syllables in Multisyllabic Words

Eventually, novice readers develop the need for decoding and blending separate syllables. Teachers focused on syllables in interesting ways. Lani tapped rhythmically with her pen to show the number of parts in a word. Others repeated word parts with distinct crescendos. Some covered each consecutive syllable by pointing or masking. Body movements, too, fell in pace with syllabification, particularly head nods. All of these provided numerous, yet analogic, signs to the young readers for the more complex structures they had to read.

Mini-Lessons Inside the Act

Most often the scaffolders did not deviate from their scaffolding. However, every once in a while, they took a few seconds to do a quick, personal mini-lesson. This one begins with a focus on initial consonant strategies and ends with meaning cues. The novice has miscued *golf* for *croquet.*

TEACHER: Do you think it's *golf*?
STUDENT: Yeah.
TEACHER: Look at the beginning letter. G- G- Golf? Do you think it's—
STUDENT: No.
TEACHER: No, I don't think so either. How *does* it start? Cr- Cr- o- o-. It's called *croquet.* That's a hard word for us, but we play that game in the summer. See the picture.

Praise for the Trying

Kara, Hannah, and Julie all spoke of the difference in what they affirm for the fluent and what they affirm for the novice. For instance, when Kara provided praise to her novice reader, that reader had just finished inaccurately reading a section of text. The child had miscued; however, the miscue was a meaningful substitution. That is, it still made sense, even though it was not correct.

When the teacher was asked why she praised an inaccuracy, she affirmed, " 'Cause she's a low reader, and anytime I get the chance I say, 'All right! You're doing good! Keep going!' " In other words, Kara was celebrating the approximations—just as Brian Cambourne (1988) suggested. Her novice had fluently moved through a portion of text with a *keep-going strategy*; that is, she replaced a word with a meaningful substitution and kept going. Meaning had not been distorted, and the child had read both fluently and independently. The teacher then praised what the reader had done—and at the same time *intentionally* overlooked the miscue.

Monitoring Graphophonics: For, with, and by the Reader

Often the best ways to discover the strategies a reader is using is simply to ask him. This can be helpful information for scaffolding decisions. For instance, in this transcribed episode notice how, when the novice reader successfully finishes a sentence, Kara inquires about her strategies, for she wants to know if this emergent reader has moved beyond just the picture as a cue:

STUDENT: *(reading)* "I like books on my floor." *(reads quickly, confidently, and very fluently)*
TEACHER: How did you know that was floor? *(leans forward a bit to focus more toward the child than the text)*
STUDENT: *(responds with the hint of a proud grin)* F-L *(points to the letters and then reaches to the bottom of the page to turn)*

When we later watched the video, Kara explained: "Just checking again. 'Cause she is using picture cue a lot. You can tell, 'cause when she gets to a word she doesn't know, that's the first thing she'll go to, is picture."

Notice she says, "Just checking," which would mean "Just assessing," or "Just monitoring." And Kara found out that the reader was applying a graphophonic onset strategy. She now can assume that she will not have to model this strategy for this reader. But maybe she will consider leading her toward rimes.

At another time, when Jane was watching the footage and was asked why she chose to provide the word after using an ineffectual (S-S), she responded, "Because sounding it doesn't lend itself to that one." So again we see this ongoing assessment followed by informed facilitation. This time, Jane resorted to reading the word for the child. She did not want to waste time on an ineffectual cue.

Just like Kara, other teachers sometimes need to validate their own assumptions regarding a reader's behaviors and intentions. To do this, they check in with the reader. Notice what Linda learns about Joey in the following.

Joey read "I will eat, too" for the sentence "I want to eat, too," which prompted Linda to ask, "Can it be *will*?" as she focused the reader toward graphophonic noticing behaviors.

"Huh-uh," Joey responded.

"Why can't it be *will*?" his teacher asked, leading the reader toward graphophonic analysis.

"Because it doesn't have an *I* in it," the reader responded.

"Okay, so look at what it does have," his teacher nudged. *(And she then takes him back to the beginning of the sentence to reread.)* "And I w- t-? Say the ending sound. *(And she reads again for him.)* And I w- n- t"

So after Linda leads the Joey toward the reliable consonant sounds in the word, this reader picks up the proffered cues, and correctly rereads: "I want—and I want to eat, too."

"What was that word?" the teacher monitors.

"Want," the reader responds and then reads on.

Lani passes the monitoring on to her student when the reader stumbles on the word *squeeze* and tries sounding it out—to no avail. Notice how Lani nudges the novice forward in his reading using a variety of strategies:

TEACHER: Okay, you've tried sounding it out. What's the next thing you might want to do?

STUDENT: Look at the picture. *(but then is stuck again because that cue doesn't work either)*

TEACHER: Okay. Hm-m-m. It doesn't tell you much does it? What is the next thing you might try?

STUDENT: Skip it.

TEACHER: Okay. *(speaking softly now and nodding her head in affirmation)*

Actually, it is nearly impossible to scaffold without monitoring, because it is the monitoring that drives the scaffolding. But the goal is to eventually nudge the reader into monitoring his own reading. In so doing, you will be working yourself out of your scaffolding job!

A Fine Balance

Obviously, graphophonic cues are of utmost importance, for without the sound-related print on the page, we would have nothing to read! But to simply bark at words cannot count as reading, because reading must first and foremost be a meaningful process. And the more word-centered we make it, the further away from chunking we lead a child. Yet when we keep meaning in the forefront we and our students succeed. However, just as important as graphophonic and semantic-syntactic cues are the pragmatic cues we offer readers. The following chapter investigates ways in which pragmatic cues can make or break a reading relationship.

Grist for Discussion

Investigate the following scaffolding transcript from a reader who has now moved from preword into word reading. At first the teacher selected a book that was not challenging. This was the second selection and far more appropriate for scaffolding.

First mark all the teacher's graphophonic cues. Then decide whether each was or was not an effective cue. And finally, discuss what you would have done differently. (The text being used is *The Reason for a Flower* by Ruth Heller [1983].)

When this reader begins to read this new text, the teacher sits back and folds her arms, seemingly confident in the reader's independence.

TEACHER: Let me see this . . . I think it starts out . . . Read the title.

STUDENT: *(reading)* "The Reason for the Flower. This one has become a plum. The Reasons for a flower. Birds and bees, and these—"

TEACHER: Let's go back there and get this one. *(reaches over and moves the marker to the spot of focus in the book, while the student stays right with her)* Angelo, please sit down, please. *(Since the teacher was first involved with another reader for quite a while and then worked for a while to find something that was challenging for this child, she is getting nervous about the behavior of those at their seats, who could at this point be testing her concentrated involvement.)*

STUDENT: *(reading)* "Sip nac-ter."

TEACHER: Let's look at that again. *(Says this quickly, almost as though she is bothered by the error, but what is really the problem is probably the fact that some kids are starting to move about the classroom—AND it is the end of the school year, so everyone is antsy. The teacher reaches over to slide the marker to the spot but does not put her hand over this little girl's, as she did with the emergent reader. Instead, she keeps her hand alongside of the book. She does, however, lean forward to get into the act a bit more.)* Let's go back to that word. There is a short *E* in there. Something that the bees sip from flowers.

STUDENT: "Nectarine."

TEACHER: Nectar. *(quickly points to the word)*

STUDENT: *(maintaining autonomy in turning the pages, unlike the emergent reader, and reading)* "Nectar from the flowers and as they search for more and more polen *(uses a long* O *in* pollen*)* from the flower before goes—"

TEACHER: That's a short *O* on that. *(Lets her finger move over the top edge of the page enough so that she can focus the child's attention on the short* O. *Then quickly withdraws and sits back again, completely away from the reader and the text.)* And it's po-o-o- llen. *(elongating the short* O *sound)*

STUDENT: *(reads on)* "to the next one they explore. Some pollen travels in the breeze without the help of birds or bees, and very often makes you sneeze. From an- other."

TEACHER: No, it has an *A* in front of it *(reaches across the top of the book again to quickly point to the* A*)* so its—? *(stops mid-sentence in upward inflection to invite reader in)*

STUDENT: *(trying to decode)* "ann- other" *(reader repeats previous behavior)*

TEACHER: anther, anther *(and teacher tells the word)*

STUDENT: *(reading)* "anther on a" *(reader stops to investigate the word* stamen*)*

TEACHER: That's a long *A* in there. You're going to hear the *A*.

STUDENT: *(reading)* "stamen."

TEACHER: Right! That has the short *I (reaches forward and motions toward the next word, anticipating the reader's need, yet does not touch the book this time)*

STUDENT: *(reading)* "stigma on a style."

TEACHER: And those words are written in a different way, weren't they? Those letters were written in a different order on the page. (*referring to the book's irregular formatting or layout style*)

STUDENT: *(reading)* "Pollen grains must travel and stay a little while. And then you'll see the reason for each flower even weeds. The reason for a flower is to manufacturing—"

TEACHER: Manufacture, good, good! *(Although the reader came close to this word, she still miscued, yet the teacher praised her—and then corrected her.)*

STUDENT: *(reading)* "Seeds that have a cover of one kind or another. Some grow inside a juicy fruit, and it's not odd to find them growing in a pod. The largest one is a coconut. Seeds travel far and wide. Some even like . . . " *(reader goes on to read the remainder with no scaffolding)*

Chapter 7

Pragmatic Relationships That Influence Cueing

I could not remember when the lines above Atticus's moving finger separated into words, but I had stared at them all the evenings of my memory, listening to the news of the day, Bills to be Enacted into Laws, the diaries of Lorenzo Dow—anything Atticus happened to be reading when I crawled into his lap every night. Until I feared I would lose it, I never loved to read. One does not love breathing.

HARPER LEE,
TO KILL A MOCKINGBIRD

A few chapters back I mentioned the three attributes of the pragmatic cueing system: *field, tenor*, and *mode*. The field, the *environmental influence*, is important because it relates to everything in the reader's physical space, including the objects that surround him. The mode, the message system, is important because it is the vehicle through which the reader receives the message. This means that mode includes the text he is reading. Several times I discussed these aspects, which can make or break a relationship.

Now finally, we come to tenor, which may possess the most influential cues, because it involves the living relationships within the act; that is, the transactions that occur between human beings. This chapter investigates this important area.

The Dance Within the Relationship

Through the camcorder lens I watched Julie as she slid up, elbow to elbow, beside novice reader Ralisha, a first grader who was subvocalizing her way through a version of *The Little Red Hen* during Sustained Silent Reading.

Keeping her finger poised to mark her place in the text, Ralisha raised her eyes to the teacher's, creating a kind of ethereal connection between the two.

"May I?" interrupted the teacher. Ralisha nodded, her smile mirroring that of her teacher, who reached forward to grasp the right-hand edge of the book. Synchronistically, Ralisha released her own grip to allow the mutual act of book holding to unfold.

It was no surprise that, as Ralisha moved on through the story, she and her teacher worked in harmony. Through the lens of the camera their harmonic transactions took on the characteristics of a literacy dance, one in which teacher and student traded and shared control of the situation through both the melodies of their voices and the rhythms of their gestures. Similar to other dances, this literacy dance was often guided by gesture. Even the most simplistic adjustive response made by the teacher seemed to carry the novice reader over potential, as well as realized, hurdles. Both individuals shared ownership of the process as the reading relationship grew.

These relationship cues that teachers offer influentially shade and hue every scaffolding event. They are describable, but usually tough to measure. Maybe that's why so little has been written related to the *metamessages* (the messages about the messages) that abound within a teacher-student reading relationship. There are a few who have dissected, described, and documented relationships; some even involve children and schools (Noddings 1984, 1992; Kohn 1993, Kozal 1991). But few mention reading relationships.

Such sensitive behaviors will never become a part of any scripted lesson from some company's how-to manual because pragmatic cues must be *internalized* and *spontaneous* in order to evoke an optimal reading relationship—which this chapter makes evident. For one thing, scripted lessons are taught to a group of students, not to individuals. Moreover, it is difficult to imagine a scripted lesson that indicates smiles, hand pats, or the effective *finger dances* described in the following. This chapter is important because it examines the more intangible, somewhat ethereal relationship qualities—ones that we all know exist—whether or not they can be measured!

This Definitely Isn't Fluff!

I originally pegged this section for an earlier appearance in the book—right up front—because it is significantly related to reading success—and failure. But without the presentation of semantic-syntactic and graphophonic cues, I felt some readers might consider it "fluff." Trust me! It is not fluff. And with the structures of the previous two chapters as its introduction, I hope that readers will realize that the substance of this section is what drives the entire process—the relationships and successful scaffolding. Indeed, human relationship cues are the primary energy, the underriding vitality of any teacher-reader dyad.

A Heart Focus

In the following I discuss what happens when teachers lead from the heart. Obviously, we do not put our heads in the cupboard, but heart focus is the main topic on the table. And rightly so, because without heart a reading relationship loses its energy, its focus, its meaning, its value, and, of course, its harmony. Heart is not fluff; it's actually a dimension of intelligence. It's time we started giving it the place of honor that we know it deserves.

The Metamessages of Gestural Signs

Information is conveyed by the meanings inherent in articulated words. It is the message. It is rational. However, researchers (Grinder and Bandler 1975; Tannen 1986) suggest that we are also sending/receiving something else, which they call the metamessage. This other entity is actually communicated about relationships. It involves attitudes, events, and the content of what's said.

> Whereas words convey information, how we speak those words—how loud, how fast, with what intonation and emphasis—communicates what we think we're doing when we speak: teasing, flirting, explaining, or chastising; whether we're feeling friendly, angry, or quizzical; whether we want to get closer or back off. In other words, how we say what we say communicates social meanings. (Tannen 1986, p. 16)

And this addresses only voiced gesture. But what about bodily gestures—how we communicate with our hands, our arms, our eyes, our mouths, and, sometimes, our whole body? These metamessages were evidenced throughout the mediation footage, just as they would be in any living relationship.

Our body and voice gestures—voice inflection and intonation, hand movements, body stance—all cue students in significant ways. On the videos teachers' voices displayed excitement, pleasure, humor, and kindness. Occasionally they also showed negatively voiced cues, such as impatience (especially when interrupted by another child in the class), complacency (especially when they were getting tired), and frustration (especially when readers underperformed to their teachers' expectations). Readers read these messages, just as they read the more obvious articulated ones.

Bodily movements and voice often carry strong and overriding metamessages. Think how differently a reader will receive us if we are harsh, whining, angry, fearful, and halted, or sincere, gentle, compassionate, and joyful. We certainly are not going to sell any product, reading or otherwise, with negative metamessages.

The Influence of Mirroring on Relationships

Those who have spent years and thousands of dollars studying gesture (Grinder and Bandler 1976; Robbins 1986) have information that is so influential that large corporations hire them to scaffold sales representatives. These gesture specialists call our attention to "mirroring" techniques, which appear to have relevance to all relationships—even those between teachers and their students. It's all about rapport.

Anthony Robbins incorporates these techniques into a program he calls NLP (neurolinguistic programming), developed from the gestural research of Grinder and Bandler. This is also, by the way, the breakthrough technique that Barry Kaufman (1979, 1995) used with his autistic son, Raun. In NLP, Robbins (1986) suggests:

> One of the best ways to achieve rapport is through mirroring or creating a common physiology with that person. That's what the great hypnotherapist Dr. Milton Erickson did. He learned to mirror the breathing patterns, posture, tonality, and gestures of other people. And by doing that, he achieved a totally binding rapport in a matter of minutes. People who did not know him suddenly trusted him without question . . . While the words are working on a person's conscious mind, the physiology is working on the unconscious. That's where the brain is thinking, Hey, this person's like me. He must be okay. And once that happens, there's a tremendous attraction, a tremendous bond. And because it's unconscious, it's even more effective. (pp. 234–35)

Effective Scaffolding Through Mirroring

I watched as the most effective scaffolding brought Robbins' words to life. Teachers mirrored a child's voice tone, pitch, rate, and volume. They mirrored the child's eye contact and body language, facial expressions, and hand gestures. And then, in a kind of harmonic ballet, students mirrored back the teacher's gestural behaviors until the two could only be explained as one, united by relationship.

When Robbins is asked, "What would happen if we could mirror everything about another person?" his answer explains the impact of mirroring on a reading relationship.

> People feel as though they've found their soul mate, someone who totally understands, who can read their deepest thoughts, who is just like them. But you don't have to mirror everything about a person to create a state of rapport. If you just start with the tone of voice or a similar facial expression, you can learn to build incredible rapport with someone. (pp. 234–35)

I watched such rapport unfold as teachers mirrored students and students mirrored teachers. Kara sat with her hand holding her head; eventually her reader sat with her hand holding her head. One removed her hand and the other mirrored that behavior—again and again. Another teacher, Lani, presented a teasing grin to her reader; the reader tossed one back at his teacher, back and forth, back and forth. Kara's students were so good at mirroring the rhythms of her fingerpointing that the dyad could change the author of the pointing without missing a beat.

Gestural influence on a reading relationship is difficult to measure; therefore, research skirts this important variable. Yet, those of us who have ever had a relationship with anyone at anytime know that it is very often gestural behaviors that set our emotions and intentions into action, that make or break the connection. Gesture's emotive influence is significant; and its power in bringing focus and harmony to the dyad is unsurpassed. It's always especially fascinating to see how it is used to gain control of a situation.

"Who's Building Whose Building?"

The title of an article by Dennis Searle, "Scaffolding: Who's Building Whose Building?" (1984), is a metaphor for Who's in control? and is an important issue in a reading relationship. The ongoing flow of control from teacher to student and back again is what moves the learner from dependency to autonomy, and what moves a sensitive teacher from *doing-to* toward *doing-with*.

These one-on-one transactions are a very special venue in which optimal learning can take place. They occur between living, breathing human beings and display a different essence than interactions via computers, books, and other sign-bearing systems. Human transactions carry a spark that interactions with books, or any other nonhuman entity, will never possess. This spark is set ablaze through opportunities in ownership, control, leadership, authority, power, and strangely enough, among this cluster, a could-be opposite: caring.

Leading from a Self-Agenda: An "I" Stance

Sometimes we find the mediator asserting a position of power or authority, which we will call the "I" stance (Buber 1970), meaning the scaffolding adult has an agenda that he is imposing on the reader. Holding such a perspective, the mediator himself acts as author of scaffolding events. As such he makes decisions based upon his own goals and all that shapes them, whether they be educational, philosophical, personal, or political. Through this lens he interacts with the learner, imposing his own view of the way in which the process should proceed.

Guided by a Reader-Agenda: A "Thou" Stance

When the mediator experiences the perspective opposite her own, she is within a stance of caring, which will be called the Thou state of being (Buber 1970). Nel Noddings (1984) describes this state most eloquently:

> When I receive the other, I am totally with the other. The relation is for the moment exactly as Buber has described it in *I and Thou*. The other "fills the firmament." I am not thinking of the other as object. I am not making claims to knowledge. We enter a feeling mode, but it is not necessarily an emotional mode. In such a mode, we receive what-is-there as nearly as possible without evaluation or assessment. We are in the world of relation, having stepped out of the instrumental world; we have either not yet established goals or we have suspended striving for those already established. We are not attempting to transform the world, but we are allowing ourselves to be transformed. (pp. 32, 34)

Far from the "I" stance, in this "feeling mode," one must actually "transform" by relinquishing self. That is, the teacher becomes the child before her, feeling his feelings, thinking his thoughts. It moves us out of imposition and into reception.

United in Sharing: A "We" Stance

At times, a kind of union of the "I" and "Thou" occurs. It is by far the most interesting, for it is the time-place when the mediator, carrying his or her formed intentions, joins the learner, carrying his or her formed intentions, in what Csikszentmihaly (1990) would call a "flow" experience. Together they spiral the learner toward growth in what might be called an attentional synchronicity. This is the "We" stance. During the mediation process, the "I" leaves that stance to move into the shoes of the learner, into "Thou," but then eventually both individuals flow into a "We" synchronicity, an upward movement of growth, an ultimate relationship. A magical moment.

Writing Reciprocity: Honoring Children's Writing Through Authentic Publication

Children want to write when we place value on their compositions. Earlier I mentioned one channel for this: poetry charts. But it's important for kids to be honored through other forms of authentic publication, too. Kids need to know the grand variety of publishing possibilities the real world offers. This breeds not only proficiency in a variety of forms but also intention and responsibility.

For example, just before the 1991 war in the Middle East, the children were uneasy, and many used writing as a kind of cathartic outlet. Luke, who'd been struggling with literacy before this point, wrote a beautiful poem that the city's newspaper chose to publish on January 15, the day the war began. I can't even begin to explain the impetus this publication had on Luke's literacy. I will say that before long, Luke was reading *Charlotte's Web* fluently.

From interaction to transaction then becomes a spectrum of possibilities for the mediator, one along which she moves back and forth between self and other.

This means that scaffolding can evolve from situations in which the teacher is the one in control, demonstrating such authoring or leading, to those where the mediator must *remove his own shoes to stand in the shoes of the child*. Somewhere in the middle is the how-when-where of this dyad, a fall into flow, a union of opposites, a time-space for growing, for synchronicity. Throughout, the issue is one of control—taking it, giving it, and sharing it.

Vehicles for Control

Sometimes control is maintained through an object or a particular behavior, which then becomes the vehicle for control. It is interesting how many control devices can be found in any classroom, and certainly within any mediation act. Most of us watch these tools or behaviors being used and never stop to think about them in this manner. Yet, viewed within the mediation act they tend to demonstrate who's in control.

The Book as Source of Control

For instance, every teacher in this study used the text as a source of control. They would reach over and take hold of the book when they felt they needed to author more of a particular situation. Or they would merely grab a corner of the text. Scaffolders were often in charge of turning the page. But that's just one of their control behaviors.

Patty used a marker and the book for control. This is quite obvious within the transcription, a portion of which follows. Here, Patty is preparing to have the novice student read the text (the bullets indicate where the teacher extends control):

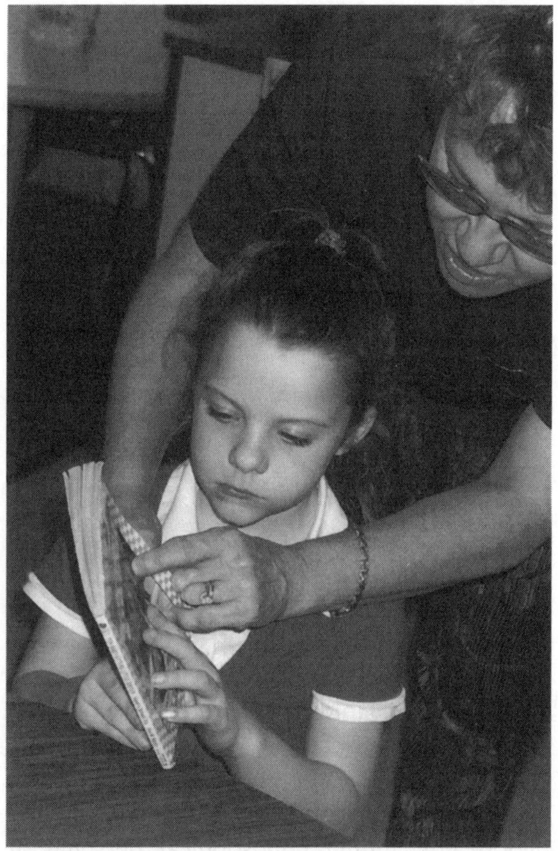

Teacher and reader share control of the text.

TEACHER: • *(prepares for the reader to read by turning to the next page of the book)*
• (*holds down the left page, and reader again backs off, folding his hands in his lap*)
• *(begins to discuss the reading with him, sliding the yellow marker under the first line of the page to be read)*
We're gonna try to read a little more about Sean and Maura. This is the book that the children way, way across the ocean would be reading in their first grades. *(looks briefly at the reader and relinquishes control)* Okay. Go ahead. *(Offering the marker to the student. As the reader moves forward to take control, he now unclasps his hands to hold the page with his left and the marker with his right. His body moves forward and, in control, he begins)*

Although Patty passes control at the end of this episode, we can see how throughout the mini-event she was very much in control of the book, the marker, and as a related consequence, the child. We can also see that the reader was reading his teacher well, for the minute she invited him to "Go ahead," the youngster simultaneously unclasped his hands and took control of the book.

Other teachers used different control objects. Lani held a pen and would come forward with it in an extension-of-self manner when she wanted the floor. And just as a musician in an orchestra would, Lani's student responded accordingly to the entrances and exits of her pen. It's really quite fascinating the ways in which we learn to dance within relationships.

Touch as a Control Vehicle

Some teachers took the reader's hand or arm to stop him or to keep him focused while they spoke. This demonstrates touch as a control vehicle. When Julie lost her reader's attention, she rubbed his back a little, using touch as a control device. However, touch was used in a wide variety of ways, and not just to gain attention. It was used to comfort, to interfere, to slow the tempo, and to celebrate. But each behavior demonstrated a type of control.

Teachers who clapped their hands in celebration were still controlling the situation. Those who reached forward to comfort a struggling reader were still trying to keep that child from a place of discomfort. Touch can work wonders, but it can also offend or frighten students who do not want that particular kind of control. It's important to understand that touch differs depending on the culture, the child, and the situation. And so does body stance.

Body Stance as a Control Vehicle

Whole bodies are also vehicles for control. If it was obvious to me peering through the lens of a camcorder, it must have been obvious to the reader that when a teacher was sitting back with her arms folded, it meant the child had free reign. Or, as in Kara's case, it could be observed that when she sat with her hand under her chin, rather than near the book, it was usually a time when the reader was confidently and competently moving along.

There are probably hundreds of these control vehicles in every classroom and relationship, if we put on the spectacles to view them. One cannot help but wonder which comes first, teacher relinquishing control or reader fluency? Or is it a sensitive balance?

Leading: Pulling Students Through Print

Most teachers almost cheered their novice students through print with their words of praise and affirmation. But they also demonstrably pulled them through. Both Hannah and Kara keep their pointer finger moving out in front of the reader's place in text so that, unless the child had a problem, they were always slightly ahead of him—pulling, leading. Even when students segmented graphophonically through an unknown word, the teacher covered up all but the beginning of the word, but when the reader uttered the uncovered part, the mediator moved her finger even farther forward than the next segment/syllable.

At one point, Hannah demonstrated a most obvious leading behavior when she turned to the reader and motioned, palm up, fingers closing and pulling forward. She was gesturing, "Come on." In response to Hannah's leading, the child immediately tried again.

Although this "Come on" gesture was unique to Hannah, other teachers used leading or guiding behaviors, also. Some were voiced and some were gestured; however, each had a similar purpose—that is, to pull the reader through the print. Such leading behaviors are control devices.

Control: A Sensitive Balance

Most teachers moved back and forth between teacher control and student control; that is, they traded it. This was very common, and could qualify as an *interaction*; that is, first one had control, and then the other did. The teacher might be seen leaning back, but if the child had trouble, she'd lean forward, help him over the hump, and then lean back again. In these episodes we often heard the teacher saying, "Okay, go ahead" or she asked a question at the end of a page or a section of print. They worked *after* each other, a slightly different context than *with* each other. First one, then the other. We see that in the following scaffolding event.

The teacher is leaning across the table on her elbows explaining the book to the child. She demonstrates a relaxed body stance, but is still holding the book and pointing to the pictures as she talks. The student occasionally looks at her and shakes his head in response to her questions while continuing to hold the marker.

The teacher does a short introduction to the page and then physically turns the book toward the child and releases control. The reader places the marker under the first line and begins in much the same word-marking manner as before. The teacher now sits with her left arm resting on top of her right, leaning slightly forward—yet relaxed, interested. The child is now in control of the book, the marker, and the reading act.

This was definitely a supported read; however, there is a difference between this and the actual *sharing* of control. One must work in greater harmony to actually share control.

Sharing Control

There are times when a teacher and the child work so closely together that it is difficult to distinguish their separate actions. A dancing dyad, they seem to move as one. There is a harmony to such episodes. The following is an example of this flow brought forth primarily through gesture. It begins with student autonomy as the reader proceeds through print independently. But gestural harmony evolves between Julie and her fluent reader as they move through a very challenging book for a first grader and along the way to a "We" state of being.

As we peer in to observe this event, we see the reader holding the left bottom side of the page, as she finishes it, while the teacher holds the right side of it with her right hand. However, as the student reads the last word on the page in a subdominant key to let a listener know "There is more the come," she also moves her left hand to the opposite page and within an eighth note of time, their hands move in the harmony of page-turning, the reader with left hand, scaffolder with right. The simultaneous gesture brings them to the new page with both teacher and student now holding the left page of the book. Neither appear aware of the synchronicity of this page-turning but the student again reads on.

This was a shared control—a dance led by both partners. Each took over in response to the other, but occasionally we lost sight of the lead—a time when the two became one.

A similar synchronicity occurred when teachers unobtrusively slid in to add intonations and inflections to a child's somewhat sterile read. At first, I could hear two voices, one expressive, the other not, yet joined in the same rhythms. But before long, the intonations and inflections, too, had synchronized so that two had become one.

The Struggle for Control

Sometimes, we see a struggle for the reins of control. The subtleties of these acts might be difficult for the on-site observer to detect, but through the replaying and slow playing of video, they tend to unfold in a revealing way. A teacher herself noticed one of the more obvious struggles on the footage. It occurred when her novice reader brought a well-rehearsed book to the session that he wanted to read, but it was not one of the teacher's designated choices. Needless to say, he did not want to give up his self-selected text. Each time Julie tried to talk about the text *she* wanted him to read, he would slide his book over, move it to his lap or even point to the pictures using his book, *instead* of his finger!

Laughing about the episode during post-viewing, Julie said that had she and her reader not been caught up in a research protocol that used challenging text, she would have of course allowed the reader to use his own book. But instead, the event's beginning became a struggle for control.

There were displays of book control within every teacher-student transaction. Some appeared as struggles. Some did not. Some behaviors were more common than others. Within the many dyads, I watched partners perched in a turn-position, waiting for the other partner to cue the "Okay, turn the page" signal. For example, Lani said, "Okay, let's go on," but then when the child started to turn the page, his teacher stopped him by keeping her hand on the previous page, while at the same time allowing other pages to rest upon her other arm. This is done to hold separate the next section to be read—one that she still wants to discuss. Taking control, the teacher then turns the page back to where they were before and draws the reader's attention to her agenda. The reader then releases the book and sits back.

Here we saw the struggle for control played out through gesture using the vehicle of a book. But it is also executed through voice, such as when one partner attempts to enter into the discussion by inserting a "But— But—" or when the teacher interrupts the student's graphophonic strategies to mediate by cuing the next sound or sounds in the word being read. Nevertheless, it is when these interrupters are ignored that we no longer need to ask, "Who's in control?"

Relinquishing Control

Some teachers waltz in and out of that kingdom of control. That is, if the reader is doing fine, they allow him to experience autonomy. Sometimes this rings through in the words of the mediator. For instance, one teacher said, "Okay, I'll let you continue." This is an obvious statement of having had control but giving it up. As a matter of fact, the "Okay" response—a relinquishing-control signal—was common to *all* teachers. However, body gesture has a language of its own and can demonstrate very clearly who has control and who does not, as well as when someone is giving it up.

Sometimes the mediator and reader slide from the flow of a shared situation into one of individual ownership. In so doing, they move from a twosome to two "one-somes." That is what happens in the following exchange between Kara and her novice reader (at the bullet [•]). We join them as the novice reader is trying to figure out the word *shoes* in a patterned text, *My Messy Room*, and is focusing on the sentence "I like shoes":

STUDENT: Sh-

TEACHER: Sh- Hm-m *(slides her fingers through the rest of the word)* "I like . . . " *(rereads, leaving off with upward pitch)* Let's see, jumping over it worked for us last time. *(points to the beginning of the sentence, distinctly signifying each word as her finger hopscotches across the page)* So let's try that.

TEACHER AND STUDENT: "I like blank" *(Both reading together until they say the word* blank. *This time the teacher does not seem to use an invitational pitch, but just flows through as though the actual word was really* blank*; although not a single beat is missed,* • *the teacher stops reading at this point, and the child continues. The scaffolder relinquished control.)*

Harmonic Balance

This issue of control is an important one. Inviting reader autonomy paves the path for approximations. Each of the teachers in this study moved in and out of control during mediation. Certainly, harmonic balance could be observed in varying amounts, sometimes beginning when a scaffolder stepped back to serve the child's intentions. According to Noddings (1984), it is those who can sensitively experience a Thou stance who will then transact in a more *caring* and effective manner.

In Flow

It was quite obvious when the teacher and student had become consumed within the enjoyment of this captivating activity, reading. Csikszentmihaly (1990) discusses that kind of enjoyment of an activity through a lens that focuses on the act of listening to music. His thinking can easily be expanded into the process of learning to read, for according to Rosenblatt (1978), Nell (1994), and Csikszentmihaly himself, reading is much like listening to music; that is, they are both aesthetic experiences and both can evoke flow. As a matter of fact, Csikszentmihaly (1990) suggests that "every mental operation is able to provide its own

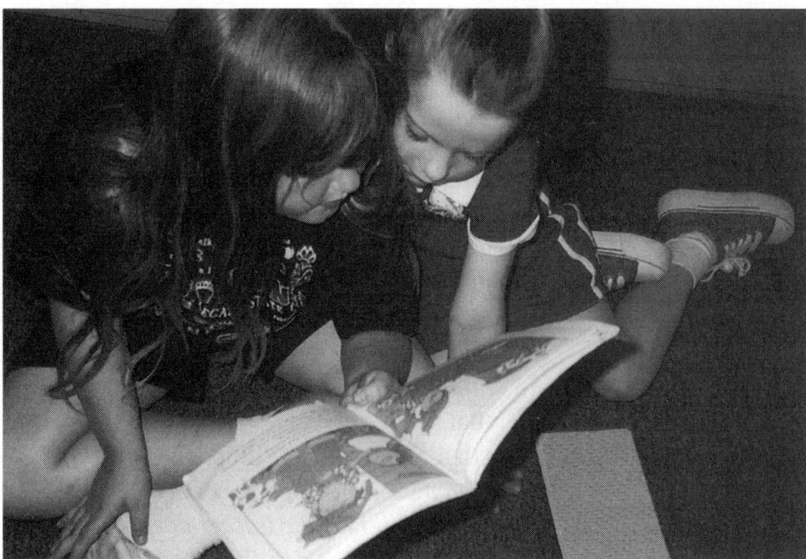

Two girls, united as one, in the flow of text.

particular form of enjoyment. Among the many intellectual pursuits available, reading is currently perhaps the most often mentioned flow activity around the world" (p. 117). And if he weren't a scientist, he'd probably say, "It's magical!"

By *flow* this researcher means the loss of self to the activity, that is, something in which one finds pure joy, a time "when our minds become one . . . it's a real pleasure" (p. 63). This flow is "an egoless thing. . . [that] . . . just happens. And yet you're more concentrated." Furthermore, this "loss of sense of self separate from the world around it is sometimes accompanied by a feeling of union with the environment" (pp. 62–63). These are the words of a renowned researcher who has closely studied the behaviors and effects of those experiencing flow. Joy and pleasure are integral to such experiences, and that is why we need to weave our reading relationship with threads of pleasure.

The Niceness of Reading

When we make reading a playful, joyful activity, we draw on its *ludic* (Nell 1994) nature. Jane, a teacher with several years experience, spoke of the necessity of preserving this ludic nature of reading. For her, the skills of reading came in second place. First, came the love. She said:

> If a child is sitting down to read you a story, you can't make a lesson out of everything in the story. You have to preserve just the activity of the *niceness of reading* the story to the teacher . . . If we were doing something else, some activity after the story, where we were picking out words, like a beginning *L*, then that would be a lesson in itself. I think that that is probably my philosophy that way. The activity is not to teach her every word that she does not know. It's just to use the strategy that comes the quickest for her and just go on and enjoy the story.

Indeed, this enjoyment shines through in Jane's reading relationships. It was demonstrated from the very way in which she held the text to the way in which she joyfully lived through the text's content with the kids. And it was also this joy in textual experience that prompted Jane to keep the flow going, always providing the reader with a great deal of support. In Jane's words, "if you stop for everything, the kids won't like it and won't enjoy the experience and then there's no point in doing it." No doubt Allington and Goodman would agree. To Jane, the primary objective of the experience was to develop a love for reading, a feeling about books and reading that she hoped would live on, long after the kids left her classroom.

We all love to do that which we love to do, and the more we love it, the more we do it. And with it comes more and more and more experience, *not practice*. In the end, all that self-selected experience creates excited, excellent, exemplary readers! So yes, the ludic quality of reading is important.

Grist for Discussion

What pleasures do you remember about learning to read or reading classes? What teachers do you remember fondly? What were their metamessages?

Chapter 8

Cue Use and Abuse

As the teacher receives the child and works with him on cooperatively designed projects, as she resists the temptation—or the mandate—to manipulate the child, to squeeze him into some mold, she establishes a climate of receptivity . . . But the commitment, the decision to embrace a particular possibility, must be the child's. Her commitment is to him.

NEL NODDINGS,
CARING: A FEMININE APPROACH TO ETHICS AND MORAL EDUCATION

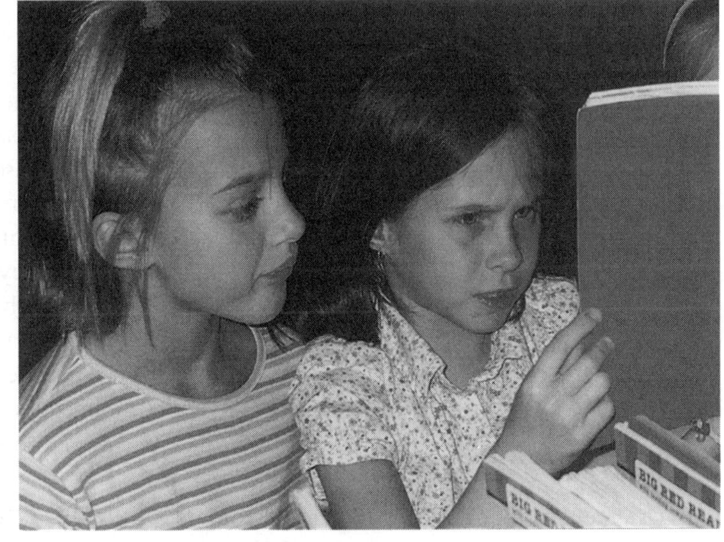

There is no scaffolding cue that works all the time for every learner. The variables are far too numerous to make any all-inclusive, homogenized statements about the way in which all kids learn. That's why I think of scaffolding behaviors as my "bag of teacher tricks," and for some kids I have to keep reaching in for another, then another, then another. I know that when the relationship is right they will open the door and let me in.

This means there would probably be noticeable differences between scaffolders, and indeed there was. Yet the greatest scaffolding differences were not between teachers, but between the ways in which each teacher scaffolded her novice and fluent readers. There is a significant difference between the scaffolding offered to a novice and that which is offered to a fluent reader. I investigated some of these differences and believe this information is noteworthy.

Differentiating Instruction for Novice and Fluent Readers

This book has already mentioned ways that teachers sometimes scaffold students of differing ability. Let's look a bit closer at some of those specific differences that could be an influence leading to effective or ineffective cueing. Think of these more as information rather than rules, because no one can be absolutely certain about what will or will not work in any given reading relationship.

Have Novice Readers Moved into the Analytic State?

Almost all teachers provided the novice reader with a noticeably greater amount more of graphophonic cueing. That is, when these novice readers were miscuing, their teachers often tried to mediate with some type of graphophonemic aid. This would indicate a focus on pieces and parts in early reading. But, have these readers moved into the analytic stage of novice reading enough to be able to profit from such cues? For instance, notice in the following excerpt, from the *My Messy Room* transcription, how the reader (struggling with the word *messy*) reiterates the sound cue for the short sound of *E*, yet she is still unable to blend even the root word *mess* into a whole (see bullet [•]), and the teacher must finally rescue her by telling the whole word:

STUDENT: m- *(continues to leave her own finger under the word in question)*

TEACHER: m- e- *(uncovering the word as she sounds through and in pointing synchronicity with the reader)*

STUDENT: • e- s- s- *(now the teacher slides her finger off the word and the child's finger remains under the last letter,* Y, *as her lips form a* W *sound)*

TEACHER: m- m- *(signals the child to back up and try again; however, when the child makes no immediate response, the teacher quickly gives the whole word cue)* Messy.

STUDENT: Messy. *(repeats the word the teacher has offered)*

The teacher modeled the individual sounds within the unknown word, and although the novice could mimic her isolated sounds, she could not blend the sounds together. This deviation away from the flow of reading may have taken a toll on meaning. In the end, the teacher did tell the child the word. This kind of sound-by-sound interruption may actually be effective, if done *occasionally*. Who knows, maybe this was the turning point for this novice. However, if lengthy interruptions for decoding consistently occur, we have to question their effect on fluency and on meaning.

More Teacher Praise for Novices

It is fairly obvious to any observer when a child is a novice reader. It is also obvious that such novices, just as novice painters or skaters, need lots of support; however, once readers—or skaters—approach fluency, we allow them much more autonomy.

Spoken supports were not only *reinforcements of praise*, such as "Good!", "Outstanding!", and "Nice job!", but they were also *keep-going* encouragements, such as "Okay," "Yeah," and "Uh-hm-m." Such affirmations let the novice know he is on the right track. They help build confidence and keep the reader focused. Maybe that's why teachers offered novices far more of both of these. (See Figure 8–1.)

Scaffolders praise novice readers considerably more than fluent readers—*over twice* as much (212 to 98). For some scaffolders, this difference was slight. For Lani, Kara, and Jane it was only a few words (less than five). But for Hannah, the difference was extraordinary! She uttered fifty-three words of praise and affirmation to the novice reader and only one to the fluent! Natasha and Julie also uttered over twenty words more for their novice readers than for their fluents.

Differences of this nature must be noticeable to the fluent readers, who are receiving less praise. Do they sense why these differences exist? I think so, because during partnering they too offer lots of praise for each small step a novice makes. Besides, the fluent readers received just as much praise when they themselves were novices.

Maybe we all celebrate the beginning of any journey more than its middle? Don't we tend to give more praise to all novices, no matter what the endeavor? It keeps them going. Gives them hope. And it sews any relationship with positive threads.

More Teacher Interruptions for Novices

I also found that, although all students were reading individually selected, unrehearsed instructional-level texts—ones in which even the better, fluent readers would occasionally stumble, teachers interrupted novices *twice* as often as they interrupted their struggling fluent readers (see Figure 8–2). That is, they allowed fluent readers to independently use strategies to maintain flow. Because they had more confidence in these fluent readers, they afforded them more patience and autonomy; therefore, as these more proficient readers struggled over challeng-

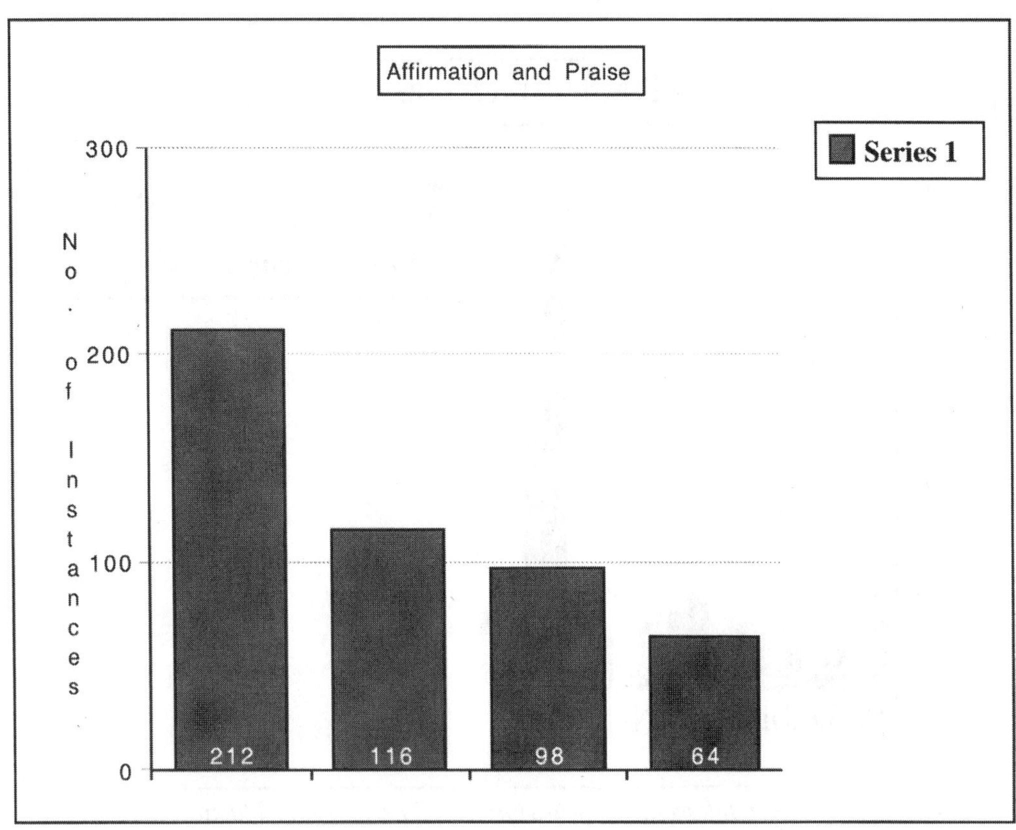

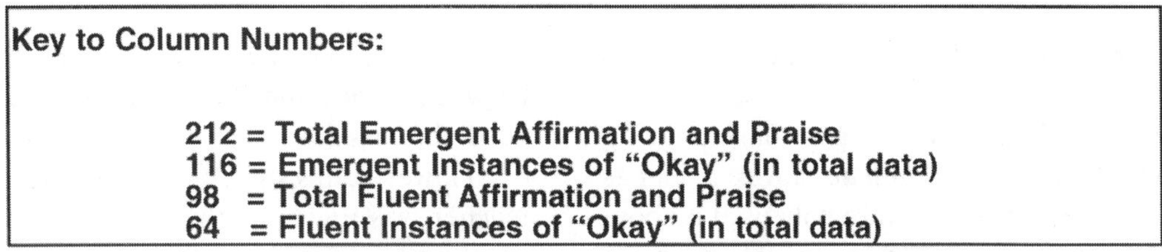
Key to Column Numbers:

212 = Total Emergent Affirmation and Praise
116 = Emergent Instances of "Okay" (in total data)
98 = Total Fluent Affirmation and Praise
64 = Fluent Instances of "Okay" (in total data)

Figure 8–1. *Total Comparisons of Spoken Praise and Affirmation*

ing sections, their teachers remained silent and unresponsive. As might be predicted, the fluent reader generally wriggled himself out of the difficulty *without* teacher mediation or interruption.

Not so with novice readers, however. Instead, it was the teacher who sometimes had to wiggle *her* way out of an overabundance of support. That is, she had to wean the dependent beginner off her smothering responses. Yet the question of when to back off while scaffolding a novice has no one right answer.

More Prereading Preparation for Novices

Being sensitive to the uncertain and immature skills of the novice reader even before the reading act, teachers prepared the novices more than they did their fluent readers. They wanted to lay the groundwork for success. Julie volunteered the following explanation: "I prepared him [the novice reader] more . . . because I know he's not an advanced reader and I sensed he was a bit nervous . . . [The fluent reader] was very confident . . . I knew that she really wouldn't need it." Such metacognitive understandings of individual scaffolding differences are important in the teacher-student reading relationship.

More Instances of Touch-the-Page Fingerpointing for Novices

To draw attention to locations in text, teachers used fingerpointing more frequently with novice readers. They touched the page almost three times more than they did with their fluent readers. For instance, Julie pointed sixty-nine times

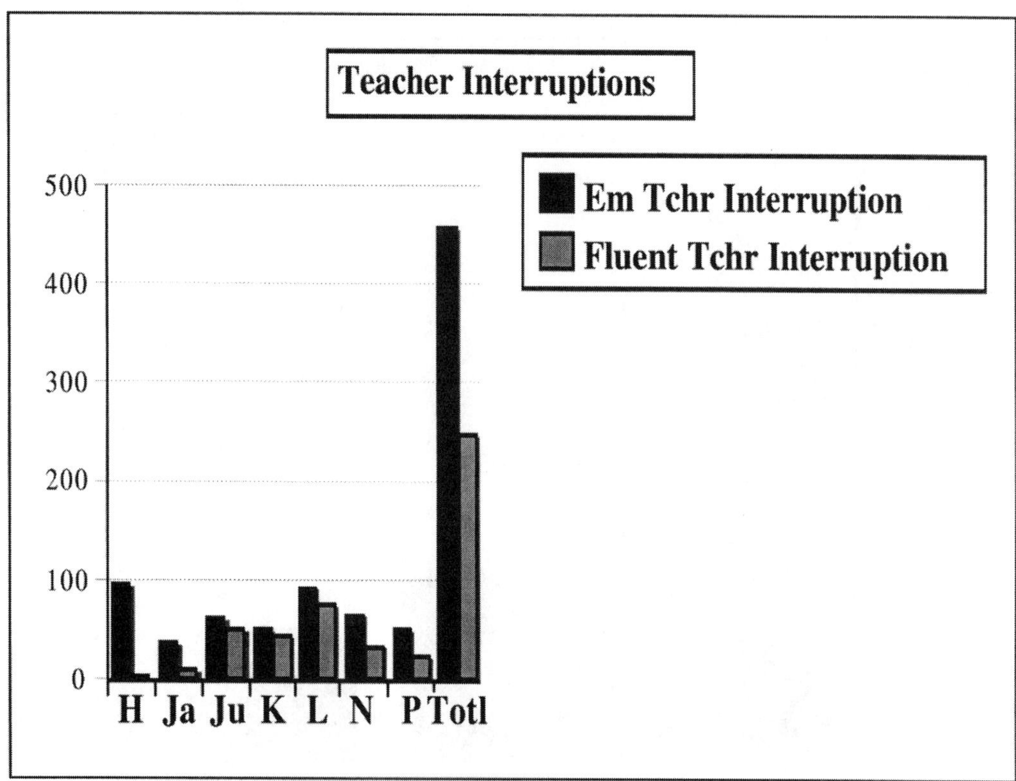

Figure 8–2. *Teacher Interruption Behaviors for Emergent and Fluent Readers*

with her better reader, but two hundred times with the novice.

Patty used this touch-the-page fingerpointing about six times as much with her novice reader as with her fluent; whereas, Kara only used it about twice as much with her novice reader. Yet we can easily see that teachers do use this marking gesture far more with less-skilled readers, even when the more-skilled are also reading challenging texts. Figure 6–1 provides a comparative view of the three individuals.

Using fingerpoint marking to focus the novice's attention is a common aspect of the reading relationship. These teachers seemed to be well aware that wordness does not happen overnight.

Greater Duration of Fingerpointing for Novices

Teachers of less capable readers would spend more time using their pointers to pull novices forward, more time showing readers where to look and what to do. Teacher fingerpointing should differ in yet another way, then. By examining the actual length of time fingers touched the page, it seemed we'd see a great difference between novice and fluent scaffolding. And indeed, this was so.

However, this still does not indicate *why* the teacher was touching; that is, whether she was pointing to the picture on the page or just attempting to hold the child's own hand in place so that it did not move beyond a miscue. Therefore, I did not consider any specific cueing systems in this investigation.

However, observing Figure 6–1 on page 93, you see that teachers do seem to spend far more time pointing at the book of the novice reader than they do the book of the fluent reader. For instance, Patty spent about six times as many seconds in touch-the-page fingerpointing with her novice reader than with her fluent; and Julie spent about three times as much.

After watching a gazillion hours of scaffolding, I began to think of teachers as conductors using their forefingers as the wands that keep the music of text flowing in harmony. Although quantities differed, teachers' finger orchestrations were definitely a common and necessary element within all reading relationships.

More Protective Teacher Body Stance for Novices

Interestingly, the entire body stance of the teachers differed, depending on the ability of their readers. Teachers' gestural behaviors demonstrated their confidence in the more able reader; they sat somewhat removed from the child, and at times even crossed their arms, as if to say, "You don't need me, so I'll just sit back and relax." Whereas, with the novice reader they sat crouched over the text and sometimes over the reader. They helped hold the book, turn the pages, and point to the words and pictures. They seemed to hang on the young learner's every breath. All teachers responded in this protective, nurturing way to their young novices. I'm certain this helped bind the reading relationship.

Differentiating the Level of a Cue

I've mentioned almost everything about cueing, except what *not* to do. I myself wondered which cues are usually *ineffective*.

Actually, there is no cut-and-dried answer to that question because its answer will always evolve out of each reader-scaffolder-text triad. Although there are some whose track record is not good, and thus should probably be circumvented, I would never say never!

There are questions that all scaffolders need to give special consideration. Do I use one cue too often? How far away from the particular teacher-student-text triad can I move before a cue is useless? Which cues rarely work?

Sometimes common sense will answer these questions for us. However, after watching all those teachers offer all those cues, and after thirty years of offering them myself, I can assure you that there are some cues that are rarely effective. The transcripts provided the evidence. Let's now investigate some of those cues.

Why Use Only First-Order or Primary Cues?

Cues can be *primary* or *first order*, or they can be *secondary*. The closer one's cue is to the inherent context or sense of a given word, the better. Consequently, a first-order cue would relate specifically to that word in its particular space and time. Cueing through meaning-analogies, past experiences, other words that sound the same, gestural motions, or anything else that *removes the reader from the specificity of that particular word* is less useful than a more strategic, more closely related cue—usually.

Conditioned Responses Are Absent When the Teacher Is Absent

The effectiveness of any cue also depends upon the context of the classroom, because children who are used to doing things in a certain fashion will respond in a predictable manner to the same predictable utterances or situations. The work of Skinner and other behaviorists bears credence for such *conditioned responses*. And humans can be conditioned into almost any behavior. This, then, clouds the field of interpretations for anyone predicting cue success, for we can never judge how effective any cue might be for a particular teacher-reader dyad—especially if we have not been a part of that classroom community before. Even so, just because a child is conditioned to say, "Sh-h" when his teacher cues him to, "Use the quiet sound," does not mean that he will independently use the quiet sound when it presents itself in other nonquiet contexts—or when the teacher is absent. That's because the quiet sound is a secondary cue. Bottom line: Use primary cues.

What Is a Primary Cue?

The easiest way to explain the difference between primary and secondary cues is through a well-known guessing game, which most of us have played at one time or another. In this game we give someone hints related to our secret word, as he tries to figure out what that word is. However, the game usually begins with the *opposite* intentions of those of a mediator; that is, players try to give initial clues that are *not* closely related. For to give a closely related clue would reveal too much, and thus give away the word and negate the challenge of the game. Eventually, however, players narrow the categories down to a place where only a few possibilities exist, and unless the guessing person has been either intuitive or lucky, he has probably remained unable to figure out the word—until his friends provide a *more closely related, first-order cue*.

Is this not also what a novice reader needs, that is, first-order, closely related cues? Not all teacher cues are primary, and some of the common ones are definitely secondary; that is, they are distantly related to the word in question. The following provides some actual examples.

Short and Long Letters

Perhaps one of the most frequent early confusions for young children stems from the use of the terms *short* and *long* in reference to vowels. Until school, children understand those two terms carry essentially some fairly standard meanings that generally relate to size. It is difficult enough for novice readers to think of the myriad sounds that some vowels can make, let alone translating through the long and short of them. That is, the reader's mind must first think what short vowel means, then how that particular short vowel sounds.

For a very long time, reading authorities have told us to just call vowels by their actual sound, rather than adding another level of interpretation. Therefore, instead of asking the child, "Do you think that vowel is short or long?" we ask, "Do you think that *E* makes an *ee* sound or an *eh* sound?" We skip the short and long business, and go straight to the sound itself. Why? Because short and long is a secondary cue, and secondary cues make our scaffolding less effective.

For example, in the following the student is reading *Owl at Home* (Lobel 1987). The section reads, "Owl is in bed. It is time to blow out the candle . . . " but the reader is stuck on the word *time* after correctly reading that which precedes it. She only makes the initial sound in the word, then stops. So Natasha, her teacher, steps in to scaffold:

TEACHER: It does begin with a *T. (pointing)* What else do you see that you recognize?

STUDENT: *I.*

TEACHER: A vowel sound? Which vowel sound does the *I* make, a short *I* or a long *I*?

STUDENT: A short *I*? *(incorrect response, which the teacher does not correct, but instead says)*

TEACHER: Ti- *(blends both letters giving* I *its long sound)*

STUDENT: Ti- *(modeling her teacher)*

TEACHER: And then the *M. (touching the letter)* Ti- m- *(sounds)*. T- ime *(onset and rime cue)* You can point. *(because novice's attention is waning)*

STUDENT: "Time. Time to . . . " *(reads on)*

Then, as Hannah's novice reader was reading the sentence, "Babykins loves to tease Daddy and make loud music," she got stuck on *tease*, so her teacher asked, "Do you know what this long *E* says *(pointing)*? Can you make a long *E* sound?"

The child responded with the short *E* sound, "Teh."

So the teacher reinforced the correct form with emphasis, "Tee-ee-ee."

The reader tried to mimic, but at first switched to short *E* again, until her teacher helped another time.

At last the reader repeats, "Tee-ee-ee."

And the teacher then compliments and just gives her the entire word, "Good! Tease."

What if the teacher had just said "Tee-ee-ee" to begin with? What if she had not brought shorts and longs into the context? Would the reader have decoded independently? Maybe.

Here you saw the confusion these readers had distinguishing short and long. Yet when the teacher made the sounds, the child replicated and used them appropriately. Essentially short and long vowels, like many other phonics issues, would be far easier to figure out if the student already knew the word. Most often, we adults only know whether a vowel is short or long because we already know the word. For instance, is the *E* in vead long or short?

The bottom line: Don't use the terms short and long. *Just use the letters' actual sounds—primary cues.*

Phonics Rules Are Not First-Order, Primary Cues

When a student is stuck on a word and we say, "When two vowels go walking the first one does the talking," we move that reader away from the particular contextual realm and into another one with rules and regulations, walking letters, and other detracting elements. More often than not, he does not decode the word any faster burdened by this rules baggage. It just becomes a distraction. And besides, most phonics rules seldom work anyway (Clymer 1963; Venezky 1970)

It is mind-boggling for a novice to check the letter patterns, decide on an applicable rule, determine if that rule incorporates a long or short application, make that application—and only then sound through the word.

The following does not include a specific phonics rule, but it does demonstrate how we teachers can get caught up in secondary sound cues. Patty is mediating her novice reader through a line of print that reads "He has food for the petshop." The reader is stuck on *shop*.

STUDENT: ". . . for the pet shh-" *(does not finish the word)*

TEACHER: What is the *S-H* sound? *(leans forward a bit and looks at his face)*

STUDENT: *(probably thought he was incorrect the first time, so this time offers)* St-

TEACHER: No, the quiet sound. What if a baby were sleeping—the mother, what might she say?

STUDENT: Shh- *(Notice that he does associate her stimulus with a particular response, probably one he's heard many times in the previous nine months.)*

TEACHER: Sh-sh- *(Repeats and reaches forward again to place her left hand over his right hand, which is resting beside the book on the table. He, within that same movement, slides his hand out from under hers.)*
So it starts with sh-. The pet what? *(Notice that she has moved into a different cueing system—one that is* not *graphophonic, yet unfortunately, it is now confounded by the previous secondary cues.)* Sh- *(offers once more for good measure)*

STUDENT: Ship. *(Notice his focus here is* not *on meaning, for he has been led toward sounds. At this point the teacher has removed her hand from the marker, so he puts his hand back up on it again. But when he realizes that he has miscued the word and that the teacher is reaching forward again, he backs off, subtly removing both of his hands from the book to let his teacher take over again.)*

TEACHER: Almost, but there is not an *I* there. *(pointing to that part of the word)* If there was an *I*, it would be *ship*. *(still stressing secondary graphophonic cues)* That's an *O*, a short *O* and that says o-o-o (*short* O *sound*). *(backs off again and moves forward with the marker after offering the final, yet primary, cue)* Pet what? *(another primary semantic cue followed by)* Shh- *(another graphophonic primary cue)*

STUDENT: Shop. *(at last)*

When this teacher stayed within the micro context of this episode; that is, when she offered "Pet what?" or the actual *S-H* sound, itself, she was using a primary cue. However, when she spoke of the "quiet sound" and "If there was an *I* it would be *ship*," or "a short *O*," she moved away from the particularity of the situation.

The proof is there: The reader produced the *S-H* sound, but when he said "ship" we knew he was not thinking in context, because there is no first grader who, in the course of his daily comings and goings, would suggest *petship*, for there is no such entity. Children know this. But when readers are myopically intentioned toward only the micro context of graphophonics, meaning often breaks down—as it did here. Meaning must remain in the forefront. As Don Holdaway contends, "The destruction of central meaning and purpose may make the task more difficult and less clear" (1979, p. 100). That is why I still cringe each time I press Play and observe this novice offer *petship*.

This deviation from meaning is what happens when we continue to encourage novices to crawl into the graphophonic elements in a word. Focusing on the rules associated with isolated sounds is about as far from meaning as we can take a young reader. Remember that before the word is actually decoded, that novice will have to retrace his tracks back toward the micro and then into macro context of what is being read. Simply: The further we go in, the further we have to come back out.

A reader who is presented with the unknown word *hope* will not stop to think, "Let's see, when an *E* is at the end of a word and a consonant precedes it, and a vowel precedes that consonant, then sometimes that vowel is what the teacher calls long, which I think means that it says its name, so let's see . . . " Notice the distance between the unknown word and the end of the reader's rumination path. Bottom line: Take the shortest route between the scaffolding cue offered and the unknown word.

"Yesterday" Cues

Some less-effective, time-related cues involve thinking backward. When someone reminds us of something that happened last week or even yesterday, our minds begin rapidly surveying cognitive pathways, trying to focus upon that to which the speaker has referred. More often than not, we have trouble moving backward in time in search of the needle in time's haystack. This is what happens when we say to children, "Remember—we had that word last week?" One teacher tried to make a *yesterday connection* by asking, "Now, what was our spelling word this week?" How could a child ever find success with such a distant cue? He will remove himself about six orders just trying to follow the teacher's lead. *Yesterday cues are never first-order cues.*

And this holds true for all cue categories: (G), (S-S), or (P). Reminding a student of some past experience pulls that reader away from the here and now of the text in hand. Bottom line: Stay in the here and now. (This is probably a good rule for life as well!)

Fill-in-My-Blank Cues

Many teachers used fill-in-the-blank (cloze) sentences that did not relate to the situational context. When the word was *watermelon*, one teacher gave the cue, "When you're thirsty you get a drink of—." Another said, "If you're not nice you're—." The child answered, "Nasty," but the word was *naughty*. Still a third, in mediating the word *skin*, had the child touch his neck and then the teacher asked him, "What are you touching?" The novice said, "Neck."

It is easy to see how misleading some of these cloze cues can be when they move beyond the (S-S) and (G) context. How much more facilitative that cloze technique would be if it incorporated a reread of the actual text, rather than some distantly related context. But these distant cloze hints are still a very common type of cue, ones that often carry the child beyond the first order and away from meaning. Bottom line: Stick with the *context* of the text being used.

Miscued Scaffolder Cues

Two common ways in which teachers miscue cues is by inviting readers to "find the little word in the big word" and to "sound it out." What if the little word that is found is the *wrong* little word? What if the unknown word is full of irregular sounds?

Which *Little Word in That Big Word?*

Although finding little words in big words is a fundamental cue for beginners (or even skilled readers), there were occasions where teachers suggested a little-word-in-big-word strategy, but decoding the little word provided minimal or even conflicting information to identifying the big word. This happened when a teacher suggested this cue for the unknown word *there* and the reader decoded, "The- er."

Later, when the teacher viewed the videotape, she lamented, "Oh, I shouldn't have used that cue." Be aware that most often the little-word-in-big-word cue probably won't work for many *one-syllable words*.

However, it frequently *does* work for multisyllable words. Even so, we always need to decide this cue's efficacy *prior* to offering it to a struggling reader. For instance, would you offer this cue if a novice is struggling with the following words: *roof*, *teacher*, *other*, *usually*, *meaning*? (Certainly grist for discussion!)

Complicating matters even more, without a gestural cue to focus the reader on exactly *which* little word he is to find, readers will frequently find *another* little word—one that is *not* sound-congruent with the big word. For instance, look at these words: *sitting* (*in*), *careful* (*car*), *another* (*not*). I cannot even begin to tell you how often this kind of misapplication occurs in first grade! Bottom line: Use gesture to denote *which* little word you mean.

Beware of Using Sound-It-Out Cues on Phonically Irregular Words

Another common miscued cue is when the scaffolder suggests "sound it out." With only about 25 percent (Venezky 1970) of our English words actually specific to their sound structure, we need to be very careful when we suggest that strategy. For example, watch what happens in the following when the reader gets stuck on the unknown word *what*:

TEACHER: Look at the word again. *(reaches forward to point to it)* Let's look at that word again. *(focuses the novice by placing her hand gently atop his to denote the spot of attention)* It has a *W*. Can you sound it out? You don't have to cover it, you don't have to cover, just— *(Doesn't want him to cover any part of the word here, as had been done previously, because this word,* what, *does not contain a regular phonological rime—*at. *It would actually work to his detriment to cover the onset. Perhaps realiz-*

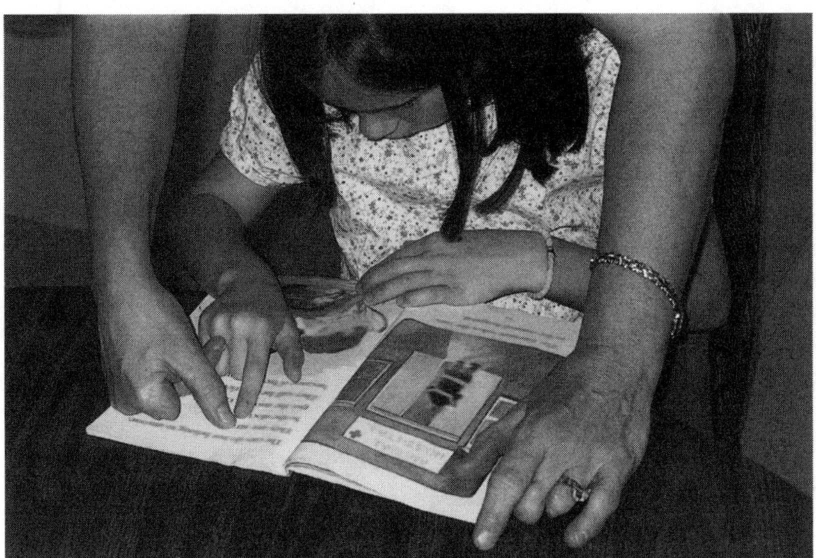

Linda masks text to reveal only the little word in the big word.

Chapter 2, a focus on the vowel sound often serves only to confuse. Bottom line: Focus primarily on consonant sounds and regular rimes.

Meaning-Analogy Cues

Using graphophonic analogies (such as consonant or rime patterns) can be an effective cue in decoding. For instance, when the word *fill* stumps the novice, we might offer, "I see *ill*." However, meaning-analogy cues may not be so helpful. Even so, many teachers use meaning-analogies and pull readers away from the here-and-now context. The trouble is, most meaning-analogies are *not* first-order cues.

Mediators such as Natasha cued, "It's like . . ." or "What's another word that means . . . ?" Usually, the child did not guess correctly and he therefore had to retrace his tracks to come back to the proper contextual time-space.

For instance, suppose the unknown word is *yellow* in the sentence "The boy has on a yellow raincoat." Just imagine how many guesses a reader might make if the scaffolder cues with "It's like the sun." (And in this case it is complicated more by the fact that most novice readers learn the *Y* sound in the latter part of their consonant repertoire.) Confused novices might offer *big*, *hot*, *round* or any one of myriad sun-related terms. That which seems so obvious to us—who know the word—may not be so obvious to the novice.

Analogies were frequently proffered at a time when the teacher seemed to have run out of other avenues. It seemed that in an effort to circumvent the Tell cue, teachers just reached for an analogy. But analogies are not first-order cues. Bottom line: Avoid meaning-analogy cues.

ing this, the scaffolder provides the word's three sounds, voicing the irregular A.*)*
Wh- a- t- *(waits for the reader to blend the proffered sounds)*

The fact that the sound-it-out cue might not work with this word seems so obvious when we read this vignette in print, but all of us, from time to time, use a sound-it-out suggestion in a situation that actually deters the reader's decoding. Maybe we should follow Adams' (1990) and others' guidelines by concentrating our efforts primarily on the more consistent (ninety-five percent-of-the-time) consonant matches. We might then scaffold with: "Reread and when you get to that hard word make the beginning and ending sounds and keep going. Then read the sentence over again and see if you know the word."

Or look at the way in which Kara does it when her novice gets stuck on the noun *socks*:

TEACHER: Hmmm? *(demonstrating a pondering stance)* What is the beginning sound first and then we'll go picture hunting. S-s-s- Hmm. *(pondering again)* What in this picture starts with *S* sound? Do you see anything? It starts with s- s- s-.

By using graphophonic and semantic cues in tandem, the reader has both the context and the dependable consonant sounds to construct meaning and decode the word. When words do not possess regular rimes, as mentioned in

Priority Cues

Some of the teachers had a priority sequence for cueing, that is, a routine scaffolding behavior; whereas, others let the situated context guide them. Natasha's cues consistently moved from (G) first and only on to (S-S) after the graphophonics well ran dry. For example, notice the reliance on one cueing system in the following when the student is stuck on *pumpernickel* in *A Chair for my Mother* (Williams 1982). All bulleted parts (•) are (G) cues; whereas, the (+) is a (S-S) cue:

TEACHER: • p- air- er . . . *(pointing)*
STUDENT: per-er-per-er-per-pernickel *(Teacher is pointing to parts and covering parts. Child continues to try to figure it out.)*
TEACHER: • Now put it all together.
STUDENT: pernickel.
TEACHER: Right here.
• You have to start right there. *(pointing to the middle of the word)*
STUDENT: pear-per- pernickel
TEACHER: Move your fingers so that you can see.
STUDENT: in *(reversing the -ni- in* nickel*)*
TEACHER: • pum . . .
STUDENT: pum . . . pear
TEACHER: • per . . .
STUDENT: per-pernickel
TEACHER: • Pumpernickel, have you ever heard of that before? *(gives it to him, so in this case the Tell is an absolute [G], but notice that she interfaces with a cue that will lead into meaning below)*
STUDENT: *(Shakes head no, and obviously that is what made this word so difficult for him. For without meaning, it was just a bunch of grunts.)*
TEACHER: + Have you ever heard of pumpernickel bread? *(Student gestures, no.)* No? Well that is what they are talking about.

Jane's routine differs from that of Natasha. This time (S-S) is the priority, for Jane relies routinely upon pictures and rereading. She rarely uses (G). We join her and her reader as she is answering a question her reader asked. Bullets (•) mark the (S-S) cues this time:

STUDENT: *(reading)* "My little sister want-wanted to play basketball, but the . . . blank was too blank."
TEACHER: Okay, but the what? Let's see what that would be.
• But the . . .
• What do you need when you play basketball?
• It has a ball and what is this? *(pointing at the hoop in the picture)*
• Do you know what this is called?
STUDENT: The hoop?
TEACHER: The hoop, right!
• But the hoop was too . . . what?
STUDENT: Hard?
TEACHER: • All right, she's getting on top of her brother, there. *(pointing)* So the hoop is too . . . *(lilting upward in invitation and waiting, but then goes on)*
• It's going to make her taller so she can get to it.
• So, the hoop is too . . . what?
STUDENT: Too high!

So for Jane, meaning is paramount. It is such a priority that she relies upon it again and again without inviting (G) cross-checking. Instead, she routinely uses the same two (S-S) cues.

It seems that by working from a menu of multiple options teachers might avail themselves of the most effective cue for each specific situational context. No doubt we would then see some variation in the patterns of proffered cues. (See Chapter 4, pages 62–63 for a large menu of cues.) In other words, we would demonstrate no routine responses to the exclusion of others. Bottom line: Vary the cues used, carefully considering each situational context.

Routine Cues

Overusing one cueing system might not be so much of a problem if it actually worked, but it doesn't. We all do this once in awhile, but let's see how it played out when one of the teachers was helping a novice. Notice how this teacher keeps repeating the same cue (at the bullets) and it just doesn't work:

STUDENT: "Almost the size of a dog. It was—" *(Teacher points at each word as child reads until he becomes baffled by the word* bigger.*)*
TEACHER: What do you think that would be?
• It was . . . *(Pointing at words, leading by rereading, and then leaving off with an upward pitch to invite the reader in. Reader is still trying to figure out* bigger.*)*
• It was . . . *(points back to words, leaving off with upward pitch again)*
STUDENT: Barking? *(reader guesses incorrectly)*
TEACHER: • It was . . . *(points back to words, leaving with upward pitch again)*

At one time or another we all tend to do what Jane is doing here. If something doesn't seem to be working, we continue to use it—only louder. What could Jane have done instead? Perhaps she could have used a (G) cue, because the unknown word *bigger* has a close sound-symbol match. She could have masked the *-ger,* or she could have sounded through the first syllable. She could have used an (S-S) cue by modeling how to skip and return, or she could have gesturally invited the reader to do that. It might have at least been worth the attempt to try another avenue, for although Jane's cues were first-order cues, they weren't working. Bottom line: If your cue isn't working, offer a different one.

Novice Readers *Do* Enjoy Challenging Text!

Many of these teachers were in schools that used a basal program for reading instruction, but this study incorporated authentic literature, that is, kids' books. Some teachers did attempt to use a basal at first, but when their novice reader read with too few miscues it eliminated the need for scaffolding. That is, novices read the basal too well! In the end, all scaffolders used authentic literature.

Several teachers later mentioned the positive influence that using more challenging text had had on, particularly, the novice reader. Sometimes this novice reader's performance outshone anything that the scaffolder might have anticipated. As a matter of fact, every single teacher commented on how well their novice reader actually performed. Jane said, "She did better than I thought she would. She's a first-grade repeater."

Two weeks later, Julie told me, "After you left she asked me to read that book again!"

Another teacher later told me that the novice was still carrying the book around with him!

These novice readers had been presented with a challenge and, dancing with their teachers, had scaled the mountain before them. As Csikszentmihaly (1990) would say of every flow experience, "It provided a sense of discovery, a creative feeling of transporting the person into a new reality. It pushed the person to higher levels of performance. In short, it transformed the self by making it more complex. In this growth of the self lies the key to flow activities" (p. 4). And reading is one of them!

Novice Readers Do *Not* Need Workbooks

Researchers continue to tell us that kids need lots of experience in reading and writing "real things" (Cunningham and Allington 1994) using connected text (Adams 1990). Workbooks are not real-world texts. Nor are they connected texts. They are contrived, a genre constructed for the purpose of, primarily, keeping kids busy and quiet. They are a school genre that robs time from sustained reading and sustained writing.

Some say workbooks are good for practice. Yet, this is not a track meet of which we speak. Bottom line: Kids need real experiences in the real-world genres using books, articles, video games, menus, letters—print matter that people use outside of school.

Differentiating Instruction Through Scaffolding Acts

It was evident that most of the mediators held novice readers in a protective stance. In most cases they sat closer. Even if they started the session seated a short distance from the reader, they eventually moved so that the novice sometimes appeared to be enfolded within the arms or body of the teacher. They touched these novices more and held their book more often than they did with their fluent readers. In some cases the body stance said it all, for with fluent readers they would sit with arms folded in a "You're on your own" cue. Whereas, with the novice reader they appeared to hover in an "I'm here if you need me" cue. They very carefully selected their texts, and more often than not, the first one selected for the novice was far too easy.

When entering the unknown we all bump along for a while until we fall in pace with the context—whether mountain climbing or reading a new text. And that's why novices usually got off to a bumpy start. But once they became familiar with the story, the spirit of success seemed to build, and it was then that some of the teachers did as Cambourne (1988) suggests, they "raised the ante." That is, they changed their instructional strategies. For instance, Hannah began pulling her finger across the words at a faster pace. And Julie

Writing Reciprocity: Modeling Writing: Its Use and Abuse

Early in this text, I told the poetry charts story describing how kids piggybacked on each other's written structures. That experience occurred the second month of first grade. It shows that forms and structures are contagious and can be caught at almost any age. Kids catch them via the environment—classroom or otherwise. If we model dozens of authentic avenues for writing, our students will follow our leads. They will become adept in multiple genres and forms.

However, if their models are workbook pages, which consume lengthy periods each school day, this too, becomes an internalized written structure. Unless we plan on our students' working for Houghton Mifflin's or McGraw Hill's workbook department, it would seem far more advantageous for us to steep students in authentic publications and compositions.

Frank Smith (1988) leads us toward many other authentic writing sources when he explains:

> Written language is for stories to be read, books to be published, poems to be recited, plays to be acted, songs to sung, newspapers to be circulated, letters to be mailed, jokes to be told, notes to be passed, cards to be sent, cartons to be labeled, instructions to be followed, designs to be made, recipes to be cooked, messages to be exchanged, programs to be organized, excursions to be planned, catalogs to be compared, entertainment guides to be consulted, memos to be distributed, announcements to be posted, bills to be collected, posters to be displayed, cribs to be hidden, and diaries to be concealed. (p. 29)

Smith fills our coffers with enough authentic sources for writing to last the entire year.What exciting possibilities! Let's replace the boredom of school writing with all that the real world has to offer!

---

focused on trying to get the reader to use more expression. She modeled it and asked him to reread to sound like the character.

Basal readers do not match readers with books. Nor do they up the ante. Only teachers can do that. One-to-one instruction requires minute-by-minute strategic decision making. It changes not only between individuals, but also within the developmental nature of any one individual. That is, even the beginning of a mediation session may look different from the end. And that's only because of the sensitive scaffolding of a knowledgeable teacher.

The Choice Is Up to You!

We have been gathering many examples of what doesn't seem to work when we mediate a novice's oral reading. On the other hand, you must by now have realized that there will never be any cut-and-dried answers to the question "What are the *best* mediation cues?" There is certainly a multitude of choices; however, considering the best/worst cues will always depend upon the specific micro or macro event within the specific situational context, and of course the teacher-student relationship. Yet, I still hope this chapter is a kind of heads-up on some scaffolding techniques that need careful consideration.

Grist for Discussion

Identify the primary and secondary cues in the following transcription. Then identify which cues worked. The student is struggling to figure out the word *uncle*.

TEACHER: Do you remember that word? (uncle) We had it a long time ago. This one here, right here. *(reaches forward and puts her hand over his to guide his attention again and then backs off)* I think if you look up on our alphabet, our alphabet sentences, you'll remember it. *(turns around to look at the top of the blackboard where the alphabet is displayed and then puts her left arm on top of her right to rest)* It's been a long time. What letter are you going to have to look for?

STUDENT: *U—*

TEACHER: Where's the letter *U*? *(Student and teacher are observing the alphabet train that runs behind them along two walls near the ceiling.)* What is the first word? *(pointing at train's word clue,* uncle*)* Remember that from way back in the fall when you read those sentences? *U - N - C - L - E. (spells it)* Remember what that sentence said? It's kind of a silly sentence. It's a silly sentence. Remember? You don't remember from that? Okay. Let's try to sound it out then. It's the short *U.* So it's gonna say u- *(She makes short* U *sound. The student is starting to play with the marker as he tries to remember, so the teacher reaches over and turns the marker in the regular position again to place it under the sentence once more. She then puts her hand beside his on the marker, but seems to be pointing to the specific word with her finger.)* Listen to what I said. *(pointing)* Listen to the sounds and see if we can put them together *u- n- c- le. (pointing to each of the letters as she sounds through the word)*

STUDENT: Uncle.

TEACHER: Right. *(Student leans forward to read the next sentence.)*

Chapter 9

Into Fluency

If they don't read much, how they ever gonna get good?
RICHARD ALLINGTON,
"IF THEY DON'T READ MUCH, HOW THEY GONNA GET GOOD?"

Reading Makes Kids Good at Reading

Fluency is a prerequisite for those who are seeking successful performance—whether that performance involves a baseball diamond, a swimming pool, or a book. Fluency may look different in each of these activities; yet there's no mistaking the fluent from the nonfluent. One gains fluent behaviors through extensive experience, regardless of what the activity is, be it knitting, playing the piano, or dancing. Reading is no different; it, too, requires extensive experience to acquire fluent behaviors.

Richard Allington (1977) once wrote an article whose title offers a key piece in the fluency puzzle: "If They Don't Read Much, How They Ever Gonna Get Good?" Most kids need to read a ton of running text; that is, whole books, articles, and the like, if they are going to become fluent. Piddling in a portion of a story with some fragmented workbook exercises once a day just isn't going to do it—especially if the text is not just right.

Readers need daily, *sustained* reading experiences—that is, experiences of lengthy duration. Some educators call this kind of endeavor *practice*. To me, practice is sports jargon. And it's about winning and losing; that is, ballplayers practice to win. Reading is about enjoying, learning, discovering—not practicing. Think about the difference between these two invitations: "I'd like you to open your books and practice" or "I'd like you to open your books and enjoy the story." The first fits into a sports mentality; the second is a real-world reader's attitude. Few in the real world *practice* reading. So we shouldn't expect fluency to flourish when we tell kids: "Be sure to take your reading book home tonight and practice."

Nor does fluency flourish on the pages of a workbook or on blackline masters. These paper-and-pencil tasks involve constant interruptions. They bounce a reader back and forth from one place to another, and students must follow basal company workbook structures to connect letters to pictures, circle words, write brief answers to someone else's questions, and fill in small blanks. Definitely not the foundations of fluency! Fluency develops through *self-directed, uninterrupted, sustained reading*—a time when readers can fall into flow and then read and read and read.

In fact, sustained reading is the best way to get those scores up! Those who read the most score higher on reading tests. Although common sense would tell us this, research also bears it out. *The Power of Reading* by Steven Krashen (1993) provides a plethora of substantiating data. Accordingly, the 2002 National Assessment of Educational Progress found that "students in classrooms that rely heavily on either trade books or on a combination of trade books and basal readers score higher on the reading tests than do students who primarily use basal readers" (Viadero 2003, p. 11). Bottom line: Kids who do a lot of reading in real books get really good at reading.

Trading the Lead: A Model for Fluent Reading

When my grandson, Cameron, began second grade he knew tons of vocabulary, could decode unknown words through use of strategies, and comprehended what he was reading. However, he was not very fluent. He read slowly in a kind of disinterested, somewhat halted fashion.

Enter Harry Potter.

Reading to Cam

When Cam found out about Harry, he wanted to be like everyone else; that is, he wanted to join the Potter "literacy club" (Smith 1988), so during the first semester of second grade he asked his mom to buy the book and read it to him. Cam's mom, Carolyn, has always read to him; therefore, this was part of the normal course of events. So after a visit to the local bookstore, Carolyn began reading the first Harry Potter book to Cam.

Reading with Cam

Several chapters into the book Cam came to spend the night at my house and brought the book for me to continue reading aloud to him. We sat down together in my big chair as he showed me where his mom had left off. I was aware that he was watching the words as I read, so after a few pages I would stop momentarily here and there for him to read the next word—a kind of cloze technique. At first I stopped on easy nouns or verbs (ones I was positive he'd know), but immediately assumed readership again after Cam responded with the word. Cam, like most kids, needed no explanation of this new game we were playing. He just wanted to keep the story moving, and he got a kick out of being a more active part in it.

However, after a while, I did not jump right back in, but instead pointed to the next words without saying anything. (I did not want to interrupt the flow of the story.) Cam knew the game was changing and he played right along, became more focused. Yet, just about the time he might have started to think he was in permanent control, I'd jump back in and he'd back off, sometimes with a little giggle.

We stopped to chat about Harry here and there, but continued our game throughout that chapter. And the next night, we did it again. Cam and I never discussed the rules of our game—we just played.

The following night, when Carolyn again sat down to read with Cam, he requested, "Do it like Grandma, Mommy."

However, I had never mentioned our little reading game to Cam's mom, so Carolyn asked her budding reader, "What do you mean? How does Grandma do it?"

Reading by Cam

It was not until that question surfaced that the details of our Harry Potter game were explicitly explained. But Carolyn caught on just as fast as Cam had, so the two of them traded control back and forth. That is, they did until a few nights later, when Carolyn noticed Cam's light was on in his room long after bedtime; and when she went up to see what her son was doing, there was Cam, sitting in bed reading Harry Potter—independently.

Catching the Flow

And Cam continued to read Harry Potter independently. As a matter of fact, that year in second grade he went through two more Harry Potter books. He and Harry had bonded—permanently. Certainly, that bonding, that incessant reading through hundreds of pages, helped take Cam into fluency, but there was something else that helped get him there—that trading-the-lead game his mom and I played with him. For in that back-and-forth experience Cam extended into our adult fluency models every time he reentered the reading act. His ears told him to keep up the pace that was already set, and thus his flow grew to sound more and more like ours.

Reading educators years ago dubbed a similar process *neurological impress* (Heckleman 1966), a support that finds the teacher reading just slightly behind the student, but stepping in to save him if he starts to fall. Actually, I learned about neurological impress in the '60s from Robert Wilson, the professor of my undergraduate reading course. He told us it was used frequently with children who had learning disabilities. But over the course of my career, I've seen similar scaffolding techniques influence all kinds of kids. Still others have developed similar simultaneous transactions, *duet reading* and *alternate reading* (Laubach Literacy Action 1994); yet, I prefer to circumvent fancy terminology and its exactness. Even kids understand when I mention *trading the lead*.

It's so easy that kids can do it with other kids. My first graders loved to trade the lead together. All they had to do was watch their teacher partner a few times in demonstration, and then they wanted to play, too. I have to giggle every time I watch beginners trading the lead with each other. It's so much fun!

Cam had a good vocabulary and strong strategies. But thanks to trading the lead and a Harry obsession, he moved right into fluency. As a matter of fact, his love of Harry continues to shine, and if sales are any indication, many other kids owe their fluency skills to Harry. The newest Potter book just came out this past week, and since then, Cam has stopped by twice with his mom and dad—both times with Harry in hand. Cam had what Krashen and his colleagues (Ujiie and Krashen 2002; Von Sprecken, Kim, and Krashen 2000) call a "home run experience" with Harry Potter!

Cam and his mom still have a triadic relationship with Harry!

Cameron's love of Harry keeps him interrogating all of us, as he negotiates the meanings of some of the well-above-third-grade, multisyllabic words. But this now-fluent reader also shares regular Harry updates, excitedly explaining the story to anyone who will listen.

"And ya know what happened next, Grandma?"

"No, Cam, tell me some more about Harry," I answer with a knowing smile.

The Attributes of a Fluent Reader

At the end of this little fluency story, we can more easily assess what makes the difference between the fluent and the nonfluent reader. First of all, Cameron had a large, *automatic sight vocabulary* and *decoding strategies* for new words. But those alone did not make him a fluent reader. He had to learn how to move through text, *audibly* reading in *syntactic chunks or phrases* at a *smooth, steady pace*. When a reader reads fluently, the process appears effortless. These are the attributes of a fluent reader. If any of these is absent, the reader will not be fluent.

Confusing Fast with Efficient

Almost everyone who writes about fluency mentions a common descriptor: *fast*. I honestly believe they do not actually mean to use that word. I think they mean efficient, but they reach instead for the easy, old standby, fast.

Fluent readers are not always fast. Instead, they vary their pace to accommodate meaning and audience; that is, they are flexible. For instance, when a proficient reader begins her sophomore biology textbook chapter on genomes, she is flexible enough in her reading to reread and even stop her reading to define a term. Proficient readers do that, yet fast readers may not.

When a first grader reads a paragraph about the differences between frogs and toads, he may slow down when he needs to more closely process text. A reader who has been trained for speed may not. So we can say that fluent readers demonstrate an internalized flexibility that serves both meaning and audience.

Therefore, please do not search for the term *fast* related to fluency attributes. It's not there. However, there are several other important attributes of a fluent reader.

Five Key Characteristics of Fluent Readers

Although reading strange or very difficult texts can effect anyone's fluency, given a readable text, most fluent readers do exhibit five common characteristics, seen on the chart below.

How can teachers move kids toward fluency? They certainly do not have the time to sit with each and every child reading Harry Potter! The remainder of this chapter answers this question, but perhaps the most essential understanding is that *fluency is more caught than taught.*

Caught, Not Taught

Skill in fluency is more caught than taught. That is, it is when novice readers have daily sociopsycholinguistic experiences that they fall into the fluent reading behaviors similar to others who they hear reading. Learning to read, like all learning, is a social process (Vygotsky 1978). Therefore, texts need to be read *to* kids to demonstrate how reading feels and sounds. Texts need to be read *with* kids to invite them into the modeled process and undergird novices with confidence. And texts need to be read *by* kids (independently), because that is when the process, itself, will pull them into fluency. Obviously, all this doesn't happen overnight!

Fluency, Not Dramatic Expression

There have been articles written that confuse fluent reading with *dramatic expression*. Some include descriptors, such as "Reads with expression," under the qualifying attributes of fluency. I feel that with all the pressures related to the present political push for perfection, teachers may misinterpret the term *expression*. That is,

Attributes of a Fluent Reader

- They possess a large, automatic sight vocabulary.
- They independently and effectively use decoding strategies.
- They read audibly.
- They read in syntactic chunks or phrases.
- They move through rehearsed text at a smooth, steady pace.

most of us who are asked to read aloud do read fluently, but we use very little dramatic expression. Therefore, I believe we need to clarify the difference between *dramatic expression* and *expressive reading*.

Expressive reading merely connotes the flow, inflections, and intonations that occur once a reader gets the hang of the process and can automatically identify words. Some also call this automaticity (Samuels 1983), which I prefer because it seems more synonymous with the smooth oral flow that mature readers exhibit—and it steers us clear of a focus on false voice, because readers need to find their *own* voice, not someone else's. We want readers to demonstrate fluent behaviors, whether or not they have the talent to sound like their favorite actor or actress.

Dramatic expression calls for a forced fluency, one that occurs when we try to be someone other than ourselves. It is about acting and audiences. Automaticity asks only that *readers be true to themselves and the text*, to read smoothly with the inflection and intonation of their own unique, self-possessed voice.

Yet, there are definitely times and purposes when we would want to scaffold students toward fabricated levels of expression. One of these serves comprehension, while the other serves an audience.

Dramatic Expression That Serves Comprehension

Sometimes, we scaffold readers toward a more refined understanding of a story's characters through our invitations to reenact more expressively. We do this more to *serve comprehension* than to drive fluency, although it tends to serve both purposes.

Watch how Jane encourages a reader to connect to a character's feelings when she offers the following invitation:

TEACHER: All right. And she said it like she meant it. If you were—if a mother was saying it like she meant it, how would a mother say that? *(pointing)* How would her mother say that, if she said it like she meant it?

Here, Jane is trying to get the reader to stand in the shoes of the mother—to understand the mother's feelings, intentions, and behaviors. This was done more in service to comprehending the feelings and intentions of a character than to encourage fluent reading.

Dramatic Expression That Serves an Audience

In my classroom we do strive to read and speak with dramatic expression, but only when the situation invites such behaviors—in plays, for instance. That's because the purpose driving the reading and speaking also drives the level of inflection we use, that is, the level of expressiveness. We always strive for fluency when reading aloud to an audience, but only dramatic purposes call for dramatic expression. Later in the chapter, I describe the ways in which I incorporate plays into the curriculum for the purpose of rereading. It is good to keep in mind that during such experiences children are encouraged to read with dramatic expression; however, they are given a multitude of opportunities to get good at their part *prior to* the performance.

Keeping Our Purposes Straight

I have to snicker just thinking of Dan Rather reading the nightly news with dramatic expression—the kind that earns a student a top score on a fluency rubric. Dan Rather paces himself. He reads audibly. He uses intonation and phrasing—and we cannot mistake his self-possessed voice. But Dan Rather is not Steve Martin!

Or better yet, let's consider a board of education meeting. Dr. Smith draws the group's attention to Article Number 6, Paragraph 2, and begins to read—fluently. But now imagine the faces of the board if Dr. Smith began to read with dramatic expressive inflection. He might receive a top rubric score, but in real life the board would surely cast a strange glance his way.

Perhaps what's most important here is that by focusing on a falsified voice for dramatic expression we could actually hinder fluency, because we would be adding another variable or spoken behavior to the fluency task. Thus, we would be making it more difficult than is necessary. This has an especially significant impact on the shy child.

Therefore, my goal is to construct literacy activities that will entice word readers to move smoothly through text at an even pace, taking in more than one word at a time, that is, chunking texts in phrases and sentences. And if kids pick up some dramatic inflection from our plays and dialogue reading, it is icing on their literacy cake. However, from my experience I know that few are headed for Hollywood, and even if they are, their talents will certainly have multiple venues in which to unfold—such as our plays. So let's focus our efforts toward a smooth pace and a self-possessed voice rather than dramatic expression.

A System's Approach

There are those who would try to simplify all of this. They contend that, if we provide children with a sound-symbol structure, reading will happen. Yet language is far more than a system of letters and sounds. It is a complex network of social semiotic systems used for the making of meaning (Halliday 1978). Readers use those complex systems of cues to construct meaning. But at the core of it all, we always find that the learner's intentions are driven by his emotions and meanings, which, in turn, supports fluency.

The More Predictable the Text, the Less Readers Fixate

When reading meaningful material, the more fluent the reader, the less the brain fixates on individual words. This allows for larger chunks to be stored in short-term memory, enabling the learner to construct macro meanings. After extensive scientific eye movement research, Paulson and Freeman (2003) found that the brain uses only what it needs to make meaning from print. Their research showed that "[the] brain took the available information and pieced it together into a seamless whole. In this perspective, *reading depends less on what the reader sees than on what the reader does with that information*" (p. 16) in the making of meaning.

The more predictable the situation, the less print the brain needs as it reaches forward to construct meaning. Sometimes it needs very little because the context is laden with meaning, and thus prediction is strong. Meaning is a driving force for fluency.

Fluency *Without* Comprehension! Yikes!

Although fluency supports comprehension, readers can be very fluent *without* constructing much meaning. Peter Duckett once told me about an experience he had in an elementary school he visited in Turlock, California, where a group of Spanish-speaking kids were reading in English. He said they could read aloud flawlessly with great accuracy, yet when he asked them the meaning of what they had just read, they replied, "Ni idea. No tenemos que comprenderlo, solo tenemos que leerlo." (No idea, we don't have to understand it, we just have to read it.)

As I said before, there is more to reading than meets the eye. It's a complex system of interacting cues, but without comprehension of what we are reading, does it even matter how fluent we are?

What the Eyes Look at During Reading

Duckett's (2003) first-grade eye movement research verifies the reaching-forward process that occurs during reading. After tracking and analyzing readers' eye movements, he found that during reading, not only are readers' eyes ahead of their voices, but also that 89 percent of reader *fixations* (stopping points) were on major components, mostly nouns and verbs, while "82 percent of the non-fixated words were function words." This is a common finding in eye movement research (Just and Carpenter; and Paulson in Duckett 2003, 53). And it's an important fluency consideration.

Focus on Major Components

This means that *most readers' visual fixations skip function words*—abstract words like *but* and *and*, words used primarily as syntactic glue in our language, words that are tough to describe until one possesses metalinguistic knowledge of English syntax.

Just as babies and new-language speakers receive and transmit messages through key nouns and verbs, Duckett's research demonstrates that readers do much the same, as they move through text, reaching for that which is meaningful and predicting the upcoming text. They seem to play a kind of hopscotch through sentences, relying mostly on the concrete, the meaningful. They focus heavily on what Duckett (2002, 2003) calls the "major components" of text.

The Use of Pictures for Sampling

Pictures are a major component for novices whose eyes move from concrete words to picture and back again, but devote more time to print. Duckett (2003) calls this back-and-forth process *sampling*, which connotes a search for meaning to accommodate a somewhat weaker graphophonic congruence. When he photographed the reading of first graders and then analyzed their eye movements, he concluded:

> In sampling pictures and print they devoted the majority of their time to the major meaning carriers in both media. In pictures they sampled from the major components (characters and objects). Within pictures the major components are key sources for information regarding who and what is central to the story as well as the actions between characters and objects. Thus, sampling the major components in pictures provides the reader with information regarding nouns, adjectives and verbs. Within print, readers knew enough to sample more frequently from the content words . . . because these words are the major meaning carriers in print. (pp. 16–17)

Syntactic Glue

This process of sampling is one and the same as that used by adult readers; albeit, adult readers are more experienced and efficient. This means that we all, young and not-so-young, do not fixate on function words, such as conjunctions and prepositions, that hold little meaning. These *functors* lack concreteness for even the mature mind. They are merely the predicable syntactic glue that helps weave the language together into sentences and paragraphs. Once we have the concrete elements, most of us are able to intuitively and accurately predict a graphophonic match that will fill in those syntactic gaps.

For example, complete this cloze sentence: *The boy ran __ ___ hill.* Easy, right? That is why the eye fixates primarily on the major components of a text's meaning, that is, its nouns and verbs, which should also be a scaffolder's grounding points.

Scaffolding at-a-Glance Reading

It is fairly evident, then, that one of our main tasks after novices drop into word reading is to move them forward into chunking larger pieces of text. When reading is word-centered, which it is for young novices, it is bumpy. It reminds me of those ball machines at a batting-practice park. Pop! Wait. Pop! Wait. Pop! The novice is examining each word carefully, ideally using all cueing systems, decoding, then examining the next, because he knows few words at a glance. And his finger keeps his place. This is all well and good—at first.

However, fluent readers are at-a-glance readers who rarely labor over a word. They no longer point, but read at a steady pace and keep a kind of beat to the rhythms of print with their intonations. For them, decoding has become automatic—unless they are reading difficult text, which requires more flexibility.

"But wait a minute," you ask. "How about those novices who have learned to fluently read books like *Brown Bear, Brown Bear, What Do You See*?"

When a novice who is transitioning between preword and word learns to reenact—or even read—a repetitive book smoothly, he cannot be considered a fluent reader, because remember, fluent reading requires a large store of automatic sight vocabulary and strong decoding strategies. What that novice has is a good memory—which is a helpful thing—but it does not make him a fluent reader. As a matter of fact, earlier I mentioned how a novice will actually slow down to read word-by-word before he moves into fluency. So it's as if on their developmental journeys into reading kids speed up at first when they copy-read, then slow down when they acquire wordness, then speed up again as the process becomes automatic. And each occurs because readers are trying to construct meaning using a meaningful process. Yet, when they drop into that smooth flow it always seems like some kind of magic has occurred.

But there is much we can do to lead readers to such magic. We can scaffold foundations in fluency prior to the reading act and we can process with students during the reading act. Let's first investigate how we can scaffold fluency prior to the reading act.

How Teachers Scaffold Fluency Prior to the Reading Act

Formal reading-group instruction usually includes a guided reading period in which prereading instruction in story structure, vocabulary, schema, strategy instruction, and such is offered to lay a foundation for the follow-up independent reading act. This prep is a real boost to fluency because it nurtures accurate predictions, and the more predictable the text, the more fluent the reader.

Writing Reciprocity: Using Writing to Scaffold Chunking

Chunking words into syntactic phrases can be scaffolded through the publishing process, and it undergirds both reading and writing. Here's what I do.

During writer's workshop, when a novice finishes a piece, I ask the child if we can publish it. Writers know I will then word-process the piece with its sentences broken into meaningful syntactic chunks (just as many beginner books do), placing but one chunk per page. I might break this writer's sentence in the following manner: "When my dad gets home / we can eat our supper." Then I create an empty window above or below each chunk so that the writer can illustrate its meaning. It's easy to see how this example could have a different pictorial context for each—one involving Dad coming in, while the other would illustrate their mealtime. Furthermore, there are now even computer programs that help with this entire procedure.

After a writer's illustrations are complete, I add a cover and title page, a few extra pages at the end for comments, and then staple. Before long, I turn that process of chunking over to the writers, placing the chunking in their hands, and thus scaffolding them further into syntactic investigations. It always seems so magical that kids never chunk leaving the end of a syntactic cluster dangling; that is, they always keep noun, verb, and prepositional phrases intact.

In no time, they are constructing their own books at home, too. And kids love to read each other's books during Read-a-Book time; and each time it happens, they are scaffolded in fluency by reading in those meaningful chunks.

By midyear we had very few kids who still needed to lean on a Shared Book Experience (SBE) in order to read that day's story. In other words, they had accrued sufficient sight vocabulary and decoding skills to go it alone, so we could use a guided reading protocol—one where prereading prep laid the text background, but then afterward, the students read independently. That's why it's important to fortify those transitioning novices with lots of background *prior* to their reading. We need to pave their road to fluency by making the text *as predictable as possible*.

Chunking: Teaching Vocabulary in Phrases

By laying these firm foundations, we are helping fluency ride on the wings of predictability. One of the ways in which I scaffolded kids into fluency through vocabulary instruction was by presenting *vocabulary-in-phrases*. That is, I did not make a list of words and introduce them one by one. Instead, I stole from their story the entire phrase in which that word resided, so instead of offering them *chair*, I copied from the text the phrase, *into Dad's big, old chair*.

This helps in several ways. First of all, it adds more cueing avenues to decoding this new word. Second, it provides a prereading model that uses the *exact text wording*; therefore, it will look and feel familiar when the novice approaches it in text. Third, it offers a variety of other venues for activities. In other words, kids can act out phrases, add a rhyming line; whatever might be a fun, yet still beneficial, activity related to the story and reading.

I myself do *not* preread this vocabulary-in-phrases for the group. Instead, I dub someone as leader, and ask the group to move to the far end of the room, read each phrase together, guess what it might mean, and then choose from a menu of related tasks, like those I just mentioned. In the meantime, I am able to work with another group.

Prereading Schema-Development Tapes

Background audio- and videotapes also ground the text in predictability. For guided-reading schema-building, readers can listen to audio- and videotapes. That is, there is not a speech-to-print match for the story, as there was when kids were first moving into word reading. Tapes by the same author can develop a taste of style, vocabulary, sentence length, phrasing, and such, thus enhancing predictability.

However, they were just as often tapes that retold the same story—just a different version. (I must have ten different versions of *The Three Bears*!) Sometimes, I ask listeners to fold a paper twice to yield four windows on front and back. Then, as they listen they can draw parts of the

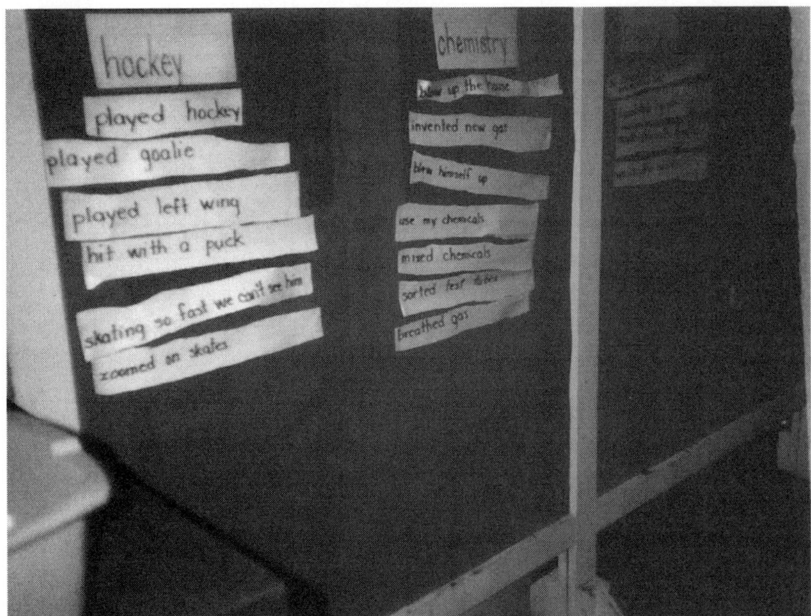

Pictured are some vocabulary-in-phases that one group in my room used in December prior to reading Morris's Disappearing Bag *by Rosemary Wells.*

Picture Walks

Picture walks remain a staple forever. They are especially helpful when any reader (even you or I) uses an expository or informational text. Prereading the pictures and the headings not only undergirds fluency, but it also supports comprehension by laying a conceptual foundation before the reading begins. Readers construct macro-contextual inferences as they make their first skim-through-text hypotheses that their reading will then validate or nullify.

What's at the bottom of all this? The more predictable we make the text, the greater its potential for reader fluency.

story. This tracking would support their developing macro context for story schema when they actually enter the reading act; it adds predictability, which nurtures fluency.

Some storytellers have tapes that follow the story line of their books, but are not exact print matches. Robert Munsch's tapes are perfect for adding predictability to his texts, because they are close to the printmatch, but do deviate, sometimes considerably. Many of his deviations are sound effects, which evoke giggles and story fun. The children absolutely love Robert Munsch's storytelling. His exciting, dramatically expressive tapes pull listeners in and tantalize them into reading each tape's bookmate. And with those terrific tapes ringing in their heads, they can't help but fall into fluency once they hit the printed page. Furthermore, they *choose* to read them again and again and again.

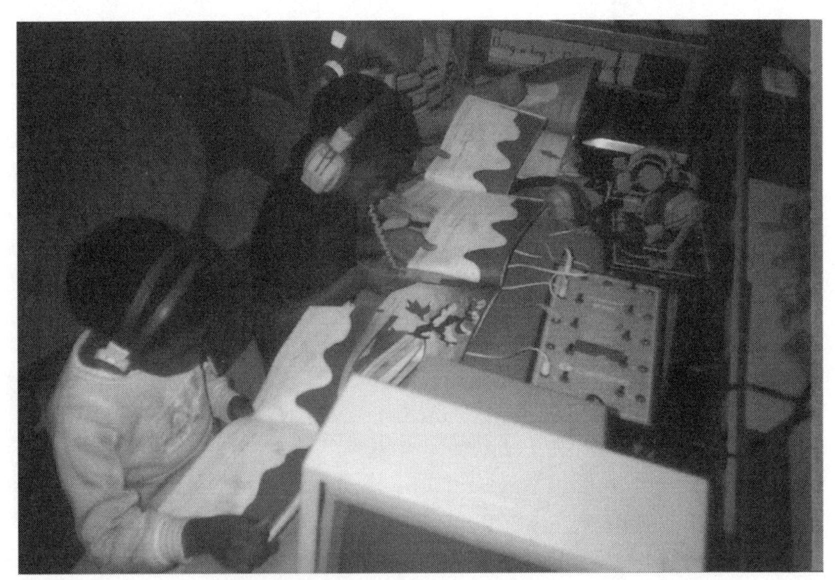

Prior to reading, a group listens via headphones to a winter story.

How Teachers Scaffold Fluency During Reading

After considering what Duckett and Paulson and Freeman have demonstrated in their eye movement research, it is an easy connection that we can make to the acts of scaffolding teachers. And it should therefore be no surprise that one of the most natural and ongoing fluency scaffolds involved *protracting* kids through the words. That is, scaffolders stayed ahead of readers, leading them, pulling them forward.

Moving Right Along

Teachers used a variety of tactics to keep kids moving along through print. They seemed to understand that drawing a youngster's attention to each and every word could be detrimental to the development of fluency, because it encourages a reader to fixate on some less important information and slows the process. As a matter of fact, I would suggest that some of the teachers' pointing ballets actually resemble the reading eye movements in pictures that Duckett (2003) shares. We need to move novices away from word-by-word reading because *we readers do not look at every word when reading*. Duckett (2003), Paulson and Freeman (2003), and Rayner (1997) have eye tracking data that make this a scientific fact.

Therefore, once a novice begins to identify words, we need to keep our pointing out ahead, pulling him, moving him forward, drawing his eyes toward major meaning components in the text and to the picture, rather than forcing him to laboriously attack, analyze, define, discuss, and murder every word. His drive for meaning should keep him focused toward larger units of language, which will in turn support the smaller ones, the words.

Keep the Pointing Focused on Major Components of Text

This suggests that teachers should guide readers toward authentic behaviors, the kind that real readers use in real life. And indeed, the videotaped teachers did just that. Most of them spent more time on the concrete parts of language. Few spent time dissecting and defining abstractions, such as conjunctions.

Furthermore, one of the most consistent scaffolding behaviors that teachers used with novices was pointing to or tapping the picture, a gestural message telling the youngster that concrete information related to sampling, cross-checking, and uncovering meaning could be found in *who* or *what* was in the picture and *what was occurring* there. The pictures major components (cues) throughout.

Demonstrating What Fluency Sounds Like

As Linda scaffolded Joey through a book that contained considerable dialogue, she encouraged him to reread parts aloud after the first read. She referenced pictures, asking, "What's he doing here?"

On one page Joey responded, "Giving him some ice cream."

"So what did he say?" Linda asked.

And Joey responded,"Here is something—some—" reading haltingly and without intonation.

At that point, the teacher entered to model fluency as she ran her finger under the words, "Here is some ice cream!" When she stopped to let Joey finish, he reread her modeled sentence with the same intonations, phrasing, and beat as that of his teacher, and continued forward in that manner—until his next unknown episode, that is.

Sometimes novices need extra modeling and another chance. Linda offered that here.

Helping or Hindering Fluency?

There are some misused, overused, and abused methods and structures that seem to surface no matter the century; no matter how boring, ineffectual, or even harmful. Some school traditions will just not go away! Nevertheless, as long as there is some choice involved, we can maneuver into what's best for kids. Choice is important for kids.

Choice Enhances Fluency

Choice makes a difference in most learning situations. That is, doing the task because the teacher said to is very different from choosing to do that task *after* considering available choices. Choice is the key initial motivating factor that creates the intentions that drive successful literacy experiences. Think about the difference in these two situations: (1) The teacher asks Maurie to reread page 16 in her reading book. (2) The teacher asks the class to get quiet because Maurie *wants* to read her part in the play—or the poem she's written—or the response she received from the Sierra Club. Maurie *asked* to do it in the second instance! The intention differed; thus the reading results will differ.

Stamping Out Round-Robin Reading Once and for All!

Perhaps one of the most intimidating situations for a student who is not fluent is reading *unrehearsed* text aloud in front of the class. It seems like—for at least one hundred years—we've known that round-robin reading in a large-group situation is not a good practice (See *Good-bye, Round Robin* by Optiz and Rasinski 1998). Yet I regularly talk to teachers and kids who are involved in it. Just the other evening a young child told me, "The boys in my room read better than the girls."

Being a female I just had to ask, "How do you know?"

He explained how the entire class reads from the same basal every day. The teacher calls on each student to "have a turn" reading unrehearsed paragraphs from each day's selection. How intimidating! And how potentially harmful to fluency! Could everyone in that classroom really be reading at that same basal grade level? Might it not be extremely difficult for some? (But I still can't believe they're all girls!)

There are dozens of times when kids might want to read something aloud. And when someone *wants* to read a piece aloud, they also want to read it fluently. We need to create circumstances in which such intentions can grow and flourish. And we need to eliminate intimidating ones, such as round-robin-reading—once and for all.

Stumbling Mumbling

We've all heard our share of stumbling mumbling readers. Stumbling mumbling occurs when a child is asked to read something he does not want to read. He does not want to read for primarily one of two interrelated reasons: (1) He's not interested; (2) The text is too difficult and he hasn't had the opportunity to prepare beforehand.

To circumvent stumbling mumbling in our classrooms and to instead encourage fluency, we need to keep a couple of things in mind. First of all, the easiest way to make text fascinating is to embed it in interesting, authentic situations or curriculum. I'll discuss this later, but right now, let's consider the other debilitating issue, using a text that is too difficult.

When the Text Is Too Difficult

As a standing rule of thumb, texts are too difficult when novices (or fluent) readers miscue more than ten times in one hundred words, that is, their word accuracy level is less than 90 percent correct (Fountas and Pinnell 2001; Clay 1979) reading unrehearsed text. Yet there were times when I knew a book was too difficult even though the reader had only a 6 percent or 8 percent miscue rate. Most often, I felt such insecurities develop when students consistently stumbled, then self-corrected their way through each page in a series of fits and starts. (Essentially, ten self-corrections would *not* count as errors.) That is, when their fluency was obviously and continually offended, my ears told me that that youngster should try another selection. After all, reading should be fun! Can something that tough be fun?

I've discussed text qualities earlier in this book, but please be reminded that certain aspects in a text's construction will make it easier to read. That is, texts are easier when they possess any or several of the following attributes: repeated patterns, rhyming words, pictures that illustrate the graphics, lots of white space, short sentences bounded at the ends of lines, large font, an ample amount of high-frequency words (Cole 1998).

Guidelines Related to Text Difficulty

Pinnell and Fountas (1999) provide us with sound guidelines related to *Matching Books to Readers*. It takes a fair amount of experience to do this adeptly, so using the Pinnell-Fountas book as a guide can be very helpful. Most of the primary teachers at my school have or share a copy and appreciate the leveled list and guidelines this book offers.

We also used the Degrees of Reading Power (DRP) computer program that can be purchased from *www.TASA.com*. Text levels are listed in DRPs, which emanate from a combination of readability formulas. TASA does the legwork that allows us to simply type in the name of a book, and within a second or two, the level appears. Neither of these resources provides every possible book, but both list most of the popular texts.

Most Internet sources and computer programs seem to offer only *grade-level listings*, and when a child is just entering the process, grade level is not a fine enough delineation. Beginners need a baby step between books, not a giant grade-level leap. Both the Pinnell and Fountas book and the DRP program provide the finer gradations that will help scaffold a novice more gently from one beginning step to the next—in other words, they consider *sublevels* within the first- and second-grade levels. Several series (Wright Group, Rigby, Celebration Press) offer texts that follow this sublevel progression. Such textual scaffolds help novices move in baby steps from one book to the next.

Additionally, Chapter 10 in *Guided Reading* (Fountas and Pinnell 1996) describes *how* to level books for novices. Pictures of text pages help show the differences described on each page. Our school's primary teachers and I organized a large multiple-copy library, and we used Fountas and Pinnell's guidelines for all previously nonleveled books. The task helped all of us acquire a sound sense of the subtle progression of text difficulty, and it also helped us to learn a bit more about why texts themselves are such an important part of the reading relationship.

Decodable Texts: A Word-Centered Approach

We know that many teachers are now mandated to use decodable texts to teach reading. Yet, why might these actually deter the process?

Decodable texts are constructed so that readers can sound out each word. Their focus is centered on sound-symbol match; therefore, meaning sometimes receives a short shrift (as illustrated earlier by Shanasti's question, "Do you think the author's trying to write a new kind of poetry?"). They follow a word-centered approach, as opposed to a meaning-centered one. At this point in this book, it seems that everyone would understand why such a word focus could deter not only fluency but also meaning—especially for readers who become mired in the micro!

We need to ask all those who triumph decodable texts, "Are we actually holding children back by using this genre? If we anchor students to words, will they flow into fluency?" And most important, we need to ask, "Where's the research on these contrived texts?" There is none.

Sounding Good!

I can't say enough about how important it is to consider the text's level of difficulty, because a novice can perform fluently in one easy book and not so fluently in another. Continually placing a reader in a situation that asks her to read text that is too difficult will be detrimental to fluency because it never allows her the chance to *hear herself reading fluently*—which is only exacerbated by the reader's waning self-esteem.

The recent push to get classrooms back into a reading series will no doubt compromise many children's chances of experiencing just-right text, because using only one book is not a broad enough choice. Series producers often suggest that the teacher use a common at-grade-level story for all students in the classroom, regardless of their reading proficiency. So those who are struggling in grade-level texts may *never* have a chance to experience fluency because they will be reading in that level all year. Many teachers, especially those in the inner cities who are depending on government grant monies, will have even fewer choices, because they are under strictures that chain them to the mandated reading series. They *must* use it.

Nevertheless, all teachers can afford students a time during the day when every reader gets to experience and be scaffolded in just-right books—*a time other than the basal slot*. Without such experiences, nonfluent readers may never understand what it feels like and sounds like to read fluently—to sound good. They will never know that reading is fun. The following ideas may help teachers find some time slots and methods for using just-right texts, and they will also address the issue of student interest—both of which lead to fluency.

Listening to Their Own Fluency

Novices need lots of opportunities to *hear themselves* read fluently. They need to get the feel of it. Hannah, in her zealous and appreciative manner, often encourages with a kind of can't-wait excitement, "Oh, read that over again for me!" And proudly, the little novice rereads the sentence or the page, pleased to make his teacher so happy, but also proud after listening to himself perform fluently. Hannah's behaviors remind me of the way in which we ask our babies to do their little stunts over and over, never boring of their blossoming talents.

Setting the Scene for Success

It's really important for teachers to be child advocates. This means that we must sometimes *mindfully maneuver* to create a child-centered situation, even in the toughest of times. It's easy to become controlled by those in high places who do not know our children. But remember, only those who are closest to the children know them best. It's up to us to set the scene for our kids' success. We need to mindfully maneuver to make our classrooms just-right places in which every child can learn to read fluently. Some ideas for helping kids achieve their own fluent reading follow.

Help Kids Select Just-Right Books

Some readers monitor themselves, they know what they can and cannot read. They wisely select just-right books that become their foundation for fluency. Others, especially beginning readers, choose books that are too difficult. They need a teacher's support to direct them. To scaffold kids in this way, teachers will need to listen to a child read and then take a moment with that reader to explain why that particular book might be especially easy, just right, or too difficult (vocabulary, conceptual load, patterning, and so on). This then presents a model that readers themselves will eventually use independently.

Once a reader can read mid-first-grade-level books with several sentences on a page, some teachers introduce the *five-finger-rule*. That is, if the novice encounters five words on one page that he does not know, he can predict that the book is probably too difficult. Thus, when kids are searching the shelves before Read-a-Book, we remind them, "Use the five-finger-rule." Then we stand back and watch as novices open books and tick off any unknown word by raising a finger. This works especially well with young children who need that sense of concreteness—at least until they get the idea of what fluency feels like. Bottom line: The book is one of the most important factors related to fluency.

Self-selection from a large library of books is a wonderful motivation to read just-right books.

Create Avenues for Developing a Classroom Library

Some readers have tons of literacy opportunities; that is, they live in a household that reads, goes to the library, and discusses literacy. Or they attend a school that celebrates a vast, up-to-date library. Other children don't have these privileges, and it is they who struggle with literacy in school (Neumann 1999; Krashen 1995). So for those who might be limited by the availability of resources and experiences, we teachers need to find ways to immerse them in print. This commonsense idea that the more children read the more likely they will become fluent is also validated by studies related to exposure to print and experiences with books (Allington 1977; Stanovich 1986; Krashen 1993; Juel 1996). How many more decades of studies do we need to make sure there's an adequate supply of good books in every classroom?

Until someone turns that wish into a reality, we teachers will have to continue borrowing from our grocery money, visiting garage sales, reaping free books from the kids' book clubs, begging for used books from the older students, connecting with Reading Is Fundamental, using online books and articles, appealing to good-

Samaritan organizations—whatever it takes. (Can you tell I've done them all!?) My colleague, Linda, and I had over 2,000 books in each of our rooms, and the school only gave us $50 a year for supplies. We do what we have to do for the kids. Right?

Create Classroom Opportunities for Reading Experience

Just before I began my investigation into teacher scaffolding behaviors, I asked Linda, "What do you think is the most important part of our curriculum for developing fluent readers?"

After some deliberation, she responded, "Read-a-Book and Share-a-Book, for sure!"

I agreed.

As I explained in Chapter 3, Read-a-Book was our daily period of engaged, sustained reading in just-right text. Even when the day's activities—school pictures, Santa's Secret workshop, physicals—found us needing to remove a piece of the curriculum, it was never Read-a-Book that had to wait. It was too important. And always by midyear, the whole group was engaged in reading lengthier texts *silently*. It really did sound like sustained *silent* reading then. But we could not change the name of something that was so much a part of us—a curricular structure that nurtured kids into fluency.

Immediately after Read-a-Book, we had our fifteen-minute Share-a-Book, a time when readers had a chance to sit in front of the group and independently read aloud what they'd read at their seats. (Sometimes they did take a scaffolding buddy with them—just in case.) Share-a-Book provided the context for *authentic rereading*! After each reader read about three minutes or so, we'd stop the performance, offer a kind word, and invite the child to take his audience comments. The listeners then offered their thoughts related to the book. Obviously, they had to learn how to, but that's another book (see *Knee to Knee, Eye to Eye: Circling in on Comprehension* [Cole 2003]).

Getting to Know the Author Helps Fluency

It's wonderful when beginning readers stumble on an author they love, much like Cameron did. For some novices, it's Dr. Seuss. For others, it's Steven Kellogg, Robert Munsch, Mercer Mayer, Syd Hoff, Arnold Lobel, Russell Hoban, Barbara Park, or Mary Pope Osborn. The author that turns a child on can also be the one who leads that reader into fluency. That's why it's important to have just-right-readability author collections from a variety of genres, both fiction and nonfiction.

Part of the reason we adults are so relaxed reading the authors we know is because their writing becomes more and more predictable as we get to know the author's style, content, and genre. The same is true for kids. After we have read ten Stephen King or Barbara Kingsolver or Tom Clancy books, we breeze right through the next and the next and the next. This happens to kids, too.

However, a brand-new text or a brand-new author can challenge even adult fluency—especially if it's written in iambic pentameter or has sixty-seven-word sentences or repeatedly offers up eight-syllable Russian names! Nevertheless, if we love iambic pentameter, and we read enough books in iambic pentameter, we learn to predict those, too, and fluency again increases.

This aspect of increasing fluency then is a no-brainer. The more we participate in a predictable activity, the more

A small group of girls experience Share-A-Book.

comfortable we become, the more able we are to predict, and the more fluent our behavior becomes. That's why there is a motto among reading teachers that goes something like this: "Never have a child read an unrehearsed text in front of the class." Preparation undergirds predictability—for both adults and kids. Give the kids a chance to know the author, know the style, know the vocabulary, know the text *before* asking them to perform.

Don't Make It Boring!

Sometimes we teachers read about scholarly methods to enhance fluency and we want to run immediately to our lesson plans and write "Repeated Reading" under Monday's reading plans. Yet, after Monday's regular guided-reading protocol unfolds, do we then command the kids to just repeat the reading? That's pretty boring.

There is an enormous difference, as well as a different result, between *lessons taught for the sake of following a directive* and *lessons integrated into authentic, meaningful experiences.* Indeed! How many adults read an article or book over again?

Actors do! Radio announcers do! Family members preparing to record an answering machine message do. Someone trying to provide evidence to win an argument does. Kids having book-fun together do. Someone celebrating an appreciation of a segment of text, or a poem, a quote, or an email does. Singers do. Lyricists do. Need I go on?

My point is that there are dozens of avenues that offer *authentic* experiences in repeated reading. Why would we ever think we'd get substantive results just by asking kids to do something over again merely because we said to? Bottom line: Create authentic situations for repeated readings.

Keeping the Beat

A year ago, I did a monthlong trek from Lukla, Nepal, up the Everest Trail to Mt. Everest Base Camp. The steadily upward daily challenge took its toll the second day, and I wondered how I would ever keep up with the ten (younger!) others in our group. Our leader kept telling us to "Breathe!" which I thought I was doing. After we had trekked for about six hours that exhausting day, we found ourselves at the base of a one-mile ascent leading to Namche Bazar. Just as I was ready to give in to my exhaustion, a sherpa began to chant, "Om Mani Padme Hum," and gradually, my pace fell in rhythm with the repeated chant—and so did my breathing. Before long, I was walking down the streets of the beautiful Nepalese trading village that sits atop that one-mile incline. And when we moved on to the mystical monastery of Tengboche far beyond Mt. Ama Dablam, I knew my pace would hold as I stayed in flow with both the rhythms and melodies of the mountains. Sometimes, we just need to catch the beat.

Scaffolding the Beat!

I *caught* the beat, the rhythm, on that trail and stayed with it throughout—all the way to base camp a week later. Catching the beat is just as important to success in the act of running, swimming, or reading. However, the beat is something that's *caught, not taught!*

How does a child catch the beat inherent in the act of reading?

Scaffolders can lead novices toward fluency, but they can't catch it for them. Every teacher pulled her novice reader through print by steadily moving her finger forward. Sometimes, when the reader came to an easy phrase, such as "into the house," her scaffolder would make a swift sweep, gesturing for the reader to read the phrase in one fell swoop. Much like those in an orchestra, whose beat is kept by the conductor, the beat for novices was kept by their teachers' pointing. Most scaffolders used some form of pointing to set the rhythms for the novice, leading them forward in steady harmony.

Now consider the amount of pointing done for fluent readers. We know it was minimal. That's because fluent readers no longer need to be pulled, for they have already caught the beat.

Catching the Beat with Music: Choral Reading and Singing

I have another suggestion that worked in my classroom and it worked on Everest Trail, too. Music! On large pieces of tagboard I copied the words to our favorite songs, the students illustrated each in posterlike fashion, and then we hung song charts all over the classroom. Partners

First graders from my room love to sing the lyrics of charted songs together.

through multiple rereadings. Shelley Harwayne (1992) says choral reading is a good way to build community, and I agree.

We always used choral reading to introduce poetry. I modeled first, and then sometimes I led, while at other times a child led. We had so much fun reading chorally in different ways: boys and girls taking line turns, soft lines and loud lines, reading only the line of your color, and so forth. It's a communal avenue for fluency.

used pointers to sing through the lines together. We also kept Raffi's books beside a tape recorder so small groups could quietly read and sing along with their favorite Canadian songster. We had songs for every play, every holiday, every unit, every birthday—on tape *and* in print. I made enlarged copies of the packaged words for Red Grammar's tapes, and Tom Chapin, too. We never tired of following along, singing, as the music played. Consider it an early version of Muzak!

Music tends to be sung in phrases, which is just what we want novices doing—phrase-reading. Over and over and over again, *songs pull kids toward fluency*, demonstrating how words are grouped. Plus, singing lyrics is always *authentic rereading*, because everyone loves to sing favorite songs over and over. Even teachers!

Like singing together, kids can read aloud together, chorally; that is, they can read together in one unison group. In this manner, the weak can carry the strong without anyone even knowing who's carrying whom. And the weaker readers soon become strong

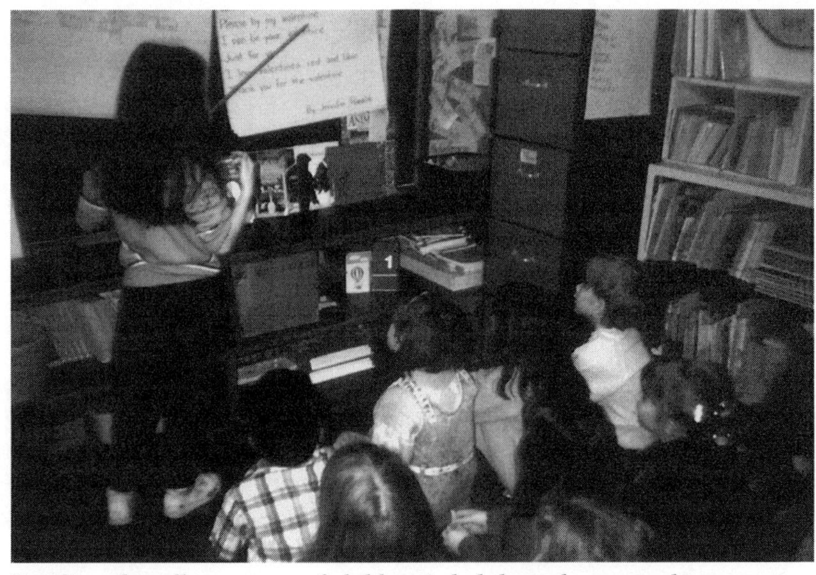

Reading chorally, a group of children is led through a poem by a peer.

Rereading Leads to Fluency

All of us love to do repeat performances of our successes. That's why golfers replay the same course, family members take the same cake to pot lucks, and vacationers return to the same resort. Young listeners love to hear the same book again and again—until their parents have it memorized. Likewise, most novice readers choose to read the same book over and over—unless it is imposed on them; that is, unless they have no choice in the matter. All that self-selected rereading is fine and good; however, if a golfer never played a different course, and a baker never baked a different cake, and a vacationer never visited a different place, life would be pretty shallow and boring.

We all need to challenge ourselves because, essentially, that is how we learn (Csikszentmihaly 1990). Readers need to challenge themselves, too. If we scaffolders lay a firm foundation for a new text we can help dissolve its challenging nature. Don Holdaway (1979) showed us a fun way to lay such firm foundations when he described his Shared Book Experience (SBE). It is yet another tactic involving demonstrations and repeated readings.

The Shared Book Experience: A Social Construct for Repeated Readings

In an SBE the teacher first reads the text aloud to the group, stopping for discussion here and there, and then she invites the students into the act for the next read—all the while having fun with the text in myriad ways. Afterward, the kids partner-read, which makes a somewhat unknown text less challenging; that is, two heads are usually better than one—and more fun!

Young children love to have fun with new stories, new books, in social situations, as opposed to sitting alone just practicing words on workbook pages, which grows old very quickly. On the other hand, kids will read and reread texts together, supporting and scaffolding each other in every conceivable manner when they have the privilege of togetherness.

I offer and demonstrate a variety of ways in which novices can play with text for the rereadings. They can take turns with sentences or pages, or they can take character parts. They can trade the lead, or they can read chorally. *The choice is theirs*—and therein lies the success of this experience.

Using Poetry to Echo Read

Our poetry charts were a great resource for *echo reading*, which primary kids love to do! This technique finds one reader (often one who is more able) reading each line first, then his partner echoes that leader. Because poetry is written in phrases and lines, it can serve as a model for chunking. Plus, poetry is often repetitious.

Regardless, charts can be constructed so that lines of short poems are repeated. Using two different colors helps direct each reader to his lines. However, we always do these first as a class, then the kids can partner and reproduce our behaviors.

Many Valentine's Day poems optimally suit our purpose. Here's an example of a short poem that lends itself to echo reading:

Valentine, valentine,
Valentine, valentine,
Won't you be my valentine?
Won't you be my valentine?
Valentine, valentine,
Valentine, valentine,
I'll be yours, if you'll be mine.
I'll be yours, if you'll be mine.

Notice the pull in this poem toward whole-sentence phrasing. And kids will do this without batting an eye, if we introduce it in joyful, social ways.

What a wonderful way to learn to read and make a friend at the same time!

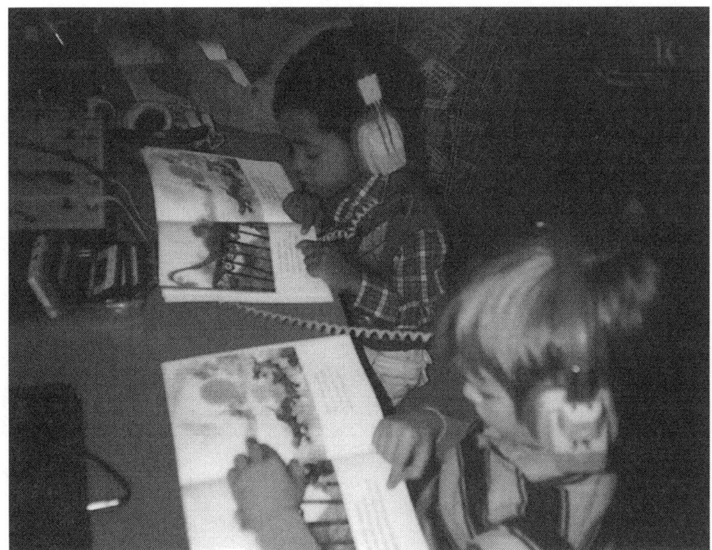

Students sit at our listening center enjoying a book together.

Dramatic Performance Aids Fluency

Every single year that I taught first grade we performed (at least) one play per month. Plays are wonderful, interdependent, fluency-developing collaborations! Granted, ours were not Cecil B. DeMille productions, and as a matter of fact, they were sometimes devoid of scenery. Yet, that did not matter to the kids. Nor did it matter to their proud parents, who always received a class-constructed invitation to attend. Even after twenty years, students still remember some of our productions. I did not develop a curriculum that involved dramatic performance for the primary purpose of fun, but it certainly helped! I brought plays into our classroom to help kids develop fluency through repeated readings and understand another genre, plays.

Sometimes I'd interject, "Could we read that sounding another way?" meaning, can someone read it with a different intonation, inflection, tone, rate, or any of the attributes of good oral reading and fluency. I did not necessarily mention all of those terms, but the kids understood because I had already modeled for them what I meant.

Listening Centers: A Key Rereading Scaffold

Sometimes, a teacher introduces a story that has a taped recording that accompanies the text. But she makes certain that, if the recording is a commercial one, it is not a storytelling version (as those of Robert Munsch), but actually follows the text word for word.

After the story has been introduced and shared by the teacher, students can use the listening center to follow along and catch the flow of the reader on the audiotape. I am careful to make certain that the text is not read too rapidly. As a matter of fact, I frequently just recorded my own tapes. That way, I could pace the tempo and prosodies to the ability of the students.

Readers love using a tape to follow along, and it provides a wonderful model of fluent reading. Students will later reread the texts with the same melodies and rhythms that were heard on the tape. They copy the fluency. And because it's fun, they ask to do it over and over. The fact that I have five shoeboxes full of these taped books speaks for itself!

Gluing character parts on the backs of masks allows kids to read while they act.

Puppet shows win the top prize for authentic repeated readings.

Puppet Shows Invite Perfection!

I planned for puppet shows most of the time, rather than staged acting. Why? Because then we could *tape record beforehand* so that everyone sounded perfect. That is, if Dujan made a mistake right in the middle of the part he was reading, no problem! I just pressed Rewind and Dujan read it again. A no-stress performance! Plus, we hid behind room dividers if the whole class was involved, or, when the group was smaller, we used the puppet theater I purchased through a grant. They simply moved the puppets while the taped recording played their reading. That way no one felt embarrassed or shy, but everyone still had to listen closely to *comprehend* and *interpret* what his or her puppet should be doing throughout the entire performance.

To add an air of authenticity, we invited parents to our performances. And for those parents who could not attend, we also videotaped so they could watch it at home.

But here's my favorite fluency factor: Everyone follows along every time we practice for the event, so that by the time we perform, practically every child can read the *entire* play fluently—even the difficult parts performed by the more fluent readers. What a confidence boon! Plus, it's a grand model for what fluent reading sounds like. And to top it off, we have a ton of fun doing it.

This group of girls decided to construct their own readers' theater play by turning a narrative into a script!

Readers' Theater: A Radio Play

Readers' theater is usually dubbed a *radio play*. That's because the focus is on reading as one would for a play; however, for readers' theater participants read their parts while sitting on small stools or chairs, but facing the audience *only* during their spoken parts. There are few or no props and scenery, which makes these dramatic performances a far easier undertaking than a full-fledged play.

About twenty to thirty years ago a readers' theater company produced packets of well-known classic tales written at a variety of reading levels from primary through high school. Many teachers still use those wonderful old scripts. Unfortunately, the company that produced them no longer exists. Yet a new company found at *www.aaronshep.com* has received good reviews from the American Library Association, Horn Book, and other reviewers. Aaron Shepard offers readers' theater scripts for stories and novels by such authors as Louis Sachar, Roald Dahl, Nancy Farmer, Sid Fleischman, Deborah Nourse Lattimore, Russell Hoban, Stephen Manes, and Eleanor Farjeon.

Nevertheless, many teachers compose their own readers' theater texts, and once the kids have experience in how it's done, they too can get involved in the creation. I always had some groups who wanted to compose and perform a readers' theater after reading a multiple-character story. They used the text they'd read to develop a script, which I then copied for each of them. Who knows—one of them may be a playwright today!

Celebrate the Trying

I once heard Barry Neil Kaufman speak and then bought his audiotape. He is the best-selling author of *Son Rise* (1979), a book (and movie) about his formerly noncommunicative, autistic son, Raun. What a wonderful, uplifting story Kaufman tells of how he and his wife accomplished the impossible. I'll always remember one of the important pieces of advice he gave us. He said we teachers must always *celebrate the trying*. Similarly, researcher Brian Cambourne (1988) tells us to *celebrate approximations*.

What these two men are suggesting is that we keep a positive spirit intentioned toward the *process* itself rather than the end product. When we expect novices to arrive at some distant district or federal goal before they are ready, they tend to disappoint us. However, if we focus on the here and now of the process, *grounded in this child, this text, this day, this moment*, it is far easier to celebrate the trying.

When we celebrate we make learning fun, kids want to do it more, they even tend to become obsessed with it. One parent shared with me, "Last night I got such a kick out of Nila reading the faucets on the bathtub! She reads everything in sight! Even the bathtub fixtures!" Just visualize this wonderful wet celebration!

For me, there will always be something magic about reading. Take that magic out of it, and you remove its essence. That essence, that call to magic, can only be caught, not taught. And it's caught through celebrations.

When a child, a teacher, and a book unite in a reading relationship, there is indeed much to celebrate. Whether the child is a novice or a fluent reader, sensitively reading the relationships provides direction and intention for both the reader and the scaffolder. Every moment unfolds a new opportunity for teaching and learning, for sensing and feeling, for giving and receiving. And that's what real teaching is all about.

Conclusion

I remember that words—written or printed—were devils, and books, because they gave me pain, were my enemies . . . And then, one day, an aunt gave me a book and fatuously ignored my resentment. I stared at the black print with hatred, and then, gradually, the pages opened and let me in. The magic happened.

JOHN STEINBECK,
IN STEVEN GILBAR, *THE OPEN DOOR*

In the end, learning to read is magical—like that magical moment when you first take off on your bike by yourself, or you roller skate across the floor—alone, or you catch on to a dance step. Reading just one day, all of a sudden, happens—just like it did for Steinbeck. First, no one in the room is reading, and then, the entire class is!

Each year I'd scaffold in the manner described in this book, and each year the kids would go over the hump in November. Sure the scaffolding helped, but it was *more than that.* There was never a year in the fifteen years that I taught first grade that I did not *expect* that magic to happen for every child. And to predict good things is to contribute to their happening. And they did!

I spent a number of years investigating exactly what those scaffolding behaviors are—what we teachers do and what we say to help a beginning reader. And don't misunderstand me, because those scaffolded cues are definitely important. But beyond all that—a magic happens. Yet, it's a magic we can help cast.

That's why research always shows that myriad methods work. The methods merely invite children to taste the magic, and then the magic takes over. If you commit to the process and believe, the magic *will* happen. It *always* does. And each time it happens, I know I've witnessed one of life's wondrous gifts, and like Byrd Baylor I say to myself, "How lucky I am to have been here for this."

References

Children's Book References

Baylor, B. 1986. *I'm in Charge of Celebrations*. New York: Charles Scribner's Sons.

Bemelmans, L. 1998. *Madeline*. New York: Penguin.

Butterworth, C. 1990. *Frogs and Toads*. Austin, TX: Steck-Vaughn.

Calmenson, S. 1989. *The Principal's New Clothes*. New York: Scholastic.

Cherry, L. 1993. *The Great Kapoc Tree*. New York: Harcourt Brace Jovanovich.

Cowley, J. 1986. *The Jigaree*. Australia: The Wright Group.

Crews, D. 1978. *Freight Train*. New York: Puffin.

Dahl, R. 2002. *Charlie and the Chocolate Factory*. New York: Puffin.

Fallon, C. J. 1981. *We Work and Play*. Dublin, Ireland: C. J. Fallon.

Grahame, K. 1988. *The Reluctant Dragon*. Illustrated by M. Hague. New York: Henry Holt.

Heller, R. 1983. *The Reason for a Flower*. New York: Scholastic.

Keats, E. J. 1999. *Over in the Meadow*. New York: Puffin.

Kent, J. 1975. *There's No Such Thing as a Dragon*. Racine, WI: Western.

Lobel, A. 1978. *Mouse Tales: The Wishing Well*. New York: Harper & Row.

———. 1987. *Owl at Home: Strange Bumps*. New York: Harper & Row.

Martin, B., and E. Carle. 1996. *Brown Bear, Brown Bear, What Do You See?* New York: Henry Holt.

Mayer, M. 1986. *Just Me and My Little Sister*. Racine, WI: Western.

Packard, M. 1993. *My Messy Room*. New York: Scholastic.

Scarry, R. 1987. *Things to Love*. Racine, WI: Western.

Sendak, M. 1988. *Where the Wild Things Are*. New York: HarperTrophy.

Silverstein, S. 1964. *The Giving Tree*. New York: HarperCollins.

Steig, W. 1993. *The Amazing Bone*. New York: Farrar, Strauss, and Giroux.

Wells, R. 2001. *Morris's Disappearing Bag*. New York: Puffin.

Williams, V. B. 1982. *A Chair for My Mother*. New York: Scholastic.

Yolen, J. 1988. *Picnic with Piggins*. New York: Harcourt Brace Jovanovich.

Professional References

Adams, M. J. 1990. *Beginning to Read: Thinking and Learning About Print: A Summary*. Prepared by S. Stahl, J. Osborn, and F. Lehr. Urbana, IL: University of Illinois Urbana-Champaign.

Allington, R. 1977. "If They Don't Read Much, How They Ever Gonna Get Good?" *Journal of Reading* 21: 57–61.

———. 1980. "Teacher Interruption Behaviors During Primary Grade Oral Reading." *Journal of Educational Psychology* 79: 371–77.

———. 1983. "The Reading Instruction Provided Readers of Differing Reading Abilities." *Elementary School Journal* 83: 549–59.

Anderson, L. M., C. M. Evertson, and J. E. Brophy. 1979. "An Experimental Study of Effective Reading in First-Grade Reading Groups." *Elementary School Journal* 79: 193–223.

Anderson, R. C., B. B. Armbruster, and M. Roe. 1990. "Improving the Education of Reading Teachers." *Daedelus* 119: 187–210.

Anderson, R. C., E. Hiebert, J. Scott, and I. Wilkinson. 1984. *Becoming a Nation of Readers: The Report of the Commission on Reading*. Washington, DC: National Institute of Education.

Bateson, G. 1972. *Steps to an Ecology of Mind*. New York: Random House.

Bauml, B. J., and F. H. Bauml. 1975. *A Dictionary of Gestures*. Metuchen, NJ: Scarecrow Press.

Bernstein, R. J. 1965. *Critical Essays on Charles Sanders Peirce*. New Haven, CT: Yale University Press.

Bruner, J. 1973. *Beyond the Information Given: Studies in the Psychology of Knowing*. New York: W. W. Norton.

———. 1986. *Actual Minds, Possible Worlds*. Cambridge, MA: Harvard University Press.

Buber, M. 1970. *I and Thou*. New York: Charles Scribner.

Bus, A., and M. Ijzendoorn. 1999. "Phonological Awareness and Early Reading: A Meta-Analysis of Experimental Training Studies." *Journal of Educational Psychology* 91 (3): 403–14.

Calkins, L. 1986. *The Art of Teaching Writing*. 1st ed. Portsmouth, NH: Heinemann.

Cambourne, Brian. 1988. *The Whole Story*. New York: Scholastic.

Capra, F. 1996. *The Web of Life: A New Scientific Understanding of Living Systems*. New York: Banton, Doubleday, Dell.

Carnine, D., and J. Silbert. 1979. *Direct Instruction Reading*. Columbus, OH: Charles E. Merrill.

Chinn, C. A., M. A. Waggoner, R. C. Anerson, M. Schommer, I. A. G. Wilkinson. 1993. "Situated Actions During Reading Lessons: A Microanalysis of Oral Reading Error Episodes." *American Educational Research Journal* 30 (2): 361–92.

Clay, M. M. 1979. *Reading: Patterning of Complex Behavior*. Portsmouth, NH: Heinemann.

———. 1985. *The Early Detection of Reading Difficulties*. Portsmouth, NH: Heinemann.

———. 1993. *Reading Recovery*. Portsmouth, NH: Heinemann

Clymer, T. 1963. "The Utility of Phonic Generalizations in the Primary Grades." *The Reading Teacher* 16: 252–58. (Article reprinted in *Reading Teacher*, 1996, 50 (3): 182–87.)

Cole, A. 1998. "Beginner-Oriented Text: A Segue for a Few Struggling Readers." *The Reading Teacher* 51 (6): 488–501.

———. 2003. *Knee to Knee, Eye to Eye: Circling in on Comprehension*. Portsmouth, NH: Heinemann.

Cole, A., and L. Schott. 1997. Is There a Sequence of Graphophonic Development in First-Grade Journal Writing Samples? Unpublished manuscript.

Csikszentmihaly, M. 1990. *Flow: The Psychology of Optimal Experience*. New York: Harper & Row.

———. 1997. *Finding Flow: The Psychology of Engagement with Everyday Life*. New York: Basic Books.

Cunningham, P., and D. Allington. 1994. *Classrooms That Work*. New York: HarperCollins.

Dawson, G., and R. Glaubman. 2000. *Life Is So Good.* New York: Penguin Putnam.

Dewey, J. 1949. *Knowing and the Known*. Westport, CT: Greenwood Press.

Doake, D. B. 1985. "Reading-Like Behavior: Its Role in Learning to Read." In *Observing the Language Learner*, edited by A. Jaggar and M. T. Smith-Burke, pp. 82–98. Urbana, IL: National Council of Teachers of English.

Duckett, P. 2002. "Miscue Analysis and Eyemovement Study." *Talking Points* 13 (2): 6–21.

———. 2003. Email correspondence.

Durkin, D. 1978–79. "What Classroom Observation Reveals About Reading Comprehension Instruction." *Reading Research Quarterly* 14: 481–533.

Durrell, D. D., and R. E. Wylie. 1963. "Phonograms in Primary Grade Words." *Elementary English* 47: 787–91.

Ehri, L. 1976. "Word Learning in Beginning Readers and Prereaders: Effects of Form, Class and Defining Contexts." *Journal of Educational Psychology* 67: 204–12.

Ehri, L. C., and J. S. Sweet. 1991. "Fingerpoint-Reading of Memorized Text: What Enables Beginners to Process the Print." *Reading Research Quarterly* 26 (4): 442–62.

Ferreiro, E., and A. Teberosky. 1982. *Literacy Before Schooling*. Portsmouth, NH: Heinemann.

Foreman, B. R., D. J. Francis, T. Beeler, D. Winikates, and J. M. Fletcher. 1997. "Early Interventions for Children with Reading Problems: Study Designs and Preliminary Findings." *Learning Disabilties: A Multi-Disciplinary Perspective* 8: 63–71.

Fountas, I., and G. S. Pinnell. 1996. *Guided Reading: Good First Teaching*. Portsmouth, NH: Heinemann.

———. 2001. *Guiding Reading and Writers, Grades 3–6: Teaching Comprehension, Genre, and Content Literacy*. Portsmouth, NH: Heinemann.

Freeman, A. 2001. The Eyes Have It: Oral Miscue and Eye Movement Analysis of the Reading of Fourth Grade Spanish/English Bilinguals. Unpublished doctoral diss. University of Arizona, Tucson, Arizona.

Garan, E. 2002. *Resisting Reading Mandates: How to Triumph with the Truth*. Portsmouth, NH: Heinemann.

———. 2004. *In Defense of Our Children*. Portsmouth, NH: Heinemann.

Ginsburg, H. P., and S. Opper. 1988. *Piaget's Theory of Intellectual Development, an Introduction.* Englewood Cliffs, NJ: Prentice-Hall.

Goodman, K. S. 1967. "Reading: A Psycholinguistic Guessing Game." *Journal of the Reading Specialist* 6: 126–35.

———. 1969. "Reading Miscue Analysis: Applied Psycholinguistics." *Reading Research Quarterly* 5: 9–30.

———. 1973. *Miscue Analysis: Applications to Reading Instruction*. Urbana, IL: National Council for Teachers of English.

———. 1982. "Reading: You Can Get Back to Kansas Anytime You're Ready, Dorothy." *In Language and Literacy: The Selected Writings of Kenneth S. Goodman*, Vol. 2, edited by F. V. Gollasch, pp. 25–29. Boston, MA: Routledge and Kegan Paul.

Goodman, K. S., L. B. Bridges, and Y. Goodman, eds. 1991. *The Whole Language Catalog*. New York: Macmillian/McGraw Hill.

Goodman, K. S., and C. Burke. 1973. "Theoretically Based Studies of Patterns of Miscues in Oral Reading Performance." *Final Report to the U. S. Office of Education*, Project No. 9–0375. Detroit, MI: Wayne State University.

———. 1980. *Reading Strategies: Focus on Comprehension*. New York: Holt, Rinehart and Winston.

Goodman, K., and Y. Goodman. 1979. "Learning to Read Is Natural." In *Theory and Practice of Early Reading*, edited by L. Resnick and P. Weaver, pp. 137–54. Hillsdale, NJ: LEA..

Goodman, Y. M., D. J. Watson, and C. L. Burke. 1987. *Reading Miscue Inventory*. New York: Richard C. Owen.

Graves, D. H. 1983. *Writing: Teachers and Children at Work*. Portsmouth, NH: Heinemann.

Griffin, J. 2001. *How to Say It from the Heart: How to Communicate with Those Who Matter in Your Personal and Professional Life*. Paramus, NJ: Prentice-Hall.

Grinder, J., and R. Bandler. 1975. *The Structure of Magic: A Book About Language and Therapy*. Vol. II. CA: Science and Behavior Books.

Halliday, M. A. 1975. *Learning How to Mean: Explorations in the Development of Language*. London: Edward Arnold.

———. 1978. *Language as a Social Semiotic*. Baltimore, MD: University Park Press.

———. 1994. *An Introduction to Functional Grammar*. 2d ed. New York: Edward Arnold.

Harste, J. C., and C. Burke. 1977. "A New Hypothesis for Reading Teacher Education Research: Both the Teaching and Learning of Reading Are Theoretically Based." In *Reading: Research, Theory and Practice*, edited by P. D. Pearson. Minneapolis, MN: Mason.

Harste, J, C., V. A. Woodward, and C. L. Burke. 1984. *Language Stories and Literacy Lessons*. Portsmouth, NH: Heinemann.

Harvey, S., and A. Goudvis. 2000. *Strategies That Work: Teaching Comprehension to Enhance Understanding*. Portland, ME: Stenhouse.

Harwayne, S. 1992. *Lasting Impressions: Weaving Literature into the Writing Workshop*. Portsmouth, NH: Heinemann.

Heckleman, R. G. 1966. "Using the Neurological Impress Remedial Technique." *Academic Therapy Quarterly* 1 (Summer): 235–39.

Heller, R. 1983. The Reason for a Flower. New York: Scholastic.

Henderson, E. 1980. "Developmental Concepts of Word." In *Developmental and Cognitive Aspects of Learning to Spell*, edited by E. Henderson and J. Beers, pp. 1–14. Newark, DE: International Reading Association.

Holdaway, D. 1979. *The Foundations of Literacy*. New York: Ashton Scholastic.

Holden, M., and W. MacGinitie. 1972. "Children's Conceptions of Word Boundaries in Speech and Print." *Journal of Educational Psychology* 63: 551–57.

Irwin, J. W. 1991. *Teaching Reading Comprehension Processes*. Englewood Cliffs, NJ: Prentice-Hall.

Jenkins, J. R., and K. Larson. 1979. "Evaluating Error-Correction Procedures for Oral Reading." *The Journal of Special Education*: 13: 145–56.

Johnson, D. W. 1978. "Cooperation, Competition and Individualistic Learning." *Journal of Research and Development in Education* 12: 3–15.

Johnston, P. 2000. *Running Records: A Self-Tutoring Guide*. Portland, ME: Stenhouse.

Juel, C. 1996. "What Makes Literacy Tutoring Effective?" *Reading Research Quarterly* 31: 268–88.

Karmiloff-Smith, A. 1986. "From Metaprocesses to Conscious Access: Evidence from Children's Metalinguistic Repair Data." *Cognition* 23: 95–147.

Kaufman, B. N. 1979. *Son Rise: The Miracle Continues*. New York: Warner Books.

———. 1995. "Son-Rise: The Miracle Continues." *Noetic Sciences Review* 34: 22–28.

Keene, E. O., and S. Zimmerman. 1997. *Mosaic of Thought: Teaching Comprehension in Reader's Workshop*. Portsmouth: NH: Heinemann.

Kohn, A. 1993. *Punished by Rewards*. New York: Houghton Mifflin.

Kozal, J. 1991. *Savage Inequalities: Children in America's Schools*. New York: Harper Perennial.

Krashen, S. 1993. *The Power of Reading*. Englewood, CO: Libraries Unlimited.

———. 1995. "School Libraries, Public Libraries, and the NAEP Reading Scores." *School Library Media Quarterly*. 23: 235–38.

———. 2001a. "More Smoke and Mirrors: A Critique of the National Reading Panel Report on Fluency. *Phi Delta Kappan* 83: 119–23.

———. 2001b. "Does 'Pure' Phonemic Awareness Training Affect Reading Comprehension?" *Perceptual and Motor Skills* 93: 356–58.

Laubach Literacy Action. 1994. *Teaching Adults: A Literacy Resource Book*. Syracuse, NY: New Readers Press.

Leslie, L., and L. Allen. 1999. "Factors That Predict Success in an Early Literacy Intervention Project." *Reading Research Quarterly* 34 (4): 404–24.

Lomax, R. G., and L. M. McGee. 1987. "Young Childrens' Concepts About Print and Reading: Toward a Model of Word Reading Acquisition." *Reading Research Quarterly* 22: 237–56.

Mason, J. M. 1980. "When Do Children Begin to Read: An Exploration of One-Year-Old Children's Letter and Word Reading Competencies." *Reading Research Quarterly* 15: 203–27.

Masonheimer, P. E., P. A. Drum, and L. C. Ehri. 1984. "Does Environmental Print Identification Lead Children into Word Reading?" *Journal of Reading Behavior* 16: 257–72.

McCoy, K. M., and D. Pany. 1986. "Summary of Analysis of Oral Reading Corrective Feedback Research." *The Reading Teacher* 39: 548–54.

Meyer, L. 1985. Strategies for Correcting Student's Wrong Responses. Technical report of Center of the Study of Reading. Urbana, IL: University of Illinois.

Miller, G. A. 1956. "The Magical Number Seven, Plus or Minus Two: Some Limits on Our Capacity for Processing Information." *Psychological Review* 63: 87–97.

Morris, D. 1983. "Concept of Word and Phoneme Awareness in Beginning Readers." *Research in the Teaching of English* 17: 359–73.

Morris, D., and E. H. Henderson. 1981. "Assessing the Beginning Reader's 'Concept of Word.'" *Reading World* 20: 279–85.

National Assessment of Educational Progress. 2002. *NAEP Reading Report*. Available from *www.nces.ed.gov/nationsreportcard/naepdata*.

National Reading Panel (NRP). 1999. *Report of the National Reading Panel: Teaching Children to Read. Report of the Subgroup*. Washington, DC: National Institute of Child Health and Human Development.

Nell, V. 1988. *Lost in a Book: The Psychology of Reading for Pleasure*. New Haven, CT: Yale University Press.

———. 1994. "The Insatiable Appetite." In *Fostering the Love of Reading: The Affective Domain in Reading Education*, edited by E. Cramer and M. Castle. Newark, DE: International Reading Association.

Neuman, S. 1999. "Books Make a Difference: A Study of Access to Literacy." *Reading Research Quarterly* 343: 286–311.

Noddings, N. 1984. *Caring: A Feminine Approach to Ethics and Moral Education*. Berkley, CA: University of California Press.

———. 1992. *The Challenge to Care in Schools*. New York: Teacher's College Press.

Opitz, M., and T. Rasinski. 1998. *Good-bye Round Robin*. Portsmouth, NH: Heinemann.

Owocki, G. 2003. *Comprehension: Strategic Instruction for K–3 Students*. Portsmouth, NH: Heinemann.

Papandropoulou, I., and H. Sinclair. 1974. "What Is a Word?" *Human Development* 14: 241–58.

Paulson, E. J., and A. E. Freeman. 2003. *Insight from the Eyes: The Science of Effective Reading Instruction*. Portsmouth, NH: Heinemann.

Pearson, P. D., J. A. Dole, G. G. Duffy, and L. R. Roehler. 1992. "Developing Expertise in Reading Comprehension: What Should Be Taught and How Should It Be Taught?" In *What Research Has to Say About Reading*, 2d ed., edited by J. Farstrup and S. J. Samuels. Newark, DE: International Reading Association.

Pinnell, G. S. 2002. "The Guided Reading Lesson: Explaining, Supporting, and Promoting for Comprehension." In *Improving Comprehension Instruction*, edited by C. C. Block, L. B. Gambrell, and M. Pressley. San Francisco, CA: Jossey-Bass.

Pinnell, G. S., and I. Fountas. 1999. *Matching Books to Readers: Using Leveled Books in Guided Reading*. Portsmouth, NH: Heinemann.

Pressley, M. 2002. "What Should Comprehension Instruction Be the Instruction Of?" In *Handbook of Reading Research*, Vol. 3, edited by M. L. Kamil, P. B. Mosenthal, P. D. Pearson, and R. Barr, pp. 545–62. Mahwah, NJ: Lawrence Erlbaum.

Rayner, K. 1997. "Understanding Eye Movement in Reading." *Scientific Studies in Reading* 1 (4): 317–39.

Robbins, A. 1986. *Unlimited Power*. New York: Ballantine Books.

Roberts, B. 1992. "The Evolution of the Young Child's Concept of *Word* as a Unit of Spoken and Written Language." *Reading Research Quarterly* 27 (2): 125–37.

Rosenblatt, L. 1978. *The Reader, The Text, and The Poem*. Carbondale, IL: Southern Illinois University Press.

Rozin, P, B. Bressman, and M. Taft. 1974. "Do Children Understand the Basic Relationship Between Speech and Writing? The Mow-Motorcycle Test." *Journal of Reading Behavior* 6: 227–334.

Routman, R. 2003. *Reading Essentials: The Specifics You Need to Teach Reading Well*. Portsmouth, NH: Heinemann.

Samuels, S. J. 1983. "Diagnosing Reading Problems." *Topics in Learning and Learning Disabilities* 2: 1–11.

Schreiber, P. A. 1980. "On the Acquisition of Reading Fluency." *Journal of Reading Behavior* 12: 177–86.

Searchinger, G. 1995. *The Human Language Evolves: With and Without Words*. Part III. PBS televison production.

Searle, D. 1984. "Scaffolding: Who's Building Whose Building?" *Language Arts* 61: 480–83.

Shea, M. 2000. *Running Records*. New York: Scholastic.

Singh, Judy. 1989. "Teacher Behavior During Oral Reading by Moderately Mentally Retarded Children." *Journal of Reading* (January): 298–304.

Smith, F. 1984. *Essays into Literacy: Selected Papers and Some Afterthoughts*. Portsmouth, NH: Heinemann.

———. 1988. *Joining the Literacy Club*. Portsmouth, NH: Heinemann.

———. 1994. *Understanding Reading: A Psycholinguistic Analysis of Reading and Learning to Read*. 5th ed. Hillsdale, NJ: Lawrence Erlbaum.

Spiegel, D. L., and C. Rogers. 1980. "Teacher Responses to Miscues During Oral Reading by Second-Grade Students." *Journal of Educational Research* 74: 8–12.

Stanovich, K. E. 1986. "The Matthew Effects in Reading: Some Consequences for Individual Differences in the Acquisition of Literacy." *Reading Research Quarterly* 21: 360–407.

Tannen, D. 1986. *That's Not What I Mean!* New York: Ballantine Books.

Time (cover). July 28, 2003.

Topping, K. 1989. "Peer Tutoring and Paired Reading: Combining Two Powerful Techniques." *The Reading Teacher* (March): 488–94.

Tunman, W., and M. Herriman. 1984. "The Development of Metalinguistic Awareness: A Conceptual Overview." In *Metalinguistic Awareness in Children*, edited by W. Tunmer, C. Pratt, and M. Herriman, pp. 12–35. New York: Springer-Verlag.

Ujiie, J., and S. Krashen. 2002. *Knowledge Quest* 311: 36–37.

Venezky, R. 1970. *The Structure of English Orthography*. The Hague: Mouton.

Viadero, D. 2003. "'Report Card' Lacking Usual Background Data." *Education Week* 23 (42): 11.

Von Sprecken, D., J. Kim, and S. Krashen. 2000. *California School Library Journal* 23 (2): 8–9.

Vygotsky, L. S. 1978. *Mind and Society*. London: Harvard University Press.

Wells, G. 1986. *The Meaning Makers: Children Learning Language and Using Language to Learn*. Portsmouth, NH: Heinemann.

Wheatley, M. J. 2002. *Turning to One Another*. San Francisco: Berrett-Koehler.

Whyte, D. 1998. *The House of Belonging*. Langley, WA: Many Rivers Press.

Wong, S., L. Groth, and J. O'Flahavan. 1994. *Characterizing Teacher-Student Interaction in Reading Recovery Lessons*. Reading Research Report No. 17. Athens, GA: National Reading Research Center.

Index